Skill Management and Organisation Strategy

Skill Management and Organisation Strategy

Swarup K Goyal

ADHYAYAN

ADHYAYAN PUBLISHERS & DISTRIBUTORS
NEW DELHI (INDIA)

Published by
ADHYAYAN PUBLISHERS & DISTRIBUTORS
4378/4B, 105, J.M.D. House, Murari Lal Street
Ansari Road, Darya Ganj, New Delhi - 110002
Ph.: 011-23263018, 011-23277156, Fax: 011-23280028
Email: adhyayanpublishers@yahoo.com

Skill Management and Organisation Strategy

Edition 2011
ISBN 978-81-8435-291-7

Printed in India

Published by Harish Chandra Yadav for Adhyayan Publishers & Distributors. Laser Typeseting at A.V. Rao and Printed at Tarun Offset Printers, Delhi

Preface

Skills management is the practice of understanding, developing and deploying people and their skills. Well-implemented skills management should identify the skills that job roles require, the skills of individual employees, and any gap between the two. The skills involved can be defined by the organization concerned, or by third party institutions. They are usually defined in terms of a skills framework, also known as a competency framework or skills matrix. This consists of a list of skills, and a grading system, with a definition of what it means to be at particular level for a given skill.

To be most useful, skills management needs to be conducted as an ongoing process, with individuals assessing and updating their recorded skill sets regularly. These updates should occur at least as frequently as employees' regular line manager reviews, and certainly when their skill sets have changed.

In order to perform the functions of management and to assume multiple roles, managers must be skilled. The skills that are essential to successful management include technical, human, and conceptual. Technical skill involves process or technique knowledge and proficiency. Human skill involves the ability to interact effectively with people. Conceptual skill involves the formulation of ideas. And, technical skill deals with things, human skill concerns people, and conceptual skill has to do with ideas.

This book will help you bridge the gap between learning skill management and applying skills to the managing job at hand. Filled with experiential exercises, examples and the latest in technology, it is a must read for management students and professionals.

Swarup K Goyal

Contents

1

Organisational Demand for Skills

In countries across the world, it is observed that supply of highly-skilled labor has increased while their employment and/or wage shares have also increased. In other words, the growth rate of demand for highly-skilled labor exceeds that of supply. Broadly speaking, there are two possible explanations for this increase in the demand for highly-skilled labor: technology and trade. It is often argued that an increase in demand for highly-skilled labor is closely correlated with technological progress. For example, rapid progress in information technology creates new demand for computer-related labor. While it is generally accepted that technological progress requires new labor skills, there are ongoing discussions regarding to what degree increased demand for highly-skilled labor results from technological progress. It is not easy to construct a theoretical model that simultaneously considers demand and supply of heterogeneous labor. Building a model which links demand for labor to technological progress is relatively simple, but taking the heterogeneity of labor into consideration is difficult.

There are also discussions on relationships between skill upgrading and globalisation. As trade between developing and developed countries increases with globalisation trends, exports from developing countries to developed countries of largely labor-intensive goods, can change the industry structure within developed countries, focusing more on skills or capital-oriented industries. The impact of globalisation on developing countries is more complicated. It is expected that demand for low-skilled labor will increase as low-skill-based exports from these countries increase.

If this increase in demand for low-skilled labor is greater than supply, wages and employment of low-skilled labor will increase. Increased capital imports from developed countries will lower domestic prices of capital in developing countries, which will generate more demand for capital. Demand for highly-skilled labor will also increase if capital-skill complementarities hold. While it is not generally accepted that capital-skill complementarities also exist in developing countries. Increased demand for capital will also increase demand for highly-skilled labor, and if demand grows faster than supply, their wages will also increase. Hence, it is an empirical question whether shares in employment and wage of highly- and low-skilled labor in developing countries will increase or not. In practice, empirical investigation on this subject seems to be difficult due to the absence of measures that appropriately reflect skill levels, and deficiencies in consistently constructed data, including indicators of technological progress and detailed components of international trade.

Competitivity in Organisational Environment

As one of the most ubiquitous condition of social life, competition is present whenever two or more actors aspire to reach the same singular goals (e. g. winning a game) or to increase their share of the same scarce resource (e.g. customers, votes, territories, etc.). While social psychology has accumulated considerable evidence about the behaviour of competing individuals within small groups as well as the correlates of intergroup competition, it falls into the realm of organisational sociology to analyse competitive relations between mesosocial voluntary associations (e. g. social movements organisations or political parties) on the one hand and corporate actors like firms, schools and hospitals (or macro-entities like nation-states and international alliances) on the other.

Such research efforts can easily be justified by considering how fundamentally the economic sector of modern societies is determined by competitive intercorporate relations, how deeply processes of political participation and regime formation are shaped by the competition between political parties, and how insufficiently historical developments would be understood without taking into account the rivalry between feudal landowners, nation-states or larger (e. g. imperial and colonial) territorial actors.

Evidently, the perennial tendency to keep the scientific analysis of these different specimens of competition within the boundaries of highly segregated special disciplines (economics, political science etc.) has hitherto hampered the development of a more generalised theory which would be applicable to all types of collective social actors alike. On the other hand, organisational research since the 60ies has produced much empirical evidence and theoretical argumentations which could contribute to such an ambitious endeavour.

In particular, several studies have addressed the question how external competitive relations impinge on organisational behaviour and intraorganisational structures and processes – by way of causal determination or at least by restraining the options for strategic choice and tactical actions.

> How does the occurrence and intensity of competition relate to the level of human resources: to the composition of organisational staff and to the level (and kinds) of required skills?

Evidently, this question has become increasingly salient recently insofar as many current (economical as well as technological and sociocultural) developments have the common effect of increasing the pace and intensity of competition faced by companies in all economic sectors.

For instance, tariff barriers and other protective governmental regulations become eliminated in the course of neoliberalist policies; new firms from emerging countries are entering markets hitherto comfortably managed by few well-established corporations; the pace of technological innovation and product obsolescence has increased; and customers and business partners have become more demanding and more ready to articulate dissatisfactions. During the 90ies, economic re- cession has contributed to a shrinkage of many markets, so that competitive intensity (particularly in the realm of prices) has increased.

Thus, many firms currently operate under conditions of "hypercompetitivity" which forces them to commit many resources to continuous environmental scanning and learning processes, to reconsider permanently all their structures, commitments, planning schemes and operational activities, and to implement time-limited fast-response strategies in order to adapt to short-term unforseen developments and events.

In addition, it can be assumed that in comparison to previous decades, competitive relations have nowadays more direct repercussions on the role of individual employees, and thus on the level of required skills. For instance, downsizing has the effect that a larger percentage of employees have to deal with customers and other extraorganisational concerns. Likewise the tendency to disaggregate monolithic enterprises into rather autonomous divisions or profit centres has the effect that more members have to adopt a commercial perspective because they have become incumbents of "boundary roles". And finally, modern lean production and "total quality" philosophies aim at committing every employee to an "entrepreneurial spirit": thus aspiring a condition where all activities of all members are continuously oriented at the firm's most salient and invariant goal: *prevailing within an environment of ever more intensive competition.*

Contingency Perspective of Organisations

Since several decades, there is a general trend that economic firms have to commit ever more attention, energy and resources to extraorganisational concerns, because environmental conditions are getting more complex, volatile and unpredictable, and more decisive for the company's chances of survival and growth. Thus, societal pressures to conform to ecological standards, nondiscriminatory practices and many other legal regulations have increased, customers and other stake-holders are better organised and more inclined to articulate grievances or even file suits, and outsourcing and "just-in-time" strategies have created a more densely-knit web of interdependencies among different firms. And most importantly: creating values for customers and clients has become the major goal around which all business activities are organised, and the implementation of such customer-oriented strategies demands that these ideas are understood and practised on all organisational levels and by every single subunit and individual employee. Given the increasing salience of all these environmental factors, firms may institutionalise a general "market-oriented" philosophy which gives priority to external adaptation at the cost of internal organisational concerns.

Since the early sixties, organisational sociology has reacted to these developments (or in some way even anticipated them) by developing "open systems" models of formal organisations: conceiving them as reactive and adaptive (and less frequently even as proactive) entities within a challenging environmental field. These approaches contrasted with earlier stages of organisation sociology which were characterised by a neglect of such environmental relations. For instance, classical *socio-technical systems theory* was focusing almost exclusively on intraorganisational aspects, especially on the role situation of the shop floor worker. Doing this, it followed the classical Marxist approach which defined the worker as the major "stakeholder" of business organisations. Extraorganisational relationships were regarded solely as the prerogative or interest of management, which was supposed to have a perspective completely different than that of ordinary workers.

While such "introverted" perspectives always tended to see its objects as specimens of a modal single type of "bureaucratic organisation", these new environmentally oriented approaches have brought a major shift toward comparative analyses: by proposing a manifold of typologies which classify organisations according to their modes of environmental relations... When Hickson tried to make an inventory of these taxonomic typologies as early as 1966, he found more than 20 highly similar variants: all of them contrasting "more bureaucratic" (formalised/centralised/specific) and "less bureaucratic (informal/decentralised/diffuse) kinds of organisational structures. Concerning the environment, all of them also stressed the same crucial dimensions: particularly the degree of uncertainty, variability and heterogeneity of environmental events and developments, or the degree to which means-end relationships of organisational behaviour (particularly in the production sector) were explicitly known. All these approaches have converged in the rather diffuse, but influential "contingency" paradigm which asserts that there is not one single "best type" of formal organisation, but a range of different types optimally adapted to different environmental configurations.

The major substantive hypothesis of contingency theory can be summarised by the simple statement that coping with high complexity engenders higher levels of informality and decentralisation. The larger the heterogeneity, variability and unpredictability of external stimuli, demands and pressures that impinge on an organisation, the more it has to develop a structure where many individuals and subunits are capable and allowed to scan the environment, to collect and transmit information, to react rapidly to changed circumstances and to participate in collectively binding corporate decisions.

Conducting one of the earliest empirical studies to substantiate these relationships, Simpson and Gulley have found out that voluntary associations with multiple goals and adaptation problems are more likely to develop a highly decentralised internal structure, and to involve a large percentage of membership in its major activities. In addition, they tend to maintain more complex processes of intraorganisational communication in order to keep up with the larger quantity of inflowing information. Later studies have confirmed that as environmental changes become more manifold, less predictable and more rapid at the same time, it becomes increasingly important that all subunits and all individual employees in the corporation are capable and motivated for change:

> "Coping with complexity and rapid, often stochastic, change requires focus on goals, responsibility, and discretion throughout the entire organisation, understanding of the company and its context and coping with the dynamics, i.e., change and learning.".

As a result control structures become decentralised, in order to empower all employees for making decisions in accordance with their own understanding of the companies interests and goals:

> "Power shifts from the hierarchy to the control of the product by all. Power is based on skill, knowledge, and experience of the matter at hand. It requires putting complex systems into a human scale, i.e., creating an understanding of the world of work in a way all members of the organisation can grasp. Employees accept the authority to make decisions related to their work as it is directed toward a shared vision of the purpose of the enterprise. It is dependent on understanding where the company is going, why it is that way, and importance of the workers' role.

Consequently, a high basic level of intelligence and skill is necessary across all categories of workers and employees, and the need for higher educated personnel rises. In particular, employees have to be able to accumulate their own experiences on the job and to engage in autodidactic endeavours of advanced training.

Transcending this one-sided focusing on "complexity", a major synthesis of an environmentally oriented organisation theory has been proposed by Lawrence who argues that all economic firms experience two types of insufficiences which engender highly divergent strategies of adaptations:

1) *Scarcity of information:* Firms have to cope with uncertainties because they have not sufficient knowledge about their environment and its future developments on the one hand and about internal means-end relationships on the other. Such uncertainties force them to keep their resources in a highly liquid condition: so that they can easily adapt to unpredictable circumstances by reallocating their capital, by migrating to other contexts, by exchanging their personnel, by buying new technology and by redefining internal procedures and organisational structures. In addition, they have to promote higher levels of functional differentiation: so that more specialised roles and subunits are available for expanding or redirecting the range of tasks and activities.

2) *Scarcity of resources:* Typically, firms operate under conditions of constraints concerning the availability of personnel, raw materials, production facilities and all other costly resources. Particularly under conditions of intensive price competitivity, they have to minimise costs and to maximise efficiency in order to survive and maintain their markets. This usually implies that existing resources are highly specified and committed: by freezing money in long-term equipment which has to "pay out" during its use, by hiring staff with highly specialised skills that have to be updated or modified by expensive training investments every other year; and by optimising production processes by working out routinised and standardised procedures implemented for long periods of time. In short: they have to give priority to goals of intraorganisational optimisation: thus reducing their potential to mobilise liquid "slack resources" when unpredicted new circumstance arise.

As both contradictory strains are usually present, each firm has to find ways to equilibrate efficiency and adaptation needs at the same time.

When uncertainties are relatively low and resource constraints high, organisations are likely to become highly formalised and centralised "machine bureaucracies"; when uncertainties are considerable and resource scarcities insignificant, they will tend toward loosely structured "adhocracies" of the "organic management type". When both strains are very intensive, they may tend toward "simple structures" characterised by small, unstable organisational units; and when both are low or absent, optimal conditions exist for the unfolding of "professional bureaucracies". Within this conceptual framework, competition can easily be characterised as an environmental condition which is difficult to cope with because it generates substantial uncertainties on the one hand and resource scarcities on the other.

Like many other approaches within the paradigm of "contingency theory", the theoretical model Lawrence proposed was heavily indebted to the "social neodarwinist" approaches which focus on ecological and evolutionary studies of "commensalistic" organisational populations. In the meantime, several students of the topic have emphasised the shortcomings of such biologist views which see organisations mainly as adaptive actors vis-à-vis a dominant environment determining their chances of survival and growth. Instead, it has been stressed that while such one-sided adaptations are unquestionably frequent and of high importance, organisational environments can also be *dependent variables*: insofar as firms

a) *Choose specific strategies* which then lead to specific correlative environmental conditions (e. g. by deciding to rely on specific products, technologies or raw materials or by cooperating with other firms).

b) *intentionally select specific environments* (e. g. by choosing plant locations, by deciding to enter certain market niches or to appeal to certain segments of customers etc.)

c) *shape actively their environments* (e. g. by buying out dangerous competitors, erecting barriers of entry, exerting pressures on governmental (regulative or subsidising) agencies etc.

In fact, contingency theory has never succeeded in eradicating the basic heretic question: Do organisations really adapt? As Baum and Singh have noted, not all organisational sociologists share the premise that organisations are adaptable social systems capable and motivated to design their structures and processes in optimal accordance with environmental needs. On the one hand, the *"Lamarckian" adaptionists"* try to demonstrate that organisations respond to external threats and opportunities by revising their internal procedures and structures – even if they do this intuitively or even accidentally: more by trial and error processes than by rational analysis and design. On the other hand, the *"Darwinian selectionists"* assert that economic evolution proceeds by a constant replacement of unfit organisations by fitter ones. They perceive firms as rather inert and/or randomly moving entities more likely to be whiped out than to adapt successfully when environmental circumstances change to the worse:

> "....even when actors strive to cope with their environments, action may be random with respect to adaptation as long as the environments are highly uncertain or the connections between means and ends are not well understood. It is the match between action and environmental outcomes that must be random on average for selection models to apply."

Consequently, studying organisational change mainly means: focusing on the differential birth and death rates of various organisational forms.

The two perspectives can be reconciled by making use of the empirical regularity that new branches often start by a selectionist phase characterised by the rapid foundation and elimination of many small firms ("r-selection"), while more mature market niches are often occupied by rather few highly experienced players which have learned to survive by coping actively with environmental problems – or simply by dominating markets ("K-selection"). Thus, in contrast to the older "contingency theory" of organisations that has given priority to the unilateral influence of the environment on intraorganisational processes and structures, newer research studies focus on more bilateral causal relationships conditioned by strategic organisational action.. More specifically: by deciding about entering new product markets, cooperating with other firms, outsourcing specific tasks, migrating to other countries, changing production technologies or modifying the skill demands of their employees, firms basically change their environments instead of adapting to given environmental conditions. The more degrees of freedom they have in making strategic choices, the more environmental-structure – relationships can be reduced to insignificance.

There is consensus that whenever we see organisations adapting to their environment, a very complicated process takes place co-determined by many intervening factors. Thus, change is not happening automatically, but has to be implemented intentionally by managerial decisions and implementations. This implies that "adaptive" strategies can well be objectively disfunctional; that they may occur as discontinuous events, with too much delay – or never at all. Concerning the causal relationships between environmental and organisational change, it is important to notice that such change does not always take place in the form of explicitly decided and implemented measures of reorganisation. Particularly when a firm is very small, change can happen without formal reorganisation measures because the few employees can easily adapt on an informal level: by changing cooperation patterns, leadership procedures and communication intensities according to current needs.

The larger an organisation, the less it can effectively change without implementing formal measures: e.g. by hiring additional employees, by subdividing or merging submits, redefining role duties and competences, or by switching explicitly to new "firm philosophies" and strategic goals. Thus, it is not surprising to find that smaller companies show much lower correlations between any variables of intraorganisational structure and any indicators of external performance.

Most often, adaptive processes cannot be realised fully, but only in a piecemeal fashion, because traditional habits cannot be broken and/or management lacks the will or power needed for a systematic implementation. Thus, Burgelmann argues that most organisational changes are "induced" processes highly compatible with existing strategies, activities and structures; while only few of them are "autonomous" measures apt to enlarge the firm's domain and to renew its adaptive capabilities. On a general level, reorganisational measures may be inhibited by the basic fact that organisations have a vital interest to be stable actors in order to be highly reliable to their customers and suppliers and in order to exploit fully the cost-saving qualities of routinised procedures. In addition, all change involves risks because the consequences of acting differently are more difficult to predict than consequences of keeping activities as they are. Thus, a major precondition facilitating organisational change is the capacity and motivation of a firm to tolerate risks: a variable highly dependent on subjective preferences on the one hand and objective capabilities (e. g. buffering slack resources) on the other.

It has also been argued that most organisations are not able to adapt optimally to their environmental circumstances because they lack sufficient knowledge about their internal capacities and shortcomings. For instance, they are not well informed about the competencies of their personnel and about the potential savings which could be realised by rational reorganisation:

> "To date, the development of tools for analysing environmental opportunities and threats has proceeded much more rapidly than the development of tools for analysing a firm's internal strengths and weaknesses."

The more informal and decentralised an organisation, the more it is prone to experience such handicaps because informality means that little systematic information about intraorganisational structures and processes can be collected, and decentralisation implies that much information remains on the level of specific subsystems, so that top managers remain insufficiently informed. Because of such shortcomings, low potentials for rational environmental adaptation has been found in samples of Canadian day care facilities and in Californian wineries.

Finally, it has to be considered that any successful adaptation presupposes a certain pool of uncommitted "discretionary resources" which can be dedicated to the required new processes of decision-making, planning and implementation. While competitive challenges may be necessary to stimulate higher levels of performance and encompassing endeavours of adaptive reorganisation, the constraints they generate for the firm should not be so heavy that organisations lose all capacities for autonomous actions. Instead, they should have the "slack" needed to conceive and try out new activities, to become temporarily absorbed by learning processes, to initiate product innovations and market campaigns which can easily fail, or to survive periods of fundamental reorganisation during which much energy is absorbed by elaborating and implementing new structures and norms. Thus, Lawrence rightly argues that organisational learning and innovation processes will be most likely when intermediate (instead of high) levels of environmental constraints (in terms of informational uncertainties and/or resource scarcities) prevail.

Impact of Competition on Organisational Behaviour

The theoretical paradigm of "contingent organisation" presupposes that organisations are forced to adapt rationally to their environment because if they don't, they would be punished by being eliminated or at least by reduced profits and weaker chances of further growth. This "social darwinist" view is based on the premise that there are heavy environmental constraints which cannot be eliminated by organisational action: so that organisations have to accept them as given structural conditions which limit (or even: determine) their courses of action. Of course, this condition is best fulfilled in highly competitive environments which offer no opportunities for "exit" strategies" (e. g. by getting governmental subsidies or by becoming a monopolist player). But as decades of organisational research have shown, larger companies have often a large variety of options for alleviating competitive pressures: e.g. by mergers, informal alliances by creating interlocking directorates, joint ventures or other arrangements of interorganisational affiliation. On the other hand, organisations can escape by migrating to specialised niches where competition is (still) low or absent. Its has been found that small firms are often more disposed to fill such new niches because they are better able to adapt flexibly their whole internal organisation. This flexibility may be seen as a functional substitute for their lower ability to cope actively with given market conditions. Thus, the whole following discussion does exclusively apply to firms which are not *escaping from,* but actively *coping with* a given competitive situation: because exit options do not exist or because they are considered as more costly or risky than remaining within the existing field of competition.

High Significance of Firm-specific Factors

A firm's capacity to be profitable on its product market is a result of many different causal factors, some of them associated with the structure of the whole industry, others with characteristics of the "industrial district" where the firm is located; but most of all: with the specific firm's capabilities and resources. Empirical studies show that such particular factors on the level of the single organisation far outweigh the influence of overall industry factors.

It has further been substantiated that from the point of view of competitiveness and profitability, the most precious assets a firm possesses are most often not its tangible resources (like land, buildings, raw materials etc.), but highly *intangible extrinsic assets* (like customer goodwill, patents trademarks and copyrights) on the one hand and *intangible intrinsic assets* (like staff skills, management capacities and efficient forms of organisational cooperation) on the other.

While many authors stress the importance of extrinsic factors (including licenses and joint ventures), others put the emphasis on the acquisition of intrinsic capacities (e.g. by collective learning). These two views may easily be reconciliated by taking time factors into account: When fundamental new action capacities have to be acquired within as very short time, there is no alternative than "buying" such capacities on external markets; when more time is available, endogeneous developments (e. g. by advanced training of employees) may be more profitable and efficient. On the other hand, a heavy reliance on external factors proves unwise when the environment is very unstable. Thus, the increase in environmental instability and volatility which has occurred in the last decades has brought a shift from external to internal assets:

> "....we have the claim that changes in the business environment have rendered the positioning approach irrelevant and that the only sound basis for sustainable competitive advantage is the development and exploitation of those resources and capabilities which are, or will become, the core competences of the organisation. Indeed, the claim is made that core competences are more critical than the external environment as a basis for strategy determination, because the environment is in too much of a state of change to base any strategy on it."

Price Competition and Quality Competition

As consumers always want "the best offer for the lowest price", firms have a certain leeway to which extent they compete by lowering prices or by raising the "quality" of their products or services.. While in most cases, a mixed strategy will prevail, price competition certainly dominates when products cannot be differentiated qualitatively (e. g. in the case of gasoline or standardised silicon chips); and quality competition is stressed when prices are not flexible (e. g. because of interfirm cartellisation or governmental regulations).

Generally, it is difficult to cope with intensive price competition and high quality competition at the same time, because these two conditions demand highly divergent measures of adaptation. Thus, price competition often forces firms to downsize in order to reduce costs at the short-term; but because dismissals most often lead to less personnel in the R & D sector, the firm's capacities to innovate are weakened and its chances for longer-term perspectives of survival and growth may be reduced. In other cases, high price competition induces firms to substitute higher-paid skilled personnel by cheaper unskilled employees: thus reducing their general capacities to deliver high-quality products and to implement strategies of quality improvement..

Leaving aside such exogenous contingencies, it can generalised that price competition and quality competition are correlates of two diametrically opposed market structures.

a) *Price competition dominates in "stable markets": characterised by "mature", basically invariant products and consolidated, steady consumer demands:* As the products- as the technologies used for fabrication - remain basically the same, market rivalry of suppliers focuses on price competition. Thus, survival and market shares become highly dependent on rationalising processes and minimising costs.

   Vice versa, high price competition imposes a need to focus on a small range of highly standardised mass products, on highly institutionalised production procedures and on consolidated, "mature" market conditions: so that all organisational processes can be streamlined in a cost-minimising way. Insofar as price competitors are innovative, they will focus on process rather than product innovations.

Environmental stability is most important when the costs of expensive capital investments have to be regained.

— "A cost leadership strategy works best under conditions of environmental stability in which neither customers nor competitors substantively alter their aggregate behaviour. Such environmental stability serves to ameliorate the risk associated with large fixed investments in process and plant needed to sustain low unit costs with mature products."

As a consequence, successful price competitors are likely to maintain rather bureaucratised structures characterised by extensive formalisation and centralised decision making procedures:

— *"The characteristic organisational structure of cost leaders is a highly centralised machine bureaucracy, with a key role played by the technical specialists who design the manufacturing and logistic systems. Important structural decisions regarding capacity and technology are made centrally. Relatively few substantive decisions are made by lower or middle management, who are charged with following plans, maintaining the large investment in plant and equipment and running facilities to take full advantage of scale economies."*

Given their high needs for intraorganisational stability, price competitors are more likely to search new market outlets for given production lines than to change procedures in order to keep existing markets.

b) *Quality competition reigns in dynamic environments in innovative and un-consolidated markets:* At the other extreme, there are highly volatile markets characterised by new products rapidly changing because of technological innovations on the one hand and constantly shifting market conditions and consumer preferences on the other. Under these conditions, competition focuses on optimising product quality as well as the quality of customer services: goals which demand continuous efforts in environmental scanning, knowledge acquirement and technological innovation

— "If management regards the environment as stable or static, attention will be highly focused on rationalisation, productivity, and profitability. Within the automobile industry, this strategy is often referred to as 'Fordism.' If management regards the environment as characterised by change and turbulence, it will give high priority to competence development and the abilities to adjust, develop, and innovate. Within the automobile industry this strategy is often referred to as 'Toyotism.'

Given two firms facing the same current market conditions, they can nevertheless follow divergent strategies according to their horizons of time.

The short-term oriented firm A will prefer price competition for optimising its sales in the face of current competitors and for maximising this year's profit; while firm B will prefer product development and innovation in order to conquer additional markets and/or to remain competitive in the middle- and longer-term future.

Consequences of Price and Quality Competition

On a most general level price competition and quality competition diverge highly in the degree of specificity of the adaptation problems to which they give rise.For economic enterprises of any kind, price competition may generate extreme worries, but it is always a precislely defined problem apt to evoke rationally designed copping strategies:

— The problem itself can easily be identified in objective measurable terms: there are competitors trying to produce the same product with less costs and sell it more cheaply.

— There is a highly consensual, determinate way how the problem shall be solved: (reduction of costs), and

— Coping strategies can be rationally chosen because

a) it is often known ex ante that certain measures are apt to reduce costs and/or

b) when a measure is taken, its effect on costs and prices can quickly be assessed.

When competition is about "quality" (of products or services), the situation is usually much more diffuse:

— 'Higher quality" is an imprecise multidimensional concept; its real meaning is not objectively defined, but depends on the perceptions and evaluation of the customers.

— It is not very clear in which way the problem shall be solved: there are innumerable steps to be taken to change products and services: e.g. to shorten the delays in shipping, to increase the spectrum of available variants, to lengthen the lifetime of products, to establish better support line etc etc. – and nobody can know exactly how investments in these different aspects will pay out

— The causal effects of the measures taken cannot be easily assessed. For instance, when improved products are better sold, this may be caused by a series of intermingled factors (e. g. because in the meantime, the brand has become more popular or the customer preferences have changed).

If measurements are possible at all, unrealistically high investments in technology, organisation and personnel have to be made in order to establish the necessary procedures:

> "....increased resources are necessary to measure the quality of output or the performance of agents. Sorting, grading, labelling, trade marks, warranties, licensing, time and motion studies and a variety of other techniques to measure the performance of agents are all, albeit costly and imperfect, devices to measure the characteristics of goods and services and the performance of agents. Despite the existence of such devices the dissipation of income is evident all around us in the difficulty of measuring the quality of automobile repairs, in evaluating the safety characteristics of products and the quality of medical services, or in measuring educational output. The problems of evaluating performance are even more acute in hierarchies because of the difficulties of achieving low cost measurement of the multiple dimensions of an agent's performance."

Quality Competition

The high prevalence of quality competition is illustrated by a transnational company survey encompassing eight European regions, where Schienstock et. al have found that "high product quality" was the foremost factor to which most firms attributed their advantage in competing with rival enterprises. Similarly, Chaston and Mangles have found that the most important influences on performance included optimisation of employee productivity, development of new products, investments in continuous improvements of product quality and measurement of customer quality expectations. But the term "quality" has assumed a much broadened meaning than in the past. While in traditional industrial competition, the term referred almost exclusively to intrinsic attributes of the physical product (e. g. its durability, its precise and reliable functioning etc.), it now tends to encompass all stages of a firms activity: from the criteria applied in the choice of raw materials and production procedures (e. g. ecological considerations) right to the support services offered after customers have bought it and set it in operation. The raising salience of post-selling quality performance has been illustrated by the aforementioned comparative study which has found that about 40% of all firms defined "after sales services" as their essential competitive advantage.

Ubiquity of Price Competition

When trade relations become global, price competition becomes more ubiquitous because local and regional protection break down. In particular, most firms from highly developed countries like Switzerland are increasingly challenged by cheaper competitors from low-wage countries. In the past, many Swiss firms could reduce competitiveness by producing high quality products, because no other firms in other countries were able to reach the same levels. In fact, the label "Swiss Made" was a long time sufficient to provide the reputation of high quality – a collective reputation from which all singular branches and companies could profit without having to generate and their own individual reputation. Thus, the rather high competitive success of many Swiss firms in foreign markets may at least partially be attributed to the "structural competitiveness" of Switzerland as an "industrial district": i.- e. as a territory endowed with many advantageous traits vis-à -vis other geographical regions.

In the last decades, more and more firms from more and more countries acquired such capacities, and given the lower level of wages in most world regions, many of them are no better disposed to keep selling prices low. As a consequences, most firms have recently experienced an environmental change in a way that they are now forced to cope with intensive quality and price competition at the same time.

This trend has also been substantiated in the Finnish Tampere region:

> "Companies in the Tampere region concentrate on high quality niche markets in the first place. They see quality and time of delivery as their competitive advantage. These niche markets, however, do not present a safe segment any longer. More companies from all over the world have learned to produce high quality. What is now needed is to produce high quality and user-friendly products at a reasonable price and to deliver them on time."

In order to escape the cumulative pressures of quality and price competition, firms are forced to outperform competitors in other respects: by being quicker than other in introducing new products or by being more flexible to react to changed customers needs:

> "Nowadays companies from all over the world can manufacture products of high quality at low costs, sell them for a reasonable price and deliver them within a short time period. Success within the global market mainly depends on the capability of companies to rapidly and continuously produce new products and services; innovativeness is the number one factor in global competition."

Factors Influencing a Firm's Capacity to Cope with Competition

Firm Size

Since the time of Karl Marx, it is common wisdom that the evolution of private capitalism tends to produce larger enterprises, because big firms are better able to survive in economic competition. Within the Fordist paradigm of industrial organisation, this relationship has primarily been elaborated with respect to *price competition*: Thus, it has been argued that for many different reasons; larger firms are better able to minimise costs by realising of "economies of scale": e. g. because they can exercise monopsonic power on suppliers or because they are better able to make use of highly routinised mass production technologies (which result in an downgrading of required skills). More recently, it has been observed that larger firms have a similar edge in exploiting "economies of scope": associated with the basic fact when producing good A, a firm may have lower costs of producing related goods B,C,D..

For the case of *quality competition* instead, contradictory theoretical argumentations have been proposed. On the one hand, Piore and Sable have asserted that small firms practicing craft-like production styles are better able to cope with the newer trends towards customised high-quality products, because they have more flexibility to adjust outputs (quantitatively and qualitatively) to such new demands. On the other hand, it is also widely acknowledged that larger firms have higher capacities to develop large amounts of specialised knowledge and skills, and to maintain collaborative relationships with universities or other innovation-oriented institutions.

In addition, they can engage in risky innovative endeavours with less fears because conventional procedures can be maintained at the same time (within other subunits of the same organisation).

> "....larger organisations, although less likely to attempt core changes in the first place, are less likely to die during a core change attempt. Largeness can buffer organisations from the disruptive effects of core change by helping, for example, to maintain both old and new ways of doing things during the transition or to overcome short-term deprivations and competitive challenges that accompany the change attempt."

Empirically, various studies have shown that larger companies are more likely to innovate, Thus,. The Finnish study in the Tampere region has shown that firms above 200 employees are much more prone to innovate by introducing new products as well as new production procedures).

On the other hand, larger firms are often characterised by traditional Taylorist structures which go along with a high percentage of unskilled labour – a factor hampering innovativeness in many respects. Thus, it has been observed that while large firms cultivate develop and maintain highest expertise and skills in most areas, they are often not capable of exploiting it fully for their own purposes. Instead, many experts – frustrated by lacking opportunities to realise their ideas and be promoted – leave the firm in order to found new "spin-off" enterprises. These small new firms then are often developing and licensing innovations (which then might be bought back later by the larger firms).

Additionally, several empirical studies have shown that while larger firm may be more capable of providing the capital and human resources necessary for improvements or innovations, they are often heavily handicapped by rigid internal structures and a tendency to focus more on internal than on environmental matters.

Thus, larger firms have been found to maintain a lower degree of market orientation and to show signs of complacency and inertia which makes them unfit for risky measures of change. Their mere structural complexity leads to reduced capacities for information processing and slower speed in executing formally decided measures and plans.

By contrast, smaller firms can be expected to react more flexible to environmental stimuli of any kind, because more employees occupy boundary roles, because their structures are less bureaucratised, and their communication systems less complicated:

> "Small is beautiful. It is much easier for the new venture founder to attend to the myriad of details in running a totally competitive business unit as long as it is still small with only a handful of employees. Perhaps, one of the reasons new ventures are able to blossom early, is the fact that the very nature of their smallness permits adaptability and rapid response."

Consequently, while larger firms may draw more advantages from their institutional embedments and their capacity to control salient environmental factors, such advantages may be more than offset by their smaller capacity to maintain intensive environmental relations:

> "Although large firms can dominate commodity markets based on cost or financial advantages, larger industrial manufacturing concerns may be at a disadvantage, compared to smaller firms, in their ability to learn from their market environment due to lessened contact between senior managers and customers as well as customer contact personnel. This lessened level of contact can lead to internally focused operations and production/technical orientations that may fail to adjust to changing market conditions. This internal focus, combined with significant sunk costs and bureaucratic inertia,

> could render large firms more vulnerable to changing industry conditions because of the difficulty they have modifying strategy."

This reasoning also implies that size is an intervening variable moderating the relationship between firm strategies and achieved performance. Thus, when a small firms focuses on a market-oriented strategy, it is more likely to gain significant competitive advantages than a bigger firm, because it is better able to adjust its whole internal organisation to the external strategic needs. Thus

> "...market orientation may provide small firms with a potential competitive advantage over larger firms where layers of management and bureaucracy make understanding customers more difficult and also increases the difficulty of promoting a cohesive customer-oriented culture."

Many larger firms try to exploit such advantages by segmenting themselves into smaller divisions, thus combining the functional advantages of smallness and bigness at the same time:

> "The creation of small profit centres reduces the growth of organisational bureaucracy yet allows the firm to respond quickly to changes in the competitive environment. Firms that have adopted the confrontation strategy cannot afford either the extra costs of unnecessary bureaucracy or he slowing of the firm's reflexes that such a bureaucracy causes. By keeping the effective firm size small. empire building becomes almost impossible, and a firm can maintain its ability to adapt quickly to changes in competitive conditions."

Finally, it has to be considered that quality competition offers to many small firms excellent chances for survival and growth which are less available to larger enterprises. Many firms try to reduce competitive pressures by migrating to less contested niches. They typically do this by developing and producing highly specific products addressed to highly specified customer segments. The smaller the firm, the more probable that it finds such a highly specific small niche which offers a sufficiently large and stable base of subsistence. The bigger firms need larger markets which are less likely to be uncontested (or to compete simultaneously in different market niches which are unlikely to be all equally uncontested).

Niche specialisation means that a firm tries to exploit quasi-monopolistic rents by conquering a leader position within a narrowly defined field. This usually implies that it commits all resources to raise the quality standard of its production and products by optimising its technology and organisation and by internalising highly professional skills.

Expanding or Shrinking Markets

For three different reasons, firms operating on expanding markets are better able to react rationally to competitive challenges and to implement successful adaptive change

1) When niches contract, innovative behaviour is hampered by the prospective than whenever it fails, the organisation risks to be whiped out completely. On the other hand, expanding markets provide "buffers" because even when experimental new procedures turn out bad, the mere market expansion makes it probable that the company still can still survive. Corroborating this hypothesis, Baum and Singh have found that competing Day care and nursery schools were more successful in environmental adaptation under expansive than under contractive conditions.

2) During phases of growth, organisations are usually quite free to enlarge existing and/or build new structures and the recruit additional personnel in strict accordance with their changing needs. In addition, expanding firms have also better chances to upgrade their skills by hiring highly qualified employees, because they can offer se- cure jobs and promising careers. And finally, their employees may be better motivated to engage in advanced training because given their long-term employment, they can reasonably expect that such investments will pay out.

   During periods of decline and contraction however, adaptations are hampered by factors of many sorts: e g. by ossified habits and traditions, by lacking flexibility of leadership, by legal norms inhibiting the dismissal of employees, by poor opportunities to hire qualified personnel etc.

   Thus, Freeman and Hannan have found that expanding schools enlarge their administrative component quite in pace with their growing absolute size, while shrinking schools tend to keep their clerical apparatus too large.

3) Expanding markets allow for more specialisation. When firms are operating on *expanding* markets, they have better chances to survive in highly specialised niches, because it is more likely that such specialised niches are also submitted to growth. Thus, they are better equipped to commit their resources irreversibly to highly specified purposes: so that they can maximise their efficiency in a way compatible with very intensive price competition.

   On the other hand, they are also well able to survive when they sacrifice efficiency for remaining more flexible and innovative, because when markets expand, inefficiencies are not punished so harshly as in shrinking environments. Thus, they have more leeway to follow very different strategies, so that they will develop highly divergent procedures and organisational forms (high statistical dispersion). In *shrinking* markets, firms do better to keep their resources in a more liquid, reversible condition, because they may face the contingency of having to give up their traditional product lines altogether and to switch to completely new products (and corresponding markets). But exactly this strategy may be blocked because price competition is so high that firms have to be completely committed to highly routinised, efficiency-oriented procedures.

4) It has also been observed that expansive and contracting conditions have highly divergent influences on the average level of skills.

When firms have to downsize their staff because they are competing with little success (and/or within shrinking markets), they may still be forced to upgrade the skill level of their labour force (either by selectively dismiss unskilled personnel or by substituting less skilled by more educated employees.

The reason is that the total organisational activity has to be allocated to fewer heads, so that each average worker has to be able to cope with a larger variety of different tasks. Consequently it is more likely that any role also contain more complex problems which necessitate to hire workers with a higher basic level of knowledge and skills. In a Canadian case study conducted by Bob Russell, this increased role polyvalence has been found to be the major factor for higher skill demands in reorganising firms.

Thus, when firms switching to lean production procedures may need higher skills, this may not be primarily caused by increased task complexity and higher qualifications demanded for functioning in "empowered teams". Instead the more trivial reason may lie in the "horizontal expansion of jobs" (each comprising a larger spectrum of rather undemanding single tasks).

Expanding markets instead provide optimal opportunities for implementing standardised procedures and for buying capital-intensive mass production technologies – so that roles can be more specialised and taylorised and a shift toward lower skilled personnel may be observed.

Age of the Organisation

For two reasons, it may be expected that older organisations are less likely to react adaptively to competition On the one hand, older organisations are more likely to have highly consolidated and rigidified structures, so that they are less disposed to react to any external stimuli with internal change and innovative procedures. Miller argues that as organisations age, their very early success makes them assume more simple structural forms which may diminish their capacities for future adaptive change:

> "....a troublesome paradox exists: the sources of dangerous simplicity may underlie initial success and, thus, may be doubly difficult to combat. Indeed, it is very hard to distinguish between the concentration and passionate dedication so necessary for success and competitive advantage and the simplistic fixations and extremes that lead to failure."

Thus, Baum and Singh have found in their comparative study of daycare facilities that older organisations were more likely to experience disruption when their markets niches changes.

Secondly, older organisations are less likely to succumb because they enjoy higher "social legitimation" and because they are more integrated into supporting institutional environments. For instance, they are more likely to enjoy a high public reputation, to be supported by highly loyal employees, to profit from a high status among customers; to be embedded in supportive elite networks, to enjoy the help of public agencies, to have a high standing on the labour market, and to get bank credits when needed. As a consequence, social darwinist selection processes in economic markets don't guarantee the "survival of the fittest", because with increasing age, survivors are increasingly protected from direct impacts of environmental competitive pressures.

Many older firms tend to become overstaffed without being punished immediately for these inefficiencies., This is seen in the regularity that many of them have to regain their competitive capacities by downsising when environmental competition pressures suddenly increase. Even younger organisations may share competitive weaknesses when they are "spin off's" of older firms: because they are likely to have "inherited" their mother's short-comings. Empirical studies indicate that the increasing survival chances associated with higher age accrue disproportionately to larger organisation. In fact, smaller firms seem to suffer from a "liability of obsolescence" which leads to increasing risks of mortality over time.

References

Aaker, D.A.: (1989). 'Managing assets and skills: the key to sustainable competitive advantage', *California Management Review*, 31, No. 2, pp. 91-106.

Bain, Joe S. (1968). *Industrial Organisation*. Wiley, New York.

Barnett, William P (1997). 'The dynamics of competitive intensity'. *Administrative Science Quarterly* 1. 1997.

Barney, Jay B. (1995). 'Looking inside for competitive advantage'. Vol. 9, *The Academy of Management Executive*, 11-01-1995, pp 49ff.

Thompson, James D. (1967). *Organisations in Action*. New York: McGraw-Hill.

Veliyath, Rajaram / Fitzgerald, Elizabeth (2000). 'Firm capabilities, business strategies, customer preferences, and hypercompetitive arenas'. *Competitiveness Review*, 10, 2000: 56-82. Indiana.

2

Management Skills

Management consists of the five processes, namely, planning, organising, leading, co-ordinating and controlling. Management is basically an organisation activity, the organisation of work and resources, to achieve success. The successful organisation of work and resources requires careful planning. Effective planning involves foresight of the potential obstacles and readiness to fight them. It is important to head the team and guide the team members on their way to success. While organising and leading a group of people, management plays a vital role in the achievement of co-ordination and the exercise of control.

Management is such a vast subject that it becomes difficult to restrict the definition of management to a few processes. Management is complex and critical and hence it is not right to confine its description to some management processes. Believing in the vastness of this subject, some prefer defining management as 'all that managers do'. But what does a manager do? A manager is responsible for the successful implementation of management skills. A good manager needs to adhere to the basic management principles and exhibit the basic management skills in his/her personality.

The management literature is filled with lists of attributes, behaviours, orientations, and strategies for enhancing successful performance. For example, Pfeffer identified seven key practices associated with managerial and organisational effectiveness: ensure employment security, selectively hire people, foster decentralisation and self-managing teams, institute high levels of pay based on performance, train extensively, reduce status differences and share information. Quinn identified eight "seeds" of effective management and leadership: "envision the productive community," "first look within," "embrace the hypocritical self," "transcend fear," "embody a vision of the common good," "disturb the system," "surrender to the emergent process," "entice through moral power." An international study of 6052 managers from 22 countries focused on differences in managerial attributes and identified attributes such as inspirational, self-sacrificial, integrity, diplomatic, malevolent, visionary. administrative, self-centered, status conscious, autocratic, modest, and autonomous attributes.

According to top managers in North America, Europe, and Asia. the tools associated with organisation success were: strategic planning, pay for performance, strategic alliances, customer satisfaction measurement, shareholder value analysis, mission and vision statements, benchmarking, cycle time reduction, agile strategies, self-directed teams, and groupware.

These kinds of lists are useful, but they do not identify management *skills* per se. Instead they enumerate organisational strategies, personality orientations, or philosophical approaches to management, and their implementation is usually outside the explicit control of the individual manager. Either they are complex sets of activities in which many people must be involved—for example, "ensuring employment security," "selectively hiring," or "shareholder value analysis"—or they are cognitive activities that are not behavioural in character—for example, "envisioning the productive community," "first looking within," or "avoiding malevolence." Some of the lists enumerate personality characteristics or styles—for example, inspirational, or autocratic—or they enumerate organisational practices—for example, pay for performance, or strategic planning.

The effectiveness of the attributes on these kinds of lists depends on the manager's skill in implementing them, and that means being competent in fundamental management skills. Management skills form the vehicle by which management strategy, management practice, tools and techniques, personality attributes, and style work to produce effective outcomes in organisations. Management skills, in other words, are the building blocks upon which effective management rests. Management skills are the means by which managers translate their own style, strategy, and favourite tools or techniques into practice.

These management skills have recently been included in the concept of *emotional intelligence*. Emotional intelligence (or *EQ)*, according to Goleman, consists of the skills of self-awareness, selfregulation or self-control, motivation, the ability to understand others' emotional and behavioural cues (empathy), and interpersonal skills. Unlike cognitive intelligence (IQ), which remains largely the same throughout life, EQ can be developed and improved over time with concerted effort. In fact, emotional intelligence in managers has been found to be a significant predictor of organisational success in several studies.

Managerial Characteristics and Practices

Several defining characteristics demarcate management skills and differentiate them from other kinds of managerial characteristics and practices. First, management skills are *behavioural*. They are not personality attributes or stylistic tendencies. Management skills consist of identifiable sets of actions that individuals perform and that lead to certain outcomes. Skills can be observed by others, unlike attributes that are purely mental or are embedded in personality. Whereas people with different styles and personalities may apply the skills differently, there are, nevertheless, a core set of observable attributes in effective skill performance that are common across a range of individual differences.

Second, management skills are *controllable*. The performance of these behaviours is under the control of the individual. Unlike organisational practices such as "selectively hiring," or cognitive activities such as "transcending fear," skills can be consciously demonstrated, practised, improved, or restrained by individuals themselves. Skills may certainly engage other people and require cognitive work, but they are behaviours that people can control themselves.

Third, management skills are *developable*. Performance can improve. Unlike IQ or certain personality or temperament attributes that remain relatively constant throughout life, individuals can improvement their competency in skill performance through practice and feedback.

Fourth, management skills are *interrelated and overlapping*. It is difficult to demonstrate just one skill in isolation from others. Skills are not simplistic, repetitive behaviours, but they are integrated sets of complex responses. Effective managers, in particular, must rely on combinations of skills to achieve desired results. For example, in order to effectively motivate others, skills such as supportive communication, influence, empowerment, and self-awareness may be required. Effective managers, in other words, develop a constellation of skills that overlap and support one another and that allow flexibility in managing diverse situations.

Fifth, management skills are sometimes *contradictory or paradoxical*. For example, the core management skills are neither all soft and humanistic in orientation nor all hard-driving and directive. They are oriented neither toward teamwork and interpersonal relations exclusively nor toward individualism and technical entrepreneurship exclusively. A variety of skills are typical of the most effective managers, and some of them appear incompatible.

Basic Management Skills

Management thinkers have time and again stated the immense value of able managers and leaders for the success of a firm. Managers equipped with right sets of managerial skills and qualities motivate employees to give their best. Managerial skills are sets of qualities and attributes in the personality of managers that enable them to effectively manage the working of a firm. Good managerial skills can create a world of difference in the efficiency and performance of a firm. Discussed below are some of the most important management skills that are required in today's managers.

Leadership

This is one of the most important management skills. Leadership comprises of the efficient organisation of the resources in achieving a company goal. Leadership involves the management of human resources with an assessment of the strengths and weaknesses of each member of the team. It is about leading the people and guiding them towards the accomplishment of a common goal. Leadership includes a just allocation of work to the resources, planning of the implementation of tasks assigned and helping the team with task completion.

Team Building

This is another basic management skill that includes dealing with people, the most important asset of an organisation. Encouraging the team members to speak up, come up with ideas and allowing them to make mistakes and learn from them can be described as a team building skill. To build a team, one needs to foster the team spirit in all of the team members. For the team to feel motivated to work, it is important for a manager to cater to their expectations, recognise their strengths and understand where they lack. The building of a team is about building the team spirit in members and maintaining it. The skill lies in knowing the team and encouraging them to take initiative and enthusiastically participate in every venture of the company.

Communication and Presentation Skills

After having achieved the knowledge of a certain domain and on having imbibed the technical skills and more importantly self-confidence needed to be a manager, what one may lack are the soft skills, which are equally important in management. The soft skills encompass the communication and presentation skills. A manager should be open to his/her team. A manager should be able to accept constructive criticism. It is important for the manager to communicate his/her plans to the team and accept the team members' inputs on the plan of action. Communication is a two-way activity and for it to remain so, a manager needs to possess listening skills. They help a manager understand his/her team members, invite their participation and earn their regard. Good presentation skills help a manager impressively communicate with the team. 'How you communicate?' is as important as 'what you communicate?' So, the presentation skills definitely matter.

Decision-making Skill

Many a time, quick decisions have to be made. In such cases it becomes necessary for a manager to grasp the situation, think about what can be done and thoughtfully analyse the consequences of the decision to be made. A problem-solving approach is also considered as one of the basic management skills. To look at a situation analytically, one needs to bear a problem-solving approach. One needs to reason every consequence and come up with the pros and cons of the decision. A manager needs to be a quick thinker. For taking the right decision, one cannot afford to panic. One has to keep his/her cool, be aware of the results of the decisions and be prepared for them. A manager can get opportunities to celebrate a business success. But it is equally probable that a manager is forced to handle the consequences of a wrong decision. Hence while it is necessary to distinguish between the 'right' and the 'wrong', it is also necessary to be ready to accept the 'wrongs' and deal with them.

Management Skills in Changing World

Change is just too rapid and ubiquitous. The development of "nanobombs" have caused some people to predict that personal computers and desk top monitors will land on the scrap heap of obsolesce within 20 years. The new computers will be a product of teachings on molecules leading to personalised data processors injected in the bloodstream, implanted in eyeglasses, or included in wristwatches. Predictions of the changes that will occur in the future are often notoriously wrong, of course, as illustrated by Charles Watson's (founder of IBM) prediction that only a few dozen computers would ever be needed in the entire world, Thomas Edison's prediction that the light bulb would never catch on, or Irving Fisher's (preeminent Yale economist) prediction in 1929 that the stock market had reached "a permanently high plateau." When Neil Armstrong walked on the moon in 1969, most people predicted that we would soon be walking on Mars, establishing colonies in outer space, and launching probes from lunar pads. In 1973 with gas lines escalating due to an OPEC-led fuel crisis, economists predicted that gasoline would sell for $100 a barrel in the United States by 1980. At the beginning of the century, the figure was around $25. Most notorious of all, of course, was the prediction by the United States patent office in 1896 that it would soon close its doors since "everything that can be invented has been invented."

Warren Bennis half-jokingly predicted that the factory of the future would have only two employees, a person and a dog. The person would be there to feed the dog. The dog would be there to keep the person from touching the equipment! Tom Peters counselled managers that, due to the chaotic pace of change, "If you're not confused, you're not paying attention." And Peter Drucker characterised the current environment this way: "We are in one of those great historical periods that occur every 200 or 300 years when people don't understand the world anymore, and the past is not sufficient to explain the future." Almost no one would argue that "permanent white water" best characterises our current environment.

Despite all this change in our environment, there is something that has remained, and continues to remain, relatively constant. With minor variations and stylistic differences, what has not changed, in several thousand years, are the basic skills that lie at the heart of effective, satisfying, growth-producing human relationships. Freedom, dignity, trust, love, and honesty in relationships have always been among the goals of human beings, and the same principles that brought about those outcomes in the 11th century still bring them about in the 21st century. In fact, human relationships are becoming more important, not less, as the information age unfolds and technologies encroach even more on our daily lives. Most of us are exposed to more information each day than we can possibly pay attention to. Moreover, no mechanism exists to organise, prioritise, or interpret that information, so it is often unclear what is crucial and what can be ignored. Consequently, the relationship we have with the sources of that information is the key sensemaking mechanism. Building trusting relationships is a critical part of coping with information overload.

It is a fact that when everything is changing, change becomes unmanageable. No one can manage constant, unorganised change. Think of being a pilot on an airplane. Everything is changing—he entire plane is in constant motion—as the plane moves through the air. Unless you can fix on something that is not changing—for example, the ground or the stars—it is impossible to fly the plane. Tragically, investigators found that John F. Kennedy Jr. unknowingly flew his plane into the Atlantic Ocean killing himself, his wife, and his sister-in-law because he lost sight of land and, consequently, lost perspective. He became unable to manage change because he did not have an established, unwavering point that helped him maintain his bearings.

We make sense of change by being able to identify a fixed, stable, permanent point that provides us with perspective. And their relationship to effective human and organisational performance has been well-documented. Later in this Introduction we share some of the scientific research that confirms the power of these management skills in accounting for effective personal, interpersonal, and organisational performance.

The problem, of course, is that what is known is not always the same as what is demonstrated. Although we have known about the principles of effective relationships for a very long time, the history of humankind illustrates that these principles have not always been practised. Especially in our current day, what we know and what we demonstrate do not always match. George Carlin described it this way:

> The paradox of our time in history is that we have taller buildings but shorter tempers, wider freeways but narrower viewpoints. We spend more but have less; we buy more but enjoy it less. We have bigger houses and smaller families, more conveniences but less time. We have more degrees but less sense; more knowledge but less judgment; more experts but more problems; more medicine but less wellness. We drink too much, smoke too much, spend too recklessly, laugh too little, drive too fast, get too angry too quickly, stay up too late, get too tired, read too seldom, watch TV too much, and pray too seldom. We have multiplied our possessions, but reduced our values. We talk too much, love too seldom, and hate too often. We have learned how to make a living but not a life; we've added years to life but not life to years. We've been all the way to the moon and back but have trouble crossing the street to meet the new neighbour. We've conquered outer space but not inner space. We've done larger things but not better things. We've cleaned up the air but polluted the soul. We've split the atom but not our prejudice. We write more but learn less. We plan more but accomplish less. We've learned to rush but not to wait. We build more computers to hold more information to produce more copies than ever but have less communication. These

> are the times of fast foods and slow digestion; tall men and short character; steep profits and shallow relationships. These are the times of world peace but domestic warfare; more leisure but less fun; more kinds of food but less nutrition. These are the days of two incomes but more divorce, of fancier houses but broken homes. These are the days of quick trips, disposable diapers, throwaway morality, one-night stands, overweight bodies, and pills that do everything from cheer to quiet to kill. It is a time when there is much in the show window and nothing in the stockroom; a time when technology can bring this letter to you, and a time when you can choose either to share this insight, or just hit delete.

Developing management skills—the skills needed to manage one's own life as well as relationships with others—is a ceaseless endeavour. These skills were largely the same a century ago as they are today. The basic behavioural principles that lie at the foundation of these skills are timeless. That is one reason why the shelves of bookstores and on-line newsletters are filled with prescriptions of how one more executive or one more company struck it rich or beat out the competition. Thousands of books trumpet some special set of prescriptions for how to be successful in business, or in life. Many of these books have made it to the best seller lists and have enjoyed lengthy stays.

Importance of Competent Managers

In the last decade or so, an abundance of evidence has been produced that skilful management— especially those competent in the management of people in organisations—is *the* key determinant of organisational success. These studies have been conducted across numerous industry sectors, international settings, and organisation types. The research findings now make it almost unquestionable that if organisations want to succeed, they must have competent, skilful managers.

For example, in one study of 968 firms, representing all major industries in the United States, organisations whose managers effectively managed their people—that is they implemented effective people management strategies and demonstrated personal competency in management skills—had, on the average, a decrease in turnover of more than 7 percent, increased profits of $3814 per employee, $27,044 more in sales per employee, and $18,641 more in stockmarket value per employee, compared to firms that had less effective people management. In a follow-up study of 702 firms, shareholder wealth was an amazing $41,000 per employee higher in companies demonstrating strong people management skills than in firms that had a lower emphasis on people management. A study of German firms in 10 industrial sectors, produced similar results: "Companies that place workers at the core of their strategies produce higher long-term returns...than their industry peers". A study of 5-year survivability in 136 non-financial companies that issued IPOs in the late 1980s found that the effective management of people was the most significant factor in predicting longevity, even when accounting for industry type, size, and profits. Firms that did a good job of managing people tended to survive; others did not.

A study by Hanson investigated the factors that best accounted for financial success over a five year span in 40 major manufacturing firms. The question being addressed was: "What explains the financial success of the firms that are highly effective?" The five most powerful predictors were identified and assessed. They included market share (assuming that the higher the market share of a firm, the higher its profitability), firm capital intensity (assuming that the more a firm is automated and up-to-date in technology and equipment, the more profitable it is), size of the firm in assets (assuming that economies of scale and efficiency can be used in large firms to increase profitability), industry average return on sales (assuming that firms would reflect the performance of a highly profitable industry), and the ability of managers to effectively manage their people (assuming that an emphasis on good people management helps produce profitability in firms). The results revealed that one factor—the ability to manage people effectively—was three times more powerful than all other factors combined in accounting for firm financial success over a five-year period! We repeat, good management was more important than all other factors taken together in predicting profitability.

Even research by the U.S. Government confirms this management-effectiveness link. The U.S. Office of the Controller of the Currency studied the reasons for the failures of national banks in the United States during the decade of the 1980s. Two major factors were found to account for the record number of bank failures during that period: distressed economic conditions and poor management. The relative impact of those two factors, however, was somewhat surprising. Almost 90 percent of the failed banks were judged to have had poor management. Only 35 percent of the failures had experienced depressed economic conditions in the region in which they operated, and in only 7 percent of the cases was a depressed economic condition the sole cause of bank failure.

Dramatic anecdotal evidence also abounds regarding the impact of effective management on workers and organisations. One of the most notable, for example, was the General Motors automobile assembly plant in Fremont, California. The plant was built in the 1950s and, at the beginning of the 1980s, was assembling the Chevrolet Nova model. The plant had a history of labour and productivity problems, however, and by the end of 1982 the performance statistics were dismal. Absenteeism was running at 20 percent. The number of formal grievances filed by employees totalled almost 5,000 (an average of more than 20 grievances per day for every workday of the year), and over 2,000 grievances were still unresolved at year's end. An average of three to four wildcat strikes per year had occurred during the previous few years, and morale, productivity, and quality of production by the 5,000 employees were the worst in the corporation. Costs of assembling the automobile were about 30 percent above the Asian competitors. In light of these data, corporate headquarters issued an order to close the plant and lay off the workers.

Three years later, General Motors signed a joint operating agreement with one of its major competitors: Toyota Motors. Much had been written about the Japanese method of managing, so General Motors asked Toyota to reopen and manage the Fremont plant. Most of the former U.S. autoworkers were rehired, and a new management team was put in place. Workers were exposed to training in high involvement work practices, and a former Ford Motor Company employee actually became the plant manager. The primary difference between the plant before it closed and after it reopened was that a new management team was in place and employee training had occurred. The workforce, in other words, remained essentially unchanged. One year after reopening, the organisation's performance data looked like this:

Absenteeism: 2 percent
Grievances: 2 outstanding
Strikes: None
Employees: 2,500 (producing 20 percent more cars)
Productivity: Highest in the corporation
Quality: Highest in the corporation
Costs: Equal to those of the competition
Product: Geo Prism—rated AAA's best car in its price range

The remarkable thing about this turnaround is that it did not take five or 10 years to produce major improvements in productivity, cohesion, and commitment. It occurred in just over a year simply by changing the way workers were managed.

These studies indicate overwhelmingly that good management fosters financial success, whereas less effective management fosters financial distress. Successful organisations have managers with well-developed people management skills. In surveys of CEOs, executives, and business owners, results consistently show that the factor most responsible for business failure is "bad management" and the best way to ensure business success is to "provide better management." Moreover, the data are clear, management skills are more important than industry, environment, competition, and economic factors combined.

Surprisingly, however, finding people who effectively manage people is not as common as might be expected. Pfeffer & Veiga concluded that: "Even as these research results pile up, trends in actual management practice are, in many instances, moving in a direction exactly opposite to what this growing body of evidence prescribes." Common sense and common knowledge are not necessarily common practice. Knowing and doing are not the same things. Being able to analyse a case, identify a problem, or recite a correct answer to a question is not equivalent to being able to actually implement effective management skills.

Improving Management Skills

It is a bit unnerving that while average IQ scores have increased in the population over the last halfcentury, emotional intelligence scores have actually declined. In the population in general, people are less skilled at managing themselves and managing others than they were 50 years ago. While average IQ scores have jumped approximately 25 points, EQ among young people and adults has fallen. Moreover, whereas the "technological float" has shrunk dramatically—that is, the time between the introduction of a new technology and its being copied and revised is constantly decreasing and is now measured in weeks rather than years—the "human float" has changed very little. It still takes about the same amount of time to develop behavioural skills and human competencies as it always has. No short-cuts or quick fixes have emerged, and the effort and practice that are required to become more emotionally intelligent and interpersonally skilled is substantial. Progress regarding how to cope with and manage issues relating to other people has not kept pace with technological progress, and it remains the biggest challenge for managers.

The good news is that improvement in developing management skills has been found in both students and managers who have been exposed to a curriculum such as the one advocated in *Developing Management Skills*. For example, MBA students showed improvement of from 50 to 300 percent on emotional intelligence skills over the course of two years by enrolling in two courses based on the approach to developing management skills presented here. A greater amount of improvement occurred among students who applied these skills to multiple aspects of their lives outside the classroom, and people who were more competent to begin with made the most progress. In addition, a cohort of 45 to 55 year old executives produced the same results as the MBA students. That is, they also improved dramatically in their management skills even though most were already experienced in senior managerial positions.

On the other hand, exposure to a traditional cognitive-based curriculum without exposure to management skills development does not correlate with improvements in EQ, management skills, or career success. For example, Cohen summarised the results of 108 studies of the relationship between performance in college courses (as measured by grade-point average) and subsequent life success. Life success was measured by a variety of factors, including job performance, income, promotions, personal satisfaction, eminence, and graduate degrees.

The mean correlation between performance in school and performance in life in these studies was.18, and in no case did the correlation exceed.20. These low correlations suggest that school performance and successful performance in subsequent life activities are related only marginally.

The data, in other words, appear quite compelling. Attending school merely to achieve high grades in cognitive courses, while important, is not sufficient for management, career, or life success. Going into debt for a formal education or achieving an additional set of letters behind your name without also developing and improving your management skills will be an unfortunate lost opportunity. That is why we feel so strongly that in the management curriculum of universities, students should be exposed to a learning model such as the one we describe here.

An Approach to Skill Development

Successful management development, of course, is more than just following a cookbook list of sequential behaviours. Developing highly competent management skills is much more complicated than developing skills such as those associated with a trade (for example, welding) or a sport (for example, shooting baskets). Management skills are linked to a more complex knowledge base than other types of skills and inherently connected to interaction with other (frequently unpredictable) individuals. A standardised approach to welding or shooting free throws may be feasible, but no standardised approach to managing human beings is possible.

On the other hand, what all skills do have in common is the potential for improvement through practice. Any approach to developing management skills, therefore, must involve a heavy dose of practical application. At the same time, practice without the necessary conceptual knowledge is sterile and ignores the need for flexibility and adaptation to different situations. Therefore, developing competencies in management skills is inherently tied to both conceptual learning and behavioural practice.

The method that has been found to be most successful in helping individuals develop management skills is based on social learning theory. This approach marries rigorous conceptual knowledge with opportunities to practice and apply observable behaviours. It relies on cognitive work as well as behavioural work. Variations on this general approach have been used widely in on-the-job supervisory training programs, and they are common in executive education programs and corporate universities—less so in business schools.

This learning model, as originally formulated, consisted of four steps:

(1) the presentation of behavioural principles or action guidelines, generally using traditional instruction methods;

(2) demonstration of the principles by means of cases, films, scripts, or incidents;

(3) opportunities to practice the principles through role plays or exercises; and

(4) feedback on performance from peers, instructors, or experts (Figure 1).

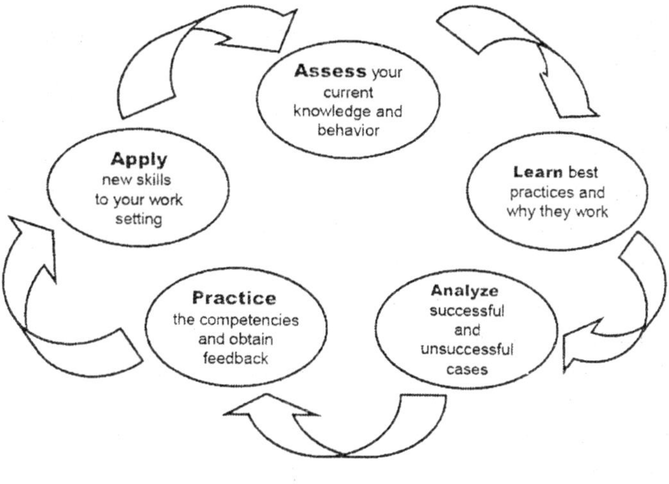

Figure 1. Developing Managerial and Leadership Competencies: The Learning Model

Our own experience in teaching complex management skills, as well as recent research on management skills development among MBA students has convinced us that three important modifications are necessary in order for this model to be most effective. First, the behavioural principles must be grounded in social science theory and in reliable research results. Commonsense generalisations and panacea-like prescriptions appear regularly in the popular management literature. To ensure the validity of the behavioural guidelines being prescribed, the learning approach must include scientifically based knowledge about the effects of the management principles being presented.

Second, individuals must be aware of their current level of skill competency and be motivated to improve upon that level in order to benefit from the model. Most people receive very little feedback about their current level of skill competency. Most organisations provide some kind of annual or semiannual evaluation (for example, course grades in school or performance appraisal interviews in firms), but these evaluations are almost always infrequent and narrow in scope, and they fail to assess performance in most critical skill areas. To help a person understand what skills to improve and why, therefore, an assessment activity must be part of the model. In addition, most people find change uncomfortable and therefore avoid taking the risk to develop new behaviour patterns. An assessment activity in the learning model helps encourage these people to change by illuminating their strengths and weaknesses. People then know where weaknesses lie and what things need to be improved. Assessment activities generally take the form of self-evaluation instruments, case studies, or problems that help highlight personal strengths and weaknesses in a particular skill area.

Third, an application component is needed in the learning model. Most management skill training takes place in a classroom setting where feedback is immediate, and it is relatively safe to try out new behaviours and make mistakes. Therefore, transferring learning to an actual job setting is often problematic. Application exercises help to apply classroom learning to examples from the real world of management. Application exercises often take the form of an outside-of-class intervention, a consulting assignment, self-analysis through journal writing, or a problem-centered intervention, which the student then analyses to determine its degree of success or failure.

In summary, evidence suggests that a five-step learning model is most effective for helping individuals develop management skills.

Table 1 outlines such a model. Step 1 involves the *assessment* of current levels of skill competency and knowledge of the behavioural principles. Step 2 consists of the presentation of validated, scientifically based *principles and guidelines* for effective skill performance. Step 3 is an *analysis* step in which models or cases are made available in order to analyse behavioural principles in real organisational settings. This step also helps demonstrate how the behavioural guidelines can be adapted to different personal styles and circumstances. Step 4 consists of *practice* exercises in which experimentation can occur and immediate feedback can be received in a relatively safe environment. Step 5, finally, is the *application* of the skill to a real-life setting outside the classroom with follow-up analysis of the relative success of that application.

Table 1. A Model for Developing Management Skills

Components	*Contents*	*Objectives*
1. Skill assessment	Survey instruments Role plays	Assess current level of skill competence and knowledge; create readiness to change.
2. Skill learning	Written text Behavioural guidelines	Teach correct principles and present a rationale for behavioural guidelines.
3. Skill analysis	Cases	Provide examples of appropriate and inappropriate skill performance. Analyse behavioural principles and reasons they work.
4. Skill practice	Exercises Simulations Role plays	Practice behavioural guidelines. Adapt principles to personal style. Receive feedback and assistance.
5. Skill application	Assignments (behavioural and written)	Transfer classroom learning to real-life situations. Foster ongoing personal development.

Research on the effectiveness of training programs using this general learning model has shown that it produces results superior to those based on more traditional lecture-discussion-case method approaches. In addition, evidence suggests that management skill training can have significant impact on the bottom-line performance of a firm. The U.S. Postal Service completed a study a few years ago in which 49 of the largest 100 post offices in America were evaluated. An important question in the study was, "How can we make post offices more effective?" Productivity and service quality were both monitored over a period of five years. The two major factors that had impact on these effectiveness measures were (1) degree of automation, and (2) investment in training. Two kinds of training were provided: technical training (operating and maintaining the equipment) and management training (developing management skills). The study found that management training was more important than technical training in accounting for improved productivity and service in the post offices, and both kinds of training were more important than having up-to-date equipment in the post office. Low-tech offices outperformed high-tech offices when managers were provided with management skill training. In short, its five-year study convinced the U.S. Postal Service that helping employees to develop management skills was the best way to improve organisational effectiveness. This is consistent with the conclusion drawn by Eric Greenberg, Director of Surveys for the American Management Association, upon summarising the lessons learned from years of surveys of American managers:

> "Where companies increased their training activity, the chances were much, much better that they were going to increase their operating profits and that they were going to increase their shareholder value. Product quality, market share, and productivity all tend to rise as training budgets go up. Companies that don't make the investment are apt to see disappointing results."

More than a quarter century ago, Mintzberg made a similar point about the curriculum needed in business schools. Things have not changed.

> Management schools will begin the serious training of managers when skill training takes its place next to cognitive learning. Cognitive learning is detached and informational, like reading a book or listening to a lecture. No doubt much important cognitive material must be assimilated by the manager-to-be. But cognitive learning no more makes a manager than it does a swimmer. The latter will drown the first time he jumps into the water if his coach never takes him out of the lecture hall, gets him wet, and gives him feedback on his performance.

A senior executive in a major consulting firm similarly observed:

> The higher up the organisation you go, the less relevant technical knowledge becomes. It is important for your first couple of promotions, but after that, people skills are what count.

A recent graduate from a Big Ten management school also reported:

> I can't believe it. I went for my second interview with a company last week, and I spent the first half-day participating in simulation exercises with ten other job candidates. They video-taped me playing the role of a salesman handling an irate customer, a new director of personnel putting down a revolt by the "old guard," and a plant manager trying to convince people of the need to install a radically new production process. Boy, was I unprepared for that!

The message behind these personal observations is clear: from almost every perspective, competence in personal, interpersonal, and group skills is a critical prerequisite for success in management. Strong analytical and quantitative skills are important, but they are not sufficient. Successful managers must be able to work effectively with people. Unfortunately, interpersonal and management skills have not always been a high priority for business school students and aspiring executives.

Leadership and Management

One of the most popular models of leadership is based on the "*Competing Values Framework,*" an organising framework for leadership and managerial skills. It was developed by examining the criteria used to evaluate organisational and managerial performance. Extensive research has been conducted on this framework over the past two decades, and a brief explanation will help clarify the relationship between management and leadership skills. You should be aware that the framework has been used on several continents to help managers and organisations improve their effectiveness, and a data base of more than 40,000 managers has now been compiled. In order to be an effective manager, in other words, individuals must be competent in (1) clan skills, (2) adhocracy skills, (3) market skills, and (4) hierarchy skills.

Clan skills include those required to build effective interpersonal relationships and develop others (e.g., building teamwork, communicating supportively). Adhocracy skills include those required to manage the future, innovate, and promote change (e.g., solving problems creatively, articulating an energising vision). Market skills include those required to compete effectively and manage external relationships (e.g., motivating others, using power and influence). Hierarchy skills include those required to maintain control and stability (e.g., managing personal stress and time, solving problems rationally).

In Figure 1, the two top quadrants in the Competing Values Framework—clan and adhocracy—are usually associated with leadership. The two bottom quadrants—market and hierarchy—are usually associated with management. In other words leadership has traditionally been used to describe what individuals do under conditions of change. When organisations are dynamic and undergoing transformation, people at the top are expected to exhibit leadership (i.e., pay attention to clan and adhocracy issues). Management, on the other hand, has traditionally been used to describe what executives do under conditions of stability. Thus, management has been linked with the status quo (i.e., pay attention to market and hierarchy issues). In addition, leadership has sometimes been defined as "doing the right things," whereas management has been defined as "doing things right." Leaders have been said to focus on setting the direction, articulating a vision, transforming individuals and organisations, and creating something new. Managers have been said to focus on monitoring, directing, and refining current performance. Leadership has been equated with dynamism, vibrancy, and charisma; management with hierarchy, equilibrium, and control.

However, the recent research is clear that such distinctions between leadership and management, which may have been appropriate in previous decades, are no longer useful. Managers cannot be successful without being good leaders, and leaders cannot be successful without being good managers. No longer do organisations and individuals have the luxury of holding on to the status quo; worrying about doing things right but failing to do the right things; keeping the system stable instead of leading change and improvement; monitoring current performance instead of formulating a vision of the future; concentrating on equilibrium and control instead of vibrancy and charisma. Effective management and leadership are inseparable.

The skills required to do one are also required of the other. No organisation in a post-industrial, hyper-turbulent, 21st century environment will survive without executives capable of providing both management and leadership.

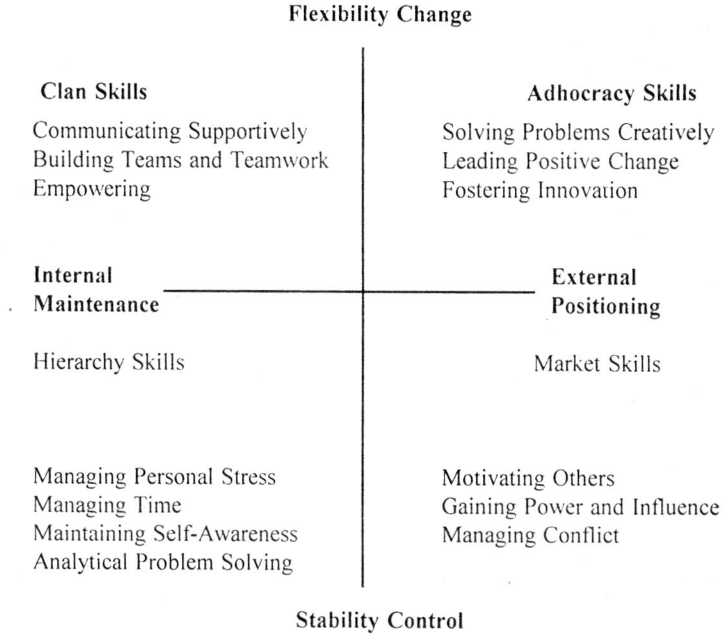

Figure 2. Leadership and Management Skills Organised by the Competing Values

Leading change and managing stability, establishing vision and accomplishing objectives, breaking the rules and monitoring conformance, although paradoxical, all are required to be successful. Figure 2 illustrates one major reason for this assertion. By staying the same, we tend to get worse.

Managerial Skills and Knowledge in Management

Various experts describe today's global economy as one in transformation to knowledge economy. Information systems and information technology have become at the beginning of the 21st century the most important factors for economy functioning in developed countries. However, it is not only the information systems and information technology, but actually working with information itself, which convey the change of thinking and creation of value in modern approaches to business and management.

These changes are reflected in current economy. The utilisation of resources is being shifted from current capital strategic resources to strategic resources in the form of information, knowledge, creative thinking and innovation. Skills and knowledge belong to critical factors of production. Enterprises can gain competitive advantage by implementing continual and on-going innovations and the managerial skills and knowledge are in the centre of this process of innovations.

Many times these facts are underestimated by small entrepreneurs and overlooked by support programs for development of this size of entrepreneurship. Small enterprises, as part of small and medium enterprises (SME), form considerable part of state economy and they are also considered an important source for development of economy. Development and support programs for small enterprise should also focus on the area to help of skills and knowledge.

Whether these assertions are justified and the neglect of managerial skills by small enterprises affects their success are the questions which we would like to cover in this contribution.

Level of Management of Small Enterprises

Small enterprises are part of larger category of small enterprises and medium enterprises. They all together form 98.8% of all companies in European Union. They are considered to be the engine for society development. Because of higher flexibility they can achieve competitive prices when manufacturing smaller batches. Small and medium enterprises (SMEs) play significant part in employment and professional training of young people. Compared to big companies, they employ more women, young people and part-time employees. SMEs are closely connected with the region than large employers and therefore have significant influence on further the region's development. Fiscal decentralisation of the regions of Slovakia creates pressure on municipalities and mayors, who must pay a closer look on actual needs of all employers doing business in the particular region.

Only this ways the mayors can secure loyalty of these employers and support them in their business. SMEs as the largest employer have gained in this new view considerable influence on decisions regarding their actual needs.

In the transitive economies like in Slovakia, there is relatively smaller share of small and medium enterprises. Government efforts are trying to speed up the change of the size structure with various support programs and instruments.

Recently, the most significant changes that influenced the business environment are:

— establishment of new tax system – flat tax of 19%
— speeding up of the procedures needed to start business
— change from defined benefit to defined contribution pension plans
— slight improvement of communication with tax offices

Although the growth of gross domestic product shows record values and there is improvement of business environment, situation of Slovak business environment is still neither easy nor ideal.

Problems of Small Enterprises

Several conducted researches prove that there is a range of problems with small and medium enterprises. Based on studies in USA, there is a prevailing notion that "small enterprises simply do not work." Even though there are conditions for entrepreneurship and new enterprises are established, the rate of failure is on high level too. "Within any given year, close to one million small enterprises are founded. Sadly, at least 40% of those businesses fail within the first year. The failure rate over time is nothing short of staggering. Of the one million started the given year, more than 800,000 (80%) of them will be out of business within 5 years and 96% will have closed their doors before their 10th birthday" says Michael Gerber. Is small entrepreneurship too risky? Is there a way to be in business with small enterprise and succeed?

The results of empirical studies of small enterprises show that failure and bankruptcy of enterprise is caused more by internal problems inside the enterprise rather then by outside generated problems. Small enterprises do not create enough force to survive and overcome daily problems in the long run.

Same experiences gained Gerber from his own consultancy practice, who coined the following entrepreneurial myth: „The fatal assumption is – you understand the technical work of a business, you understand a business that does that technical work “.

Gerber points out to the fact, that small enterprises are mostly founded by technicians, specialists or professional in certain field. For example, an accountant or a carpenter “know their onions” but have little information and experience in the field of management. They can perform their work on professional level, but seldom do they entrust their enterprise in the hands of manager, or try to acquire this knowledge by themselves. They run into problems with management of their enterprise because they concentrate all attention just to their specialised field of expertise. The management and managerial skills are neglected.

Similar results come out of Slovak study, where the second most significant reason of not wanting to be in business were missing skills and experience needed for conducting a business.

Knowledge in Management

Basic knowledge in management is needed at initial stage of running an enterprise and also later during the development stage. At the beginning, the management of the enterprise is carried out by the sole founder/owner, who must perform all the actions needed with doing the business. Crises occur when the enterprise is successfully expanding and the entrepreneur is not capable of running it due to lack of needed knowledge and managerial skills. Initially entrepreneur devoted to the enterprise to much of own energy and later on simply “runs out of breath”. With this attitude he/she can not cover all areas of the enterprise, i.e. due to the enterprise expansion. He/she lacks needed managerial knowledge and skills of running and further developing the enterprise.

Manager of the enterprise should be generalist and gain basic skills and knowledge in managerial functions such as planning, organising, leading and controlling. Manager also should have an overview of finance, marketing and market development, competitions and so on. If he/she does not pay enough attention to these issues, eventually he/she can not delegate responsibility for particular areas and will fail under the burden of undiscovered and emerging problems. These areas become with the growth of enterprise more complex and intricate and demand more attention.

Baldwin summarised these areas, which should be in attention for the small enterprises:

- insufficient use of consultancy services
- lack of quality
- unwillingness to delegate responsibilities
- key personnel leaving the enterprise
- personal issues concerning the owner/manager

These problems become more important factors causing failure of small enterprises, mainly as the enterprise grew older. According to Baldwin's research, enormous number of bankrupt enterprises – 71% answered that one most significant internal factor for bankruptcy was lack of general and financial management knowledge.

The inadequate level of management together with the missing market for the product causes the failure of enterprise. Managers do not have enough experience, knowledge or vision how to run the enterprise. Even though the managers gain experience with the growth of the enterprise, knowledge and vision remain in shortage and that causes the enterprise to fail.

Managerial abilities, Roles and Skills

Being manager is not an easy task due to the work with the people. From all production factors people are the most intricate to manage. Not everybody feels at ease in managing people. Nonetheless, there are certain personal abilities, which can predict the future efficiency and success of manager. Scholars from Faculty of management in Slovakia tried to identify necessary abilities, roles and skills managers should possessed:

- *Creativity* – ability to search and find new solutions
- *Intuition* – be able to predict future development from own experience without analysis
- *Goal-oriented* – be able to set real goals and respect the goal's hierarchy

- *Responsibility* – sense for achieving set goals and objectives
- *Self-confidence* – belief in own strength and ability to achieve goals
- *Initiative* – an effort to look for new possibilities and solutions for reaching set goals
- *Independence* – the courage to make decision based on own judgment
- *Cautiousness* – be able to make decision under stress and unsure conditions
- *Scrupulosity* - support social values and norms
- *Discipline* – self-control and regulation of own behaviour
- *Persistence* – tenacity needed to overcome barrier when achieving goals
- *Optimism* – orientation towards positive goals and things in connection with faith in success
- *Fantasy* – creation of visions and imaginations about future

Every man has hidden potential of certain kind inside. It is important how one can utilise this potential. Manager needs to use and influence behaviour of people around to reach the goals of the enterprise. In doing so manager use the managerial functions – planning, organising, leading and control; while "playing" the following roles in the enterprise :

- *Interpersonal roles* – Figurehead, Leader, Liaison
- *Information roles* – Monitor, Disseminator, Spokesperson
- *Decision making role* – Entrepreneur, Disturbance handler, Resource Allocator, Negotiator

In fulfilling their duties managers use managerial skills. These skills directly affect the results of the manager, but they can be learned and gained by training. The criteria for dividing the skills can vary but these are considered to be the basic managerial skills, which are needed for an effective managerial work:

- *Technical* – ability of manager to use specific methods and techniques in doing the managerial work. However these technical skills are not related to technology, such as skills of engineer. The technical skills for managers represent the usage of methods like break even analysis in planning or ability to prepare for and conduct a structured interview.

— *Interpersonal* – people are most valuable resource of any enterprise and manager needs to know how to lead people. Abilities include motivation of workers, solving work conflicts, communication and working with people. Therefore interpersonal skills are essential on every level of management.

— *Conceptual* – these skills are must for middle or top manager. This is the ability to "grasp the whole picture".

— *Communication* – manager needs information for decision making. Ability to disseminate and receive information is thus important tools for manager. It is not only verbal communication, but the manager should be able to distinguish non verbal signals, mood and feelings to filter the right information.

Technical/professional knowledge alone is certainly needed to make the "technical side" of doing the business work, but is not sufficient for successful development of the enterprise. The growth of small enterprise leads to new situation, which require managerial skills. Acquiring of managerial skills is not a simple task, because it means to apply theoretical knowledge into praxis. On one hand graduates from college miss the practical experience; on the other hand, the hard workers with long-term praxis many times have not yet covered new theoretical knowledge. Only by intersecting theoretical knowledge with experience from praxis it is possible to gain managerial skills.

These are the basic sets of skills of a manager, which might be hard to translate into some learning framework for small enterprises. At first it is necessary to point out that any attempt to identify universal key skills needed for small enterprises can not be complete and straightforward due to following reasons:

— The population of SMEs is vast and diverse (from small hot-dog stand to teenage millionaires)

— In connection to the size emerges the level of "development stage" – the older the enterprise gets, the more complex and sophisticated it becomes and there is need for a "better" skills set

— In connection to area of business – various types of industry have different needs for intensity of knowledge (old industrial vs. new knowledge economy)

But at least it is possible to outline how the small entrepreneurs should educate as their business grows in different phases of business development and point out the basis skills every manager should posses.

Phases of Development of Small Enterprises

Phases of development occur in every evolution and it seems intuitively acceptable. Newton says that the tradition goes back to Edith Penrose's classic The Theory of the Growth of the Firm. The phases can be summarised as follows:

— Pre start-up / actual start-up
— Survival
— First growth
— Expansion
— Global perspective

Pre start-up

The beginning of the life cycle is usually referred to as pre start-up. It is the period when many would-be entrepreneurs ponder about the possible marketability of their schemes or ideas. This pre start-up phase involves the initial consideration followed by the decision to go forwards or not. The case of positive answer requires exploration of recourses, opportunities and requirements followed by formulation of some guiding vision which is subsequently deciphered into business plan. This of course involves some assessment of the market for the would-be entrepreneur's product or service and a consideration of sources of financing.

The managerial skills, which these would-be entrepreneur posses, vary enormously at this phases. Some have formal management education like MBA, some may have years of practice and experience in particular field, yet other may have only idea or enthusiasm with no background experience. All of them will certainly develop their managerial skills set, although it will be clearly a various levels "of learning by doing". Working step by step with the business plan will reflect in better market understanding and chance of spotting opportunities, financial analysis will enhance financial literacy and so on. These early phases are important part of development but the entrepreneur will likely not get down to text-books to study the basics. Rather it will be self-searching wondering, checking whether I can do it, do I have the drive, ambition, vision or creativity?

Actual start-up

The following phase after pre start-up is typically the actual start-up. It might be a "spin off" from parent firm, university, government or private laboratory, or many times facilitated by small enterprises "incubator", which increases the change of survival.

Survival

Survival is the phase, where the basic management skills mixed with a "touch" of entrepreneurialism starts to kick in. A simple cash flow problem/mismanagement can burn down the most daring vision of any entrepreneur.

First growth

As the enterprise stays alive it moves to phase first growth. The enterprise needs to open to surrounding, let other people know it exists thus communicate on various levels with relevant stakeholders.

Expansion

The enterprise entered maturity. As it "grows up", it should start to take care of itself , otherwise he/she can "suffocate in diapers". In a given year, enterprises that used "Franchise format" have reported a success rate of 95 percent in contrast to almost 50 percent failure rate of enterprises who are owned independently. And where 80 percent of all enterprises fail in the first 5 years, 75 percent of enterprises using "Franchise format" succeed. Clearly there is advantage in replacing the former "cowboy" managing style with formalisation and creation of system of how things are done and should be dealt with.

Global perspective

After stabilising position in "home town or country" the vision is needed to determine which direction the enterprise should go. Seeing global perspective where export markets are the ocean in which the future glimpse will be a lighthouse towards which the enterprise can sail.

These individual phases represent the types and level of sophistication of the managerial skills at each development phase. It includes various components of the managerial skills set, such as finance, marketing, research, production and human resource.

This is simply a model based on empirical observation of sample enterprises. It provides some generalisation, but should not be taken as something strict and firm, rather just as a good "rule of thumb". In fact, the phases can overlap or merge. Some can be skipped; one enterprise can look for foreign market right from start, while other will create a solid home country foundation for future expansions on the first place.

Training for Small Entrepreneurs

Good idea, hard work, enthusiasm, qualification and knowledge in certain field are necessary to establish the new enterprise but not enough to run an enterprise. Gerber mentioned in his researches there should be three types of positions needed for running an enterprise:

— Technician

— Manager

— Entrepreneur

And so, there is need for three types of knowledge and further education for small entrepreneurs. If the person runs business on his own, he has to cover all areas – technical/professional, managerial and entrepreneurial. Most of the time, the founder educates his own just in the first one, to be professional in his field, to know the core of his business, how to produce the product or services.

But there is not necessity or even possibility to cover all these positions by one person. The first very important topic to learn is how to delegate. It is commonly known, that small entrepreneurs do not know how to delegate. Delegation is the hardest thing for most of the small enterprises owners. Sometimes is does not matter how the business grows and if new employees are hired, the owner does not like to trust and delegate the responsibilities to others. He/she likes to run all business on his/her own and carry all things by him/her self.

But delegation is a skill that is critical to business success and for a healthy work life balance. One person cannot do everything that needs to be done; he/she will get so busy and work will take over his/her personal life which causes personal unhappiness, stress and other problems.

Learn how to delegate should be priority if the owner wants to become a manager of his/her enterprise. It is the way how to do less to achieve more.

Training in Management

As the enterprise grows, there are different specific needs for managerial skills and knowledge. The need and range of different managerial skills depend on many factors and therefore an attempt to "craft" universal skill sets will never be perfect. One universal factor taken into account can be the development phase of the enterprise. Newton created a certain pyramids with different levels of managerial skills, based on his previous researches (Figure 3). These levels resemble the type of skills needed in different phases of development.

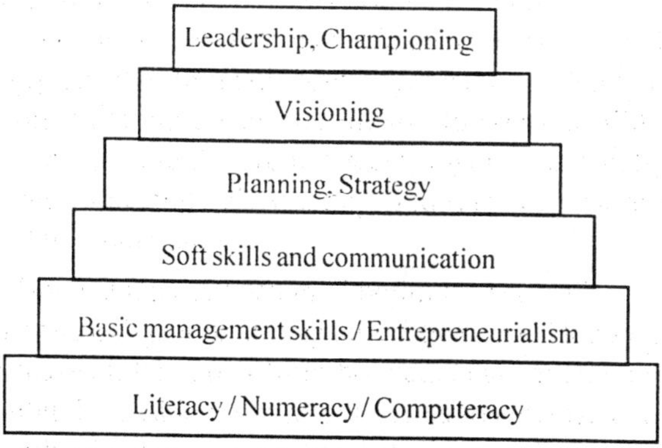

Figure 3. Pyramid of managerial skills

At the base of the pyramid is group of basic skills and competencies. At least basic "understanding" is needed in reading numbers (i.e. financial statements) and working with computer. It is hard to survive without them in knowledge economy. Many entrepreneurs include in these skills also the "technical skills" needed to produce the particular product or render the service. This is their "selling card".

Usage of managerial skills in next level includes the application of basic entrepreneurial skills to prepare business plan. Following comes to attention communication skills, which serve the following purpose:

— To secure financing from investors and banks
— Convincing potential customers of advantages of the particular product or service
— To acquire key personnel for the enterprise
— To acquire the best advice and consultancy
— To form and cultivate partnerships and alliances

Successful growth phases require that initial "fly by the seat of one's pants" decisions need to be replaced by certain form of standardisation, formalisation and procedures. Formal planning and strategy become important component of managerial skills. Later, slowly piece by piece the whole puzzle of enterprise begins to put together and visionary is in the lead. How does the enterprise see itself in future? What mission should it undergo? What enterprise culture does it want to create? Otherwise the whole journey can become a "wild goose chase".

The pyramid represents set of certain managerial skills, which are needed to manage the growth of small enterprises successfully. They should be respected by anyone who is in the small business and also by support and advisory programs for small enterprise development.

Educational Programs for Small Entrepreneurs

In Newton's survey among students and young entrepreneurs, respondents answered strongly that there should be a difference between education in entrepreneurship and management. Education in entrepreneurship should focus more on how to be innovator, visionary and creator of strategy orientation of an enterprise. It should be more about strategy, planning, forecasting, bringing new ides, notions, and visions to reality of enterprising. Education in management should focus mainly on acquiring and developing managerial skills.

On of the researches in Slovakia was carried among small and medium enterprises with the aim to map the educational system for managers (if any exists). The results were not pleasant and conclusion was that educational process for managers of small and medium enterprises is not sufficiently or at all defined. Furthermore this process would not reflect current and future trends and at the same time the characteristics of particular regions stemming from their historical evolution, current state and geographical location The methodological area needs improvement in structure, length, form and lectors and in managerial areas it is mainly management of process, especially the customer process.

The educational activities of small enterprises should focus mainly on the entrepreneurial awareness and skills in the area of marketing, information systems, tax laws and finance, acquiring new ICT skills, study of world languages (technical terminology), crafts development and protection environment and customer.

It is also the role of supporting program to help explain the difference between entrepreneurial and managerial education. The skilful worker who decides to go into business for himself/herself can be easily overwhelmed by the both types of needed skills. All he/she knows is how to make the product. He/she needs to acquire financing for the idea (with the help of entrepreneurial skills) and start running the enterprise (using the managerial skills). Starting small entrepreneurs usually posses none of them.

Systems Thinking in Quality Management

If today, after more than twenty years since the "quality revolution" started, we ask quality practitioners and quality scholars what they perceive as the core concept of quality management, we will most probably get a spectrum of answers that reflect fragmented and tool-oriented views. Had we monitored such perceptions in time, we would identify cycles of management fads, more than clear development paths. After the first, successful attempts to set the basis for the new TQM view – with the Malcolm Baldrige and EFQM Models - we had, for example, the Process Management, Process Reengineering (BPR), Self-assessment and Benchmarking periods. We also had some strange returns to the standard-based view of quality. In the recent years the scene was dominated by "Six Sigma" approaches, that focus on reducing variation (a clearly important but partial aspect of managing for quality), putting however more emphasis, quite often, on cost reduction than on customer satisfaction (a clear sign that ways are continuously sought to regain executive attention).

Truly, the technical were the most tangible and easily understandable aspects of the new TQM models. However, the most critical aspects were those related to the organisation, and the way of managing it. Unfortunately they were the most difficult to grasp, both because the way they were presented was still rough, unfinished; and because quality practitioners seldom have the necessary organisation/management skills. Probably the most significant example of unfinished transformation is that related to process management.

The intuition that, to achieve maximum quality with minimum use of resources, horizontal processes – not vertical functions – are the key, was good. But the next rational step was the understanding that processes are part of systems, and what that means. Such understanding reveals the fundamental role of *relations*. The brief annotations that we can find in both the ISO 9000 standards and Excellence Models, that "relationship among processes should also be taken into account" is the symptom of just perceiving that there is a problem, without understanding its real nature and importance. Improvement of individual processes can result just in sub-optimisation. To optimise a performance, all the processes, as well as functions, project groups, committees etc that directly or indirectly impact on such performance, should be involved. Lack of the systems view was the reason for BPR poor results.

What happened in the quality world in the 1990s was that, little by little, techniques and tools took the lead, while the organisational transformations that were supposed to be at the core of the new management philosophy were postponed, moved to the background and little by little almost forgotten. Only the issue of transforming the vertical, hierarchical organisation into a process based flat organisation remained in the agenda of the most advanced companies for a while, but quite often progressively downgraded, due to the difficulty of overcoming resistance to change and finding reasonable systemic solutions.

The outcome was that little by little top executives returned to the old mentality where quality is a matter for specialists that does not imply their own direct involvement. Those responsible for quality less and less report to the CEO and statistical more than managerial and organisational expertise is requested of them. Consultants and academics focus more on packaging and repackaging old stuff instead of continuing the innovation wave that revitalised quality management in the 1980s. A symptom of the decline is the use of the preposition "beyond" instead of "in addition to" for promoting new approaches by making the old obsolete. Many approaches claimed to be "beyond TQM", simply because the proponents had narrow views of TQM. Those who give the TQM acronym the general meaning of strategic quality management approach aimed at continuous improvement and innovation, do not feel the need to change the name of the tool box when a new tool comes in.

We have two problems, however logically connected: the fragmented and low profile view of quality management and the resurgence of technical tools (statistical in particular) as the core of quality management. The second is a consequence of the first but, on its turn, reinforces it. There must be some reasons why, in concurrence with the exaltation of Six Sigma as the icon of quality management, the word quality has almost disappeared from management journals. It is true that many CEOs, starting from Jack Welch, promoted its application, but that was in line with a technological view of quality that can be totally delegated; it did not imply any executive-led organisational transformation.

Techniques and technology are absolutely necessary, but they will not produce the necessary changes. Among the competitive factors, they are no longer the most critical. All the competitors have access to the same techniques, technologies, skills. The real differentiating factor is *to create an organisation* that is able to set out winning objectives and meet them (obviously through an intelligent use of all existing technologies).

But the fragmented view is not just a quality management problem, it is a general management problem. In fact, at the roots of the problem of approach and tool fragmentation there is *strategic fragmentation*: lack of systemic perspective, silos-type organisations, excessive specialisation. To take an example in the area of quality: the ISO 9000 Standards, by introducing the "quality management system" concept, reinforced the top management wrong opinion that quality is a separate matter, for specialists. Management for quality is an inseparable part of management instead, because quality is not a subject in itself, it is an attribute of whatever managers do.

We need then full integration of managing for quality into management, but we also need a strong injection of systems thinking into management. Only by doing that, quality concepts can be extended to the new areas that are made more and more critical by globalisation. An urgent move, given the disorderly development of the social and physical environment in which humankind is living.

Integrated View of Management

Systems thinking has emerged as the convergence point between sciences, as a fundamental way of interpreting nature and to master the ever increasing complexity of the products of human intelligence.

While analytical thinking aims at separating variables to understand specific cause-effect relations, systems thinking considers the system's global behaviour and performance as a combined effect of all its variables and – most of all – of *their mutual relations.* Analytical thinking was key to scientific development and still remains one of its cornerstones. But too much of a good thing can be dangerous. Separation of variables leads to simplification and specialisation. But sometimes it can lead to over-simplification, since specialists tend to loose the overall picture; we can preach interdisciplinary work but it seldom leads to the real capacity of reconstructing the entire patchwork from the pieces.

Interdependence among the component parts is the main factor in determining the system's characteristics, behaviour and performance. Such relations give normally rise to unique properties – the so called emergent properties - that are not reducible to any combination of the properties of the constituent parts. Sometimes emergent properties produce exceptional results, like the appearance of life or that of human beings on Earth. Similarly, in human systems, they may produce outstanding cultures and civilisations. Enterprise excellence too looks as a rare and unstable emergent property. From a thermodynamic perspective we can say that move towards higher system complexity and uniqueness means moving farther away from equilibrium. No wonder that excellence is an unstable state.

When a system interacts with its environment we define it as an *open* system. Typically, open systems interact with other systems that, together with them, form a higher level system, a *supra-system*. What is a system from one perspective is a subsystem from another perspective – and a supra-system from still another. There is a progression from cellular to multi-cellular, to ecological systems, as well as from man to social/ethnical groups to states to mankind. In a world of interactions, closed systems are quite an abstract concept, but we can consider as closed systems those whose interrelations are negligible.

Among systems, social organisations are particularly important. Higher animals have social relations, but for sure the most interesting, rich and at the same time worrying are the relations between human beings. Intelligence, capacity of choice, make human systems unique, capable of mastering and even changing the rules of the supra-system which they live in. Organisations are multi-minded, purposeful systems with properties of their own. In the past, consciously or unconsciously, mechanistic models – organic at best – were used to manage organisations. F. Taylor, H. Fayol, M. Weber theorised them. They matched their contemporary society models. Evolution of society makes such models obsolete now. In most developed environments, specially where a western type culture is diffused, even the organic model of organisations is inadequate, let alone the mechanistic; only the multi-minded, sociocultural model works. Culture is the DNA of such systems. It determines their identity and their ability to generate value for their members as well as for the external environment.

Centrality of relations is by far the main link between quality thinking and systems thinking. Quality in fact means a feature, a property, that characterises a person, an animal, an object, a situation. As such, it has neither positive nor negative implications. It gets such implications only when associated with the concept of value. It can be economic value in the case of economic relations; it can be moral or spiritual value in the case of personal, non economic human relations, it can be scientific or artistic value in the case of relations between man and nature or man-made objects. Relations are the place where qualities are perceived and value is generated or exchanged; on them quality management should then primarily be focused.

Mission and Value of Organisation

Organisations' fundamental mission is to put together people to *generate value* for defined categories of subjects (customers, users, stakeholder, the organisation itself). Not generic value, but value that will be appreciated by the target subjects, so that they will seek after it. Given the markets' dynamism, value expectations change in time and value propositions are bound to rapidly adapt to – or precede – market changes. Success in competition depends on the ability first to identify (possibly in advance with respect to competitors) attractive value, second to implement and deliver it with minimum defects (value losses) and minimum use of resources (so that the global value balance for the producer too is positive). We may say in other words, using the traditional quality jargon, that two are the fundamental conditions to be among the winners in the value-generation game: "*doing the right things*" and "*doing them right*". While the latter is the traditional purpose of managing for quality (keeping defect rate as low as possible), the former is more neglected, also because its interpretation is often trivial: whoever does not strive to do the right things? But it is far from trivial. In business, making products and services that users do not appreciate is a frequent cause for failure; public administrations are not normally allowed to go bankrupt even if they make the wrong choices, but the resulting inefficiency is a burden for the economic system they are part of.

If quality is not locked in the realm of variation and defect reduction (doing things right) but opens up to the realm of identifying and planning competitive customer value (doing the right things), the following additional benefits will be reaped:

- Top executives will more easily get involved in quality management, since new product and service planning is normally at the core of their interests.
- Systems scholars and practitioners attitude towards quality management may change, favouring the badly needed convergence between quality thinking and systems thinking

Value creation is the area where quality thinking can give the most significant contribution to systems thinking. From the systems perspective organisations are *purposeful systems*, that choose and pursue their purpose. Organisations' basic purpose should be to create value to satisfy the expectations of its target customers/stakeholders and guarantee its own sustainable development. On the other hand, the best definition of organisational quality is: *fitness for purpose*. The quality mission in the systems perspective could then be: *caring for the organisation's fitness for purpose*; specifically, caring for *fitness in generating and delivering the expected values*.

Quality is not a subject itself, it is an attribute of an object, a person, an organised ensemble of persons. Likewise, managing for quality is not an independent activity, it is part of management, with specific missions at different levels. It is not separable from the activities it refers to, and responsibility for quality belongs to the relevant operative managers. Since systems' global behaviour, their value generating capabilities in particular, depend on the complex interactions between their component parts, quality management by necessity is an integrating factor. That means that, *in opposition to the present trend that puts emphasis on this or that tool, quality management should first of all look at the system, its subsystems, its internal relations*. The main subject for quality management is the socio-cultural system: people and their relations. Within such global view, techniques, technologies, tools can find their specific allocation.

[illegible] normally formal groups, sometimes informal. In excellent organisations informal groups are numerous and important to keep organisational fitness for purpose.

Value Generation Cluster

Three elements only are represented in the figure, for simplicity. They can be either individuals or groups of individuals (sub-clusters). They co-operate to generate the expected value. From their co-operation – because of the synergetic effect typical of social systems – the value that is generated is different from the sum of the values that each individual could generate in isolation. It can be more – sometimes much more – and that is what is expected of a co-operative system; or it can be less, when people do not co-operate, when they destroy value. The synergetic (or "resonance") effect is represented in the figure by a multiplying factor N (in the central box, that represents the organisational structure involved, e.g. a process, or an *ad hoc* team). Such factor, that represents the effectiveness in generating the expected value, depends on a number of ethical/cultural factors, first of all openness, mutual respect and trust, willingness to cooperate.

Two types of relations take place within the Cluster. The first is the relation between each "element" and the organisation: a bilateral relation, represented by a couple of radial arrows for each element, pointing in opposite directions. The primary value flow is from the person to the organisation: the value that the organisation has the right to expect from any individual who freely joins it. What is a fair contribution is difficult to say since, particularly in the case of intellectual activity, defining performance standards can be difficult. But it is here that the reverse value flow, from the organisation to the individual, comes into play. People motivation to contribute to the collective value generation process is proportional to the gratification that they get in return. We can distinguish between external and internal motivation; however both important, the latter is key. Gratifications that drive internal motivation come mainly from the leadership-created environment. In the figure, the "shared values permeated environment" is highlighted: *it is the soil in which the seeds of creativity can grow*.

The second important type of relations illustrated in the figure is that between the members (elements) of the "value generation cluster" (bidirectional arrows between the elements). To enhance value generating capabilities, such relations should be based on trust, openness, willingness to share information and build knowledge together, mutual respect, empathy. Clearly, for these mutual relations too, taking such a character depends to a large extent on the values that are embedded in the environment.

Since most organisational activities require cooperation among people, the concept of value cluster can be extensively applied. Processes in particular, but also high level research groups, cross-functional committees, all should be conceived and managed as value generation clusters. A person (or a group of persons) can be (and normally is) part of different clusters. Clusters can become the building blocks of the organisational architecture. They represent a systemic solution to the problem of organisational architecture aiming at creating continuous improvement and innovation propitious environments.

References

Ackoff R. (1999), *Re-Creating the Corporation*, Oxford University Press, New York, Oxfrod.

von Bertalanffi L., (1969), *General Systems Theory*, George Braziller, New York.

Churchman C., (1997), *The Systems Approach and Its Enemies,* Basic Books, New York.

Dervitsiotis K., (2007), Guiding Human Organisations to Climb the Spiral Stages of Performance Improvement, *TQM & Business Excellence. Vol. 19, n 7 & 8.*

Gharajedaghi J., (1999), *Systems Thinking*, Butterworth Heinemann, Boston, MA

Hamel G., (2007), *The Future of management*, Harvard Business School Press, p.9.

Kast F. E. and Rosenzweig J. A., (1985), *Organisation & Management*, McGraw-Hill Inc.

Laszlo E. (1996), *The Systems View of the World*, Hampton Press, Inc., Cresskill, NJ

Nadler D.A., Gerstein M.S., Shaw R.B., (1992), *Organisational Architecture —Designs for Changing Organisations*, Jossey – Bass Publishers, S. Francisco

3

Leadership Skills in Organisations

What is leadership? It is a process by which one person influences the thoughts, attitudes, and behaviours of others. Leaders set a direction for the rest of us; they help us see what lies ahead; they help us visualise what we might achieve; they encourage us and inspire us. Without leadership a group of human beings quickly degenerates into argument and conflict, because we see things in different ways and lean toward different solutions. Leadership helps to point us in the same direction and harness our efforts jointly. Leadership is the ability to get other people to do something significant that they might not otherwise do. It's energising people toward a goal.

Without followers, however, a leader isn't a leader, although followers may only come after a long wait. For example, during the 1930s Winston Churchill urged his fellow Englishmen to face the coming threat from Hitler's Germany. But most Englishmen preferred to believe that Hitler could be appeased—so that a war could be avoided. They were engaged in wishful thinking about the future and denial that the future would be dangerous. They resented Churchill for insisting that they must face the danger. They rejected his leadership. He had very few followers. But finally reality intruded—Germany went too far and war began. At this point Churchill was acclaimed for his foresight, and became prime minister of the United Kingdom during the Second World War. During this period almost all Englishmen accepted his leadership willingly.

True leadership is sometimes hard to distinguish from false leadership, which is merely a form of pretending. Winston Churchill was a real and great leader. But there are also people who wish to appear to be leaders, but aren't actually. They say that they are leading others; they posture as if they are setting direction and inspiring others. Yet often they are merely pretending. There's an old saying that the way to become a leader is to find a parade and run to the front of it. We refer to a person "leading" a parade, but walking at the front isn't really leadership unless the person in front is actually choosing the direction! If the person isn't choosing the direction, then being at the front of the line is merely a way to pretend to be a leader.

Leadership can be used for good or ill. Hitler seemed to be a leader of the German people, but he set an evil direction. He had great leadership skills, but put them to terrible uses. Sometimes people in business use leadership skills to exploit others. Sometimes people in charitable organisations use leadership skills to benefit themselves rather than the people they are supposed to help. Leadership skills can be perverted to pursue bad ends.

Few things are more important to human activity than leadership. Effective leadership helps our nation through times of peril. It makes a business organisation successful. It enables a not-for-profit organisation to fulfil its mission. The effective leadership of parents enables children to grow strong and healthy and become productive adults.

The absence of leadership is equally dramatic in its effects. Without leadership, organisations move too slowly, stagnate, and lose their way. Much of the literature about organisations stresses decision-making and implies that if decision-making is timely, complete, and correct, then things will go well. Yet a decision by itself changes nothing. After a decision is made, an organisation faces the problem of implementation—how to get things done in a timely and effective way.

Problems of implementation are really issues about how leaders influence behaviour, change the course of events, and overcome resistance. Leadership is crucial in implementing decisions successfully.

Each of us recognises the importance of leadership when we vote for our political leaders. We realise that it matters who is in office, so we participate in a contest, an election, to choose the best candidate.

The danger that leadership will be perverted is why ethics are so important to good leadership. Ethics are the inner compass that directs a person toward what is right and fair. Only if a person has an inner ethical compass can he or she be sure that leadership qualities will not turn to evil ends.

Taking a Leadership Position

Taking a leadership position means several things: A leader must have a vision of the future for the organisation and its members.

Taking a leadership position means:

— Having a vision about what can be accomplished.

— Making a commitment to the mission and to the people you lead.

— Taking responsibility for the accomplishment of the mission and the welfare of those you lead.

— Assuming risk of loss and failure.

— Accepting recognition for success.

A leader must be able to express his or her vision clearly and in a compelling manner so that others are engaged by it.

A leader has to make a commitment to his or her vision, to the organisation, and to the members of the organisation. A leader can't be committed one day and uninterested the next. People will judge a leader by his or her commitment, and will commit themselves no more than the leader does.

A leader assumes a considerable amount of responsibility— not just for the mission that he or she urges others to accept, nor just for the organisation he or she heads, but for his or her followers, their lives and efforts, as well.

A leader assumes risk. If there is no risk, little leadership is required. If the effort is easy and certain to succeed, anyone can, and probably will, "lead" it. But where the effort entails a risk of failure, then many people will quail before the challenge and leadership is necessary to get people to make the commitment and the effort to succeed.

In most organisations, one associates high levels of leadership with high levels of authority. The chief executive of a company usually plays more of a leadership role than people at lower levels of the hierarchy in the firm. It is the same in not-for-profits and government agencies. The higher on the job ladder a person is, the more she is expected to exhibit leadership.

In the military, however, the opposite holds true, and for a very good reason. In the military the greatest leadership challenge is to get other people to risk their lives in combat. Generally, the higher one goes in the chain of command, the less exposure he has to the battlefield, and the less exposure to men and women who are in combat.

The officers who have responsibility for commanding soldiers in combat have the greatest leadership challenge, for they must get others to risk their lives. Michael Jordan's brother is an army sergeant major leading a deployment in Iraq in which he is responsible for more than 2,000 soldiers. Offered an opportunity to leave his assignment in combat, he chose to stay with his unit in harm's way. In so doing, he accepted one of the military's most significant leadership challenges.

The first responsibility in a position of leadership is to have a vision. The visionary leader must create his or her concept of what the organisation can accomplish. A business leader may be leading a few people in a department or an entire company; a military leader a small squad or an entire army. The vision may be smaller when the group of people is small; and much broader when the group of people is large, but it must be forward-looking and exciting in either case.

Visionary leadership requires:

— Creating a vision, a mission, and a strategy.

— Communicating the vision/mission/strategy and getting buy-in.

— Motivating action.

— Helping an organisation grow, evolve, and adapt to changing circumstances.

The leader must also provide a mission—what needs to be done—and a strategy, a path, for how to accomplish the mission and achieve the vision, a way for the group to get there. But having an exciting vision, an exciting mission, and a careful strategy is not sufficient. A leader must clearly communicate them. Only if people grasp the vision can they commit to it, and buy-in is crucial to motivating action. Finally, a vision cannot be rigid and unchanging; it must adapt to changing circumstances, growing and evolving. Otherwise it becomes outdated and obsolete, and loses its power to excite and motivate people.

Leaders versus Administrators and Managers

Leadership is not the same thing as being in a position of authority. It is possible to be a boss in a company without being a leader. A boss can be more of an administrator than a leader.

Conversely, an administrator can be effective in his job without being a leader. The administrator is a bureaucrat— whether in government or in business—a person who keeps careful records and sees that things are done according to the rules. On the other hand, a leader can be effective without being an administrator—leaving rules, regulations, and their enforcement to others.

Administration is not as exciting a topic as leadership, but it is almost as important. The success of organisations depends to a great degree on how well they are administered. A manager is often thought to be primarily an administrator. But a manager is not an administrator; management requires a special set of skills of its own. And being a manager is different from being a leader. So there are three roles: administrator, manager, and leader.

A manager has the broadest role, and a good manager has much of an administrator and a leader in him or her. A manager needs to set direction and inspire others to get work done (leadership functions) and he or she needs to keep records and see that rules are followed (administrative functions).

The manager is a necessary combination of leader and administrator. But leadership is the most important of the three roles.

Administrators

What does an administrator do? An administrator applies rules and regulations generally developed by top executives of an organisation. He or she keeps records and fills out forms necessary to take administrative steps.

The elements of administration are:

— Making rules and regulations
— Making decisions that apply and interpret rules and regulations
— Keeping records
— Filling out forms

Managers

What does a manager do? He or she makes plans and creates budgets that set forth in great detail how something will be accomplished and how much money and other resources (e.g., people, office space) are necessary to accomplish those plans and budgets. He decides who is going to be assigned to the necessary tasks and how they will fit into the organisation. She supervises the actions people take, ensuring that they are doing the right things, that no money is being misappropriated or wasted (we call this "controlling"), and when problems arise she helps to resolve them. Finally, by combining these tasks into a coherent whole, the manager makes the organisation operate efficiently.

Running an organisation effectively requires administration, management, and leadership. Leadership is ordinarily in shorter supply than administrative or managerial competence. Leadership is more important and more demanding for most people. Fewer people are able or willing to be leaders, so it tends to be a higher calling than administration or management.

There is a large literature discussing the differences between leaders and managers. There is also an important distinction to make between leaders and administrators. In general, a leader takes a broader view and points an organisation toward necessary, even critical, change.

The core of the criticism in the literature is that organisations of all sorts (corporations, government agencies, and not-for-profit organisations) tend to be over-managed (and/or over-administrated) and under-led. Because of over-management and over-administration, organisations are slow to make necessary changes and achieve less than what they could. This is a substantial criticism that points to the importance of leadership.

The elements of management are:

— Planning and budgeting
— Setting direction
— Organising and staffing
— Aligning the efforts of many people
— Controlling
— Decision-making and problem solving
— Motivating and inspiring people

Nature of Leadership

True leadership is special, subtle, and complex. Too often we confuse things like personal style and a position of authority with leadership.

— Leadership is not primarily a particular personality trait. A trait closely linked to leadership is charisma, but many people who have charisma are not leaders.
— Leadership is not primarily a set of important objectives. It involves getting things done.
— Leadership is not primarily a formal position. There have been great leaders who did not hold high positions—for example, Martin Luther King, Jr. and Jeanne d'Arc—and there are people who hold high positions who are not leaders at all, but administrators who don't want to rock the boat.
— Leadership is not primarily a set of behaviours. Many leadership manuals suggest that what defines leadership is things such as delegating and providing inspiration and vision; but people who are not leaders can do these things, and some effective leaders don't do them all.

Many discussions of leadership confuse any and all of the above—personality, important objectives, formal position, specific behaviours—with leadership. But leadership is more than any of the above characteristics. It's a process by which one influences the thoughts and behaviours of others in a substantial way. It may involve charisma, important objectives, a formal position, and a particular set of behaviours, but it is not limited to any of them.

Effective leaders are often very complex people. Writing about Oliver Cromwell, the Lord Protector of England during the English civil wars of the seventeenth century, a foremost historian marvelled at the complexity of his personality. "There was no single Cromwell, " he wrote, "—that is, a clear-cut individual...Instead, there was a multiplicity of Cromwells, each linked to the other by his enormous vitality...Firstly, there was the very human, simple and compassionate man, a visionary and a romantic. Secondly, there was a violent. boisterous and irascible bully. Thirdly, there was the resolute and iron willed general...Fourthly, the calculating politician, the man of expedients who had no guiding principles.

And lastly, there was...the Cromwell...who, as the interpreter of God's will, was capable of committing any atrocity." Because leaders can be so complex, we must be careful in our generalisations about leaders and their personalities. But not all leaders are such complex personalities, which is good for most of us who aspire to leadership.

Examples of Leadership

Leadership in business

In the 1980s Harley-Davidson was almost knocked out of business by competition from other firms. To survive, it needed to change dramatically. Rich Teerlink, the company's leader, was able to save the firm financially, but with the pressure off, the challenge of continuing to improve seemed even more daunting. Could Teerlink get his managers and employees to make the significant, and to many of them inconvenient, changes necessary? He did it by building a different company, one driven from the bottom up by employees rather than from the top down by managers. It's a story of successes and failures, advances and setbacks, dead ends and breakthroughs, ending in a much stronger company than before.

Leadership in Government

When Charles O. Rossotti became commissioner of the Internal Revenue Service (IRS) in 1997, the agency had the largest customer base—and the lowest approval rating—of any institution in America. Mired in scandal, caught in a political maelstrom, and beset by profound management and technology problems, the IRS was widely dismissed as a hopelessly flawed and dysfunctional organisation. Rossotti— the first business person to head the IRS—transformed the much-maligned agency. In the glare of intense public scrutiny, he effected dramatic changes in the way the IRS did business—while the agency continued to collect $2 trillion in revenue. Through heated congressional hearings, encounters with Washington bigwigs, frank exchanges with taxpayers and employees, and risky turnaround strategies, Rossotti demonstrated leadership against daunting odds.

Leaders' Political Skills

Leadership concept has been prevailing throughout the history of human. Normally researchers start it from ancient Greece philosophers and try to find its traces in the philosophic thoughts of Socrates. They make Plato's *The Republic* as the starting point about their leadership thoughts and articulate his view that the world's problems would be solved only when philosophers will become kings or kings would take up philosophy. In *The Republic* he also detailed some of the skills and other relevant characteristics of the ruling class. After that the work of Machiavelli comes as a *"literary model of sorts"* i.e. *The Prince*. Recently Keohane has proposed some better qualities to prospective leaders. He takes Machiavelli's *The Prince* as a model in terms of format for his suggestions to organisational leaders, and offers his opinions either in agreement or disagreement. He has adopted the normative approach in his thoughts same as of Machiavelli and paid attention to what leaders actually do. The key of leadership is to influence and motivate others and their ultimate objective is to boost up the productivity of organisation through people. They are in the business of capital and they have one law: the business of money to make money.

The literature of political theory reveals that at first the leadership concept was built up on the phenomenological level i.e. the society then it boiled down to a concept at the organisation level and in the end it became a practice concept for leaders. There is an attempt to theorise it for all categories and typologies of leadership without any differentiation (e.g. between leadership concept from dispositional point i.e. Transformational, Transactional, Charismatic, and from situational point i.e. Autocratic, Democratic, Bureaucratic, and Laissez-Faire) because according to Simon sometimes every arbitrary selected unit does not define a suitable level for scientific study. Much of the leadership is a social influence process. This requires a broad set of skills and knowledge of when to apply them. This is the realm of political skill and organisational politics savvy. Political behaviour is also an influencing behaviour in a sense that in this an individual attempts to influence others to achieve some ends, either personal or organisational.

Therefore it is the intention of the influencer that qualifies the influencing behaviour. Politics is an inevitable part of organisations and political skill is essential for all types of leaders. Therefore for inborn or learned political skill and understanding of organisational politics phenomenon the concept of leadership is taken here in its generic influencing role. Same is the case for all the organisational situations because every situation requires political skill. Change is the only constant factor in this world and same is the case with organisations as Berquist argues that in postmodern world, organisations have to deal with as much chaos as order and change is a constant dynamic.

Change has been an ongoing process due to environment threats or within organisational forces. It has proven to be a significant and popular mean for achieving organisational growth and corporate diversity and expansion. It is the responsibility of leaders to promote change and to create vision. Bass and Avolio emphasise that change is accomplished through the leader's implementation of the unique vision of the organisation through powerful persuasive skills, characteristics, and actions. As per demand of the change, for a more typical leader there appear to be many missing skills rather than just one. Failure of leadership in managing change seems to result from an intricate synergy of leadership deficiencies i.e. political skill and poor understanding of organisational politics.

Leadership concept surfaced in the business world in the early 19th century. The apex of the leadership is to enable ordinary people to produce extraordinary things while facing challenges and change and to constantly turn in superior performance to the long-term benefit of all the concerned constituencies. The following brief wording from many definitions is chosen to describe the difference between management and leadership: legitimate power and control vs. empowerment and change. The role of leaders in organisations has been changed entirely due to change in global environment. Now the notion of leadership is not attached with a person who only controls the employees. It is replaced with the leaders who are visionary, assist employees to plan, organise, lead and control their activities. Michela and Burke view is that leaders are hoped to initiate organisational change and to generate followers acceptance by effecting and changing their perceptions. Yeo is of the view that the development of employees in order to create a learning environment and to emphasise self-management and entrepreneurial behaviour is the responsibility of business leaders.

Leadership Scenario

In the past, patterns and characteristics of the organisation were hierarchical structures and authority, inflexibility, formalisation, centralised controls, a stable environment, and less competition within and outside. Organisations believed that change was for someone else. Most of the markets were of selling nature and the philosophy to run an organisation was to produce and dump into the market. Due to the dynamism in the environmental forces, breadth and change in consumers' needs, desires and preferences, markets has become more turbulent and volatile. In these circumstances organisations have to adopt outside-in approach and bring drastic changes. For example Cartwright and Schoenberg have reported that in 2004, 30000 acquisitions were completed globally, equivalent to one transaction every 18 minutes.

The total worth of theses acquisition was $ 1900 billion, greater than the GDP of several large countries. In this new organisational context positions and responsibilities are less static and more open-ended, and the familiar upper, middle and lower level boundaries are being redrawn and even some of them are being removed to meet the competition. In the past the emphasis has been on how leaders oversee the work of people within fixed units.

Recently leadership competence is important, assessing past impacts and current reality, matching job requirements with strategic human resource systems to address the future. The main focus is on the identification of strategies and factors that may explain the performance of individuals and organisations. Future departmental level leaders should undergo transformation from implementers to aggressive entrepreneurs. The middle level managers are playing the role of coaches and mentors instead of controllers, and top-level leaders are leading their organisations by setting direction and objectives of business rather providing sufficient resources. The lesson of the past is that leaders should identify future trends in technology, social and culture developments, demographics, economics, politics and market expectations that can influence organisation and force them to bring a change. In this scenario leadership is the art of mobilising others to want to struggle for shared aspirations. Leaders therefore must be skilled in change management process and motivate others to follow it. Hence one of their prime jobs is to predict and lead or manage change by mobilising and motivating followers and for that purpose they need political skill and organisational politics understanding.

When one goes through the leadership literature extensively he identifies that it has been produced by two camps i.e. of dispositionalists and situationalists. The leadership theories produced as the phenomenons of situation are Group and Exchange Theory of Leadership, Contingency Theory of Leadership proposed by Fiedler, and Path-Goal Theory by Evans and House. The theories of Leadership that are mediated from personality paradigm are Great Man Theory, Transactional, Transformational, and Charismatic Leadership Theories. From the past few years leaders skills has become the topic of research for theorists e.g. the work of House and Podsakoff, and of Whetten and Cameron.

In addition to influence, leadership has been defined in terms of processes, personality compliance, particular behaviours, persuasion, power, goal achievement, interaction, and role differentiation, initiation of structure, and combination of two or more of these aspects.

By and large the researchers developed their theories of leadership by focusing on one paradigm and ignoring the other. This approach can reveal the partial reality only. This integrative approach is more real and comprehensive. Political skill is an interpersonal skill that can be innate or learned and organisational politics is the combination of both personality and situation.

Interpersonal Control

Leaders in organisations are viewed as desirous of increasing their control; they can gain and exercise it if they apply their interpersonal skills properly particularly their political skill. They make decisions and consult other proposals and petitions. They motivate their team by giving incentives and sanctioning resources. They identify and share strategies that can solve organisational problems. They are determined to achieve the desired goals and for this they persuade or force others to follow a course of action. All these activities have to be performed in work setting and the scope of leadership also differs from that of most others activities. According to Keohane the issues that leaders must address have broad implications, and a large number of human beings are affected. Kotter stresses that leadership in contrast to management is the process of motivating people to change. It has been suggested that by influencing the nature of the work environment and organisational culture, leaders can have an effect on employees' attitude to work related change. The challenge then is to select and acquire a particular set of skills and actions that are prone to absorb change and resources in organisations. Thus they require interpersonal and social skills.

Research in the areas of social capital, emotional intelligence, positive psychology, and knowledge management has revealed that interpersonal relationships are critical to one's performance at work and career success. Perrewe et al. proposed that the ability of an individual to form positive interpersonal relationships should leverage their ability to cope with stressful job demands. This ability gives leaders a sense of self-confidence and personal security by developing a deep understanding and control over events. Fredrickson accentuates that it enhances individuals' psychological well-being, performance, and generates tangible benefits. It also recovers the bad experience of negative effectiveness.

Political Skills

Over two decades ago, Pfeffer argued for a political perspective on organisations that introduced "political skill" as a critical competency for effectiveness in the ambiguous and often turbulent environments of political organisations. Mintzberg also coined the term "political skill" and suggested that organisations could be characterised as political arenas, and for survival and success in such work settings the possession of "political will and political skill" is required. Mintzberg made reference to political skill as the exercise of influence using negotiation, manipulation, and persuasion. However, Pfeffer and Mintzberg work was of basic nature and they did not contribute in the conceptual or empirical development of this construct. After their work we find a gap of almost fifteen years until Ferris et al. broke the ice and made an initial attempt to more fully conceptualise, establish the construct domain, and empirically assess political skill. They have further developed and validated the political skill inventory.

Political skill is characterised by social perceptiveness and the ability to adjust one's behaviours to different and changing situational needs and the ability to effectively understand others at work, and to use such knowledge to influence others to act in ways that enhance one's personal and/or organisational objectives. Although other dimensions of social skills like social intelligence, emotional intelligence, ego-resiliency, social self-efficacy, self monitoring and practical intelligence can influence political skill, but research has demonstrated that political skill is a distinct construct with respectable psychometric properties. Issues pertaining to the derivation of political skill are concerned with whether this construct reflects a skill, an ability, or a trait, and therefore whether it is a learned competency or innate. We conceptualise that leaders can be predisposed to political skill, but it can be shaped and developed through training.

Construct Validity

Basically political skill was designed to focus on interactions in work organisations; on the contrary we also see it as conceptually unique to other social effectiveness constructs typically characterised as more general competencies affecting social interactions in a broad array of everyday contexts. There is some natural overlap of the construct domains of political skill and some other social effectiveness measures. Therefore, it is expected that modest relationships would be found between political skill and particular personality characteristics that tend to focus on social interactions, as well as with some other social effectiveness measures e.g. understanding of organisational politics.

Regarding discriminant validity, the main challenge is to demonstrate that political skill is not correlated with intelligence or cognitive ability. In psychology and the organisational sciences, cognitive ability has dominated the category of individual differences, regularly explaining substantial variance in personnel selection contexts and concerning other work outcomes. Research across several samples has revealed that there is a zero correlation between political skill and cognitive ability, thus supporting its discriminant validity.

Although there has been a proliferation of social effectiveness constructs in recent years, and there is the need to theoretically and empirically distinguish among them, it is perhaps most important to demonstrate the lines of demarcation between political skill and social skill, primarily because these two constructs sometimes have been used interchangeably and are suggested to be redundant because of similarity. However, in the research literature, scholars have made clear distinctions between social skill and political skill. Peled argued that social skill refers to the ease and comfort of communication between leaders and their employees, peers, superiors, and clients. Alternatively, Peled suggested that political skill refers to the manager's ability to manipulate his or her interpersonal relationships with employees, colleagues, clients, and supervisors to ensure the ultimate success of the project. Because both political skill and social skill have their roots in the early work on social intelligence there is bound to be some similarity in the two constructs, and perhaps reflected by modest correlations. However, we see these as two distinct constructs with different derivations and uniqueness.

With an ability to perceive others and the situation accurately, politically skilled people have an intuitive savvy and understanding of people and events in organisations. The tacit knowledge derived from such understanding helps to effectively regulate interpersonal interactions. Consequently, politically skilled individuals enjoy a sense of personal security and increased feelings of control over the process and outcomes of interpersonal interactions. Politically skilled individuals combine social astuteness with the capacity to adjust their behaviour to different and changing situational demands in a manner that appears to be sincere, inspires support and trust, and effectively influences and controls the responses of others. Trust and transparency become more important when employee perceive hypocrisy in various change processes.

Political Skill and Change in Organisations

Organisations are neither uniform nor static. They evolve over time, and so it seems reasonable to posit that all work settings will exhibit continuous and incremental changes punctuated on occasions by more episodic and radical changes e.g. mergers and acquisitions represent major and sudden change. It would be problematic if employees will not follow the change. There is a single right answer to all managerial problems. Some options may appear better than others but outcomes invariably depend upon context, timing, and implementation.

Successful leadership is a process of continual adjustment to changing environment. The leaders' need is to establish and develop distinctive skills and competencies like political skill and organisational politics savvy through their personal analysis, and then match this very skill with best opportunities for change in the organisation. Simultaneously they must be sensitive to the politicking and resistance from their subordinates.

Companies that manage change in their favour are run by leaders who have this skill, usually because of their role in establishing the organisation culture favourable to change. They make some critical and some not-so-critical decisions in this regard e.g. real delegation of power and not only the lip service, and intimating with their workers respectively. The political skill orientation is a very important variable in influencing decisions than are the leaders with out this course. Political skill enables them to scan the environment, establish sensitive controls, and facilitate internal communication before and after change. They discuss organisational matters with middle and lower level managers and also down the road with employees. Understanding of organisational politics guides them the right situation and time for decentralisation and delegation, and also sensitise on the hoarding of power. Traditions in the organisation may impede any attempt at radical change, but leaders having this "stuff" can move the organisation in the preferred direction.

Political skill reinforces individuals' belief, at a given point in time, in their ability to act as a causal agent to effect change in the intended direction on their environment and achieve what they desire. Political skill makes interactions more predictable, reducing the pressures caused by uncertainty, and in turn, enhancing perceived control over events. Thus, it is reasonable to expect that, when facing daunting challenges of change politically skilled people will find ways to solve the immediate problem or at least determine how to "get by" i.e., cope.

Politically skilled individuals not only are successful at regulating interpersonal interactions but also know exactly *how* to exert such influences in a manner that facilitates interpersonal relationships characterised by confidence, trust, and sincerity. Politically skilled people view interpersonal interactions as opportunities (vs. threats), facilitating the establishment of friendships, connections, and alliances, which in turn ensures a favourable social identity in their network by the help of which they can manipulate the environment in their favour for desired change.For example, politically skilled individuals may enjoy network centrality, enabling them to gain access to important information. Moreover, the confidence and trust placed in politically skilled individuals likely increase cooperation from others in the network. Therefore, in addition to contributing to a greater sense of *perceived* control, political skill, and the accompanying interpersonal influence, may enable individuals to gain *actual* control over events, thus helping individuals to cope with job demands fitting to organisational change.

Collectively, the literature suggests that political skill provides a unique type of control in work settings, that is, interpersonal control. With their social perceptiveness and the ability to productively use insights gained, politically skilled individuals are at a vantage point in controlling the outcomes of interpersonal interaction, enhancing their ability to cope with job demands. Through effective regulation of interpersonal interactions, political skill may act as a coping resource, thereby attenuating the negative effects of change process.

Perrewe´ and her colleagues found that political skill served as an antidote to workplace stressors, its role for the negative influences of role conflict on strain, and it also takes away the bad effects in the role overload-strain relationship. Kolodinsky, Hochwarter, and Ferris found that moderate levels of political skills were associated with higher levels of job satisfaction and lower levels of job tension, they also conclude that in comparison to more moderate levels higher and lower levels of political skill were adversely related to these outcomes. In another important study by Ahrean et al. leader political skill explained a significant proportion of variance in team performance of casework team in a large state child welfare system. Although these all are important findings and explained the prediction power of leader's political skill but more studies were needed to examine the effect of this skill on other organisational outcomes e.g. organisational change.

One of the axiom of this study is that leaders having political skill can manage change in a more effective way if they can develop a better understanding of organisational politics, as it is also about the influence processes in organisations. These two concepts are very much related to each other in a sense that through political skill one can understand organisational politics and the other way is that by developing a better understanding of politics in organisations leaders can develop and brush up their political skill. The first step in this direction is that leaders should develop a true picture of organisational life.

People are the most important ingredient of the organisations. This is the human capital that gives a competitive edge to an organisation in the presence of abundant capital and technological resources. Studies support this view that organisations are the functions of the different kinds of people; and not vice versa.

When an individual joins an organisation and becomes a part of the workplace community, he only does this to fulfil his self-interests. This supposition is presumably false that people enter in the jobs to serve the organisation. In fact the prime motive of joining an organisation is to serve one's own interests. People come to work situations with many goals and preferences. These goals invoke conflict and competition among workers to utilise the scarce resources. This competition, in turn, affects the use of power and politics in organisations. Some researchers have associated political activity in organisations with the distribution of resources or other advantages.

Consideration of the human factor involved should guide the formulation and implementation of the change process. The key to choosing the right approach to change is to keep in mind how organisations function. As a social system comprising of work, people, formal and informal systems, organisations are inherently resistant to change and designed to neutralise the impact of attempts at change. Leaders can play a critical role in selecting and planning appropriate change management approaches. They can do this job if they have organisational politics savvy by encompassing a real picture of the organisational life.

During the last two decades the concept of organisational politics has received an increased attention in management literature. This attention relied partly on the expectation of finding new answers to some old questions, such as what motivate or demotivate individuals at work and how can we explain variations in employees' behaviour and their performance in a better way. In the following part we will discuss organisational politics in some details and its relation with political skill and organisational change.

Organisational Politics

Michela and Burke argue that to change an organisation, one must first understand the organisation. Leaders' organisational politics savvy will provide them opportunity to fully understand the work settings. In term, organisational politics is built upon intra-organisational influence tactics used by organisational members to promote self-interests or organisational goals in different ways. It is usually associated with phenomenon such as power, struggles, and conflicts over the sources of power, influence, and planned and directed attempts to actualise warring interests in the workplace. A politically oriented manager might use the performance evaluation system for self-promotion or show favouritism to a personal friend. According to this definition politics is generally perceived as dysfunctional.

Therefore one can say that conflicts in workplace are almost inevitable and theories of organisational conflict are helpful in analysing the possible consequences of organisational politics. This is the political skill of the astute managers that help them to resolve these conflicts. It also has the potential to enhance growth and stability and facilitate effective decision-making and effective management of organisational change.

From the literature it is evident that organisational politics has two connotations i.e. positive and negative and both will be considered here. The common perception is that politics in the workplace is a necessary evil, unfair and irrational and thus have impression of harming the organisation and its members that led to definition of negative organisational politics. One can also define it as manipulation, achievement of goals in improper ways, and perceive it as unhealthy behaviour. Therefore, management literature considered politics relating among stakeholders as illegitimate, informal and dysfunctional. On the other hand Ferris and King found that use of influence in the organisation is positively related to the manager's positive attitude toward his employees. that is, the more an employee uses influence in the organisation, the better employee he is perceived to be and the more his performance is appreciated. Organisational politics is sometimes perceived as a legitimate fight response in times of crisis in the organisation. It is also considered as a positive process for decision-making and implementations. This is the particular domain of organisational politics where political skill of leaders can play a role for better performance of organisations which may also include leading change more effectively.

Available research on organisational politics have mainly considered it as an independent variable predicting personal and organisational outcomes such as satisfaction, organisational commitment, in-role performance, organisational citizenship behaviour, job stress, and turnover etc.. Some of the research has tried to dig out the underlying situational factors that promote the political behaviour among employees. These situational variables are ambiguous roles, policies, and discrimination for promotion and rewards. Personality has also been cited as a role player in organisational politics but it's Cheema who recently has tried to conceptualise the role of personality in organisational politics and tried to make a relationship of Big-Five personality dimensions with different categories of organisational politics.

In short, these attempts correlate organisational politics with personal struggles, conflicts, influential activities, political skill of leaders, inequity, unfairness, and effective management that result from the strong ambitions or aspirations of those who hold power in the workplace.

It is not wrong to say that based on the interactional and political skills and their better understanding of organisational politics, leaders have the ability to manage the change by reducing system uncertainty, friction and even by breaking existing political freedoms. They can also generate programmed conflicts, conflicts that raise different opinions regardless of the personal feeling of the employees, for decision making, decision-adoption, policy implementation, and change management. Fry has examined leadership as motivation to change and concluded that, to motivate followers, leaders must get in touch with their core values and communicate them to subordinates through vision and personal actions. House and Shamir and Judge and Avolio have found that leaders who display behavioural components of inspirational motivation, intellectual simulation, idealised influence, and individualised consideration are able to align their followers' values and norms and promoter both personal and organisational change. Organisational politics is all about the influence process and is also one of the important domains of the leaders. We expect that its understanding will enhance their ability to accept and implement change because leaders having political skill and understanding of organisational politics will go beyond exchanging contractual agreements for desired performance by engaging employees in the change process.

Model of Leaders' Political Skill

Drawing from the literature of leadership, political skill, organisational politics and change, a theoretical framework has emerged which explains how leader' political skill and understanding of organisational politics would influence organisational change. The proposed relationship is illustrated in Figure 1. As shown in the figure, the leaders who have political skill and savvy of organisational politics would be better equipped to manage change in a more effective, smooth, and productive way. This model also explains that a leader can be predisposed to political skill or it can be developed later through training. Furthermore it throws light on different sources of politics in organisations which means that employees and leaders can engage in it because of their personal traits or due to work situations. A close relationship is also portrayed between leader's political skill and understanding of organisational politics.

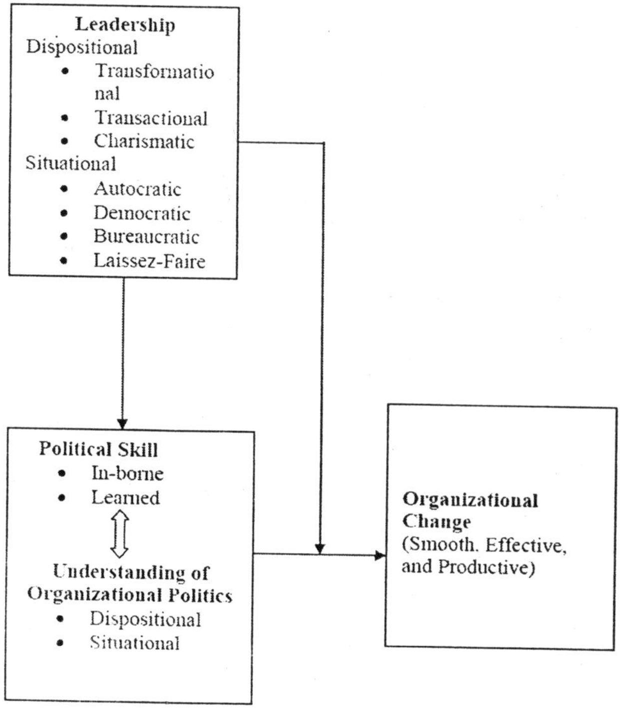

Figure 1. A Model of Leaders' Political Skill, Organisational Politics Understanding, and Organisational change

The leaders with political skill can have a better understanding of organisational politics and organisational politics savvy can provide the right assessment of the situation and can make ground for the development and exercise of political skill. These two constructs support and comprehend each other and the leaders who can deploy them simultaneously would be able to manage organisational change effectively in favour of all the stakeholders of organisation.

Leaders of organisational change should be competent and trained in the process of transforming organisations if changes are to succeed. This model specifies that this competency can stem from leader political skill and his understanding of organisational politics.

References

Ferris, Gerald R., Perrewe′, Pamela L., Anthony, William P., & Gilmore, David C., (2000), "Political skill at work," *Organisational Dynamics*, 28(4), 25–37.

Fry, Louis W., "Towards a theory of spiritual leadership," *The Leadership Quarterly*, 14(6), (Dec 2003), 693–727.

Harvey, Edward, & Mills, Russell, (1970), *Patterns of organisational adoption: A political perspective*, Nashville, TN: Vanderbilt University Press, , 181-213.

Kotter, John, P., *The leadership factor*. Free Press, New York, 1988.

Peled, Alon, (2000), "Politicking for success: The missing skill," *Leadership and Organisation Development Journal*, 21(1), 20–29.

Pfeffer, Jeffery, (1992), "Understanding power in organisations," *California Management Review*, 35, 29–50.

Weick, Karl E., & Quinn, Robert E., (1999), "Organisational change and development," *Annual Review of Psychology*, 50, 361–386.

4

Time Management Skills

Time management refers to a range of skills, tools, and techniques used to manage time when accomplishing specific tasks, projects and goals. This set encompasses a wide scope of activities, and these include planning, allocating, setting goals, delegation, analysis of time spent, monitoring, organising, scheduling, and prioritising. Initially, time management referred to just business or work activities, but eventually the term broadened to include personal activities as well. A time management system is a designed combination of processes, tools, techniques, and methods. Usually time management is a necessity in any project development as it determines the project completion time and scope.

Time management is more than just managing time. It is about controlling the use of the most valuable - and undervalued - resource. It is managing oneself in relation to time. It is setting priorities and taking charge of the situation and time utilisation. It means changing those habits or activities that cause waste of time. It is being willing to adopt habits and methods to make maximum use of time.

With good time management skills one is in control of one's time, stress and energy levels. One can maintain balance between one's work and personal life. One finds enough flexibility to respond to surprises or new opportunities. It is not how much time one has, but rather the way one uses it. The bottom line is how well one manages time. Internationally known authority on time management Dr. Alec Mackenzie in his book *The Time Trap argues* that the very idea of time management is a misnomer because one really cannot manage time in the way other resources can be managed: financial capital, physical capital, human capital, information and time. While each of the first four can be augmented, reduced, transferred or otherwise controlled, Time cannot be manipulated. Dr. Mackenzie contends that when it comes to time, one can only manage oneself in relation to it. One cannot control time as one can control other resources – one can only control how one uses it. In the world in which we live, time cannot be replaced or recreated. It is therefore not for us to choose whether we spend or save time but to choose only how we spend it.

Misconceptions about Time

There are several misconceptions which we all have about time. They affect everyone including those persons who may be considered quite successful and effective. Here are some of the misconceptions identified by Dr. Mackenzie:

— *Time management is simple* - all it requires is common sense. While it is true that the concept is simple, the self-discipline required to practice effective time management is not easy.

— *Work is best performed under pressure.* Psychological studies show this to be no more than an excuse for procrastination. One does not work well under pressure - only does the best one can under the circumstances. Pressure and challenge must not be confused. Lara's performance when the West Indies Team is in trouble has more to do with application and determination rather than pressure.

— *I use a diary, a to-do list and have a secretary to keep me organised.* One has to keep oneself organised - no one can do it for others. The trouble with the disorganised person is that he hardly has time to listen to his secretary or look at his diary.

— *I do not have the time.* The effective worker or manager often gets more work done in the earlier hours of the morning than most laggards get done in the whole day. He then no longer has to work against tight deadlines and under stress which contributes to heart problems and not unusually the ultimate reduction of time on this earth.

— *Time management might be good for some kinds of work but my job is creative.* Time management is not about routine: it is about self-discipline. Lack of discipline prevents one from being great instead of simply good.
— Time management takes away the fun and freedom of spontaneity. Is working under stress, forgetting appointments, making constant excuses and apologies to be fun? Would it not be much more fun if by better organisation one had one or two more hours every day to spend with the family, to play games, read a good book, plan for tomorrow and the day and week after or just relax?

Symptoms of Poor Time Management

Poor time management shows up by way of one or a combination of typical perceptible symptoms. Managers would do well to look for and reflect on whether they are subject to any of those symptoms with a view to take necessary corrective actions. The following are some of the indicators of poor time management:

— Constant rushing (e.g. between meetings or tasks)
— Frequent delays (e.g. in attending meetings, meeting deadlines)
— Low productivity, energy and motivation (e.g. 'I can't seem to get worked up about anything')
— Frustration (e.g. 'Oh, things just don't move ahead)
— Impatience (e.g. 'where the hell is that information I've asked him for?')
— Chronic vacillation between alternatives (e.g. 'whichever option I choose it is going to put me at a big disadvantage. I don't know which way to jump')
— Difficulty setting and achieving goals (e.g. 'I'm not sure what is expected of me')

Time Thieves

Dr. Donald E. Wetmore lists out the eleven 'inconsiderate troupe' of eleven thieves that gang up to steal some of the precious time away from productive use of managers.

1. *Poor Planning:* Failure to see the value of planning and getting impatient to get something done are the causes of poor planning. Absence of a plan of action is likely to trigger off a false start, resulting in unproductive time utilisation on the critical path of the task being undertaken. Consequently, the managers might not find enough time for completing the task.
2. *Crisis Management:* Most often, crisis management is an offspring of lack of prioritisation of tasks. As a result of the inability to distinguish between the urgent, the important and the unnecessary tasks, unimportant tasks are likely to get done first at the cost of important tasks. Consequently, the managers are not likely to find enough time to get around to the important things.
3. *Procrastination:* It is easy to put off tasks if they are not due right away. The trouble is, tasks pile up and can force managers to run into a time crunch later. Procrastination is generally triggered off by the fear of failure / success, perfectionism, wanting to do it all or incorrect priorities. It is a virtue to want to do a good job. But some people become so anxious about getting a job done perfectly that they never complete it. Managers should examine whether their efforts to get the job done perfectly are really improving things or preventing them from getting the job done.
4. *Interruptions:* Interruptions and distractions arise due to lack of planning, poor concentration and lack of control over environment. They are unnecessary thieves of a manager's time and come in many forms – drop-in visitors, telephones, e-mails unscheduled meetings, poor communications and confused chain of authority etc. Managers should be less willing to automatically give away their time just because they demand it. They should learn to avoid distractions if they are to get work done. They should work in areas where they are less likely to be disturbed and tell people when they are busy and cannot be disturbed.
5. *Not Delegating*: Wanting-to-do-all by oneself is yet another thief that could let the managers lose control. They feel that employees can never do anything as well as they can. They fear that something will go wrong if someone else takes over a job. They lack time for long-range planning because they are bogged down in day-to-day operations.

6. *Unnecessary Meetings:* If a meeting is held without a specific agenda and nothing productive comes out of it, clearly that meeting was unnecessary. Obviously, such meetings are thieves as the time is wasted and things just do not get started.
7. *The "shuffling blues":* Managers often waste much time because of disorganisation. Keeping things that they need in a specific place, eliminating clutter, making sure that they have all the materials or information that they need before starting on the task and following a day-planner or schedule will help keep the 'shuffling blues' away at the work place.
8. *Poor Physical Setup*: Not having the things that the managers need frequently within easy reach and having a lot of the things that they seldom require close-by results in wastage of a lot of time, wearing out the carpet, retrieving what they frequently need. And of course, as they pass others they will often pull them aside to steal some of their time.
9. *Poor Networking:* Quality relationships with employees and others can be a substantial timesaver as they open doors for the managers with all kinds of opportunities. Failing to develop a good network base will cause them to waste time creating what they might have had through their network.
10. *Bad Attitude:* Nothing sinks a day more effectively than having a poor attitude. It causes the managers to dwell on the problems and not the solutions and makes it possible to throw the day away. When they are burdening others with their problems and complaints they are forfeiting their valuable time.
11. *Negative People:* Being surrounded by negative people could mean the managers are spending a lot of their time listening to them but getting nothing much or purposeful from them. Obviously, avoiding such people will help the managers to minimise wasted hours and get some of their productive time back.

Saboteur Time Styles

The other aspect is self-inflicted thieves – 'saboteur time styles' that steal time. Based on the typical patterns of behaviour that tend to sabotage people's attempts at effective time management, Susan Ward classifies managers into different personality types and prescribes the following simple exercise, intended to help managers discover their standard behavioural responses to events and provide them with some clues for effective time management.

— *The Firemen* - For them, every event is a crisis. They are always seen busy dousing the fires. They find scarcely any time for anything else and do not spare a thought on time-management. Tasks keep piling up around them, while they are seen rushing from fire to fire all day.

— *The Over-Committers* – They just cannot say 'No' to anybody. They oblige and try to please everybody. All that anyone has to do is just ask, and they will chair another committee, take on another project, or organise yet another community event. Consequently, none of the tasks receives complete attention and remains half-done.

— *The Aquarians* - There is such a thing as being too "laid-back" - especially when it starts interfering with their ability to finish tasks or bother to return phone calls. Getting to things that is when they get to them is not time management; it is simple task avoidance.

— *The Chatty Kathys* - Born to socialise, they have astounding oral communication skills and cannot resist exercising them at every opportunity. Every interaction becomes a long drawn out conversation - especially if there is an unpleasant task dawning that they would like to put off.

— *The Perfectionists* – Exactitude is their watchword, and they feel that no rushed job can be a good job. Finishing tasks to satisfaction is such a problem; they need more time zones, not just more time.

Monochromic and Polychronic Views of Time

Just as a person's overall personality is made up of and represented by his or her traits, a person's time personality is made up of a series of time styles – monochronic or polychronic. It is expected that a person's awareness of the monochronic/polychronic side of personal time style affects his or her overall approach to time use, perceptions of time pressure and the amounts and order of time spent on tasks. This, in turn, affects his or her personal efficiency.

Monochronic approach to time management is essentially objective and lays emphasis on promptness, speed, brevity and punctuality. It is a very efficient and focused way to manage work and life. Monochronic time managers are those who thrive on detailed planning and organisation. They prefer to focus on one task at a time and they follow a schedule from which they don't like to deviate. They tend to get upset by distractions or interruptions and are inclined to put new tasks off until a later date, when they can be worked into the schedule.

Polychronic approach to time management is subjective and lays emphasis on inspiration, imagination, flexibility, intuition and dedication. Trust, bonding, pleasure and quality of life influence more strongly the decisions of a person who 'ticks' in polychronic time. Polychronic time managers prefer to have many projects under way simultaneously, enjoy changing from activity to activity and are unflustered by distractions and interruptions. Unlike their monochronic counterparts, polychronic managers believe they perform well under pressure.

Table 1. Monochronic vs. Polychronic Managers

Monochronic Managers	*Polychronic Managers*
Do one thing at a time	Do many things at once
Concentrate well	Are highly distractible and subject to interruptions
Take time seriously	Consider time commitments and objective to be achieved, if possible
Low context, need information	High context, have information
Are committed to the job	Are committed to the people
Adhere religiously to plans	Change plans often and easily
Are concerned with not disturbing	Are more concerned with others closeness than privacy
Seldom borrow or lend	Borrow and lend easily
Emphasize promptness	Base promptness on the relationship
Are accustomed to short-term relationships	Strong tendency to build lifetime relationships

Clearly, monochronic approach is better suited for dealing with routine and predictable tasks, while polychronic approach is better suited in dealing with things such as creating a new concept or resolving an argument. Conflict arises when managers apply a monchronic style to a situation that demands polychronic time, or managers prefer polychronic style while the situation warrants the use of monchronic style.

So how do the managers cope with a healthy need for subjective, polychronic, self-imposed time and at the same time fit in with the monochronic and objective time measures? The only way managers can figure out which method works best in a given situation is based on sound reasoning and acumen.

Five Time Zone Concept

To accelerate the ability to manage their time, managers need to strike a proper balance between monochronic and polychronic aspects of time management. The 'Five Time Zone Concept' advocated by Lewis, Justus and Storz, Moni Laui enables managers to bring about that balance. The five links in the 'Five Time Zone' approach are - vision, plans, personal organisation systems, commitment and energy.

— *Developing Zone 1 - Vision and Goals:* Managers must search for visions, not tasks. These visions are guided by their personal standards and values, and the direction they want to take. Once their visions are crystallised, they need to do some thinking to create goals from their visions and action steps from their goals.

— *Developing Zone 2 - Plans:* Having established goals, managers now can move into zone two - plans. A plan is needed to turn visions and goals into action. Writing things down and using some form of planning 'tool' are keys to successful planning. Once they have drawn up the plan, they need to review it. They should plan for high-payoff and low-payoff activities for high and low priorities.

— *Developing Zone 3 – Personal Organisation Systems (POS):* Zone three encompasses a manager's personal organisation system. Organising the desk, follow-up, paperwork, physical environment are all part of personal organisation system. The personal organisation system should focus on –

  - — Creating an interesting and relaxing work-space
  - — Providing easy access to basic tools and materials
  - — Grouping similar tasks together to optimise time
  - — Devising a good follow-up system that works well
  - — Enabling efficient handling of each piece of paper
  - — Ensuring a wider reach of people

— *Developing Zone 4 – Commitment:* The fourth time zone is the zone of commitment, in which managers correct any tendencies they might have towards procrastination. Procrastination can be overcome by identifying why one is procrastinating, breaking the mental blocks and visualising the successful completion of a task while in a relaxed state. One way to do this it to identify the real reason for the procrastination - personal, logical, emotional or ethical barrier to action. Once this has surfaced from the subconscious to the conscious, strategies can be brought into play to deal with it.

— *Developing Zone 5 – Energy:* The final factor that keeps the chain together is zone five, the energy zone. Managers must check their office surroundings, as the environment they work in can sap or strengthen their energy levels. They must also identify the prime time - the time of day when they are most energetic and alert – they can schedule high-priority, high-payoff tasks or activities for these times.

— Find your prime time

— Internal and external prime time

— Cognitive tasks for the morning

— Complete high-energy tasks in high-energy periods

— Take energy breaks

Time Management Matrix

Time management experts like Stephen Covey S R have developed a model called a time management matrix. This model enables managers to prioritise their activities and use their time more effectively. With the help of the model, they can evaluate their activities in terms of importance and urgency.

Tasks can be categorised as urgent/ not urgent or as important/ not important as shown below. Each of a manager's activities can be distinguished as one of four types, represented by the four quadrants of the time management matrix. Categorising a manager's activities in these quadrants helps him identify what is important and avoid unimportant tasks and activities. It also helps him prioritise important tasks and activities.

	Time Management Matrix	
	Urgent	*Not Urgent*
Important	*Quadrant I* Crises, Projects, accidents, etc.	*Quadrant II* Planning, exercise, relationships, etc.
Not Important	*Quadrant III* Phone calls, visitors, small talk, etc.	*Quadrant IV* Daydreaming, TV, procrastination, etc.

Figure 1. Time Management Matrix

From a study of the Time Management Matrix, the following observations can be made:

1. Activities in Quadrant I and Quadrant II may be equally important. Some activities in Quadrant II may even be more important than activities in Quadrant I, but not necessarily more urgent.
2. Activities in Quadrant I assume critical importance and top priority.
3. Spending most of the time on Activities in Quadrant I results in stress and burnout.
4. Focusing on activities in Quadrant II can reduce the activities in Quadrant I, in the long run.

5. Focusing on activities in Quadrant II will mean avoiding all unimportant activities in Quadrant III and IV.

Elements of Effective Time Management

Time goes by at the same rate no matter what one does. One can not speed it up or slow it down. Unlike the other resources that one manages, there is no way to control time. The best one can do is take charge of oneself in the framework of time, investing oneself in those things that matter most in one's life.

Effective time management requires reducing the impact of the time stealers and increasing the effectiveness of a manager in getting the things done that need to be done. The following are the important elements that combine to enable a manager eliminate distractions, interruptions and inefficiencies in the work process to make the most of time management.

Evaluating How Time is Used

The first step of effective time management is identifying how a manager is using his time. This can be done by –

1. *Activity Time Log*: The first step to managing time better is to find out how managers are currently spending their time. Keeping a Time Log is a very effective way to do this. Through an Activity Time Log, managers can make a list of the activities or tasks that they spend time on. The very act of measuring is often enough to raise their unconscious habits into their consciousness, where they then have a chance to scrutinise and change them.

Daily Activity Time Log

Start Time	*End Time*	*Activity Description*

Time Log requires that managers track all the tasks – including the routine tasks such as commuting, reading a newspaper, eating and attending telephone etc. - in a systematic way and note the successive sequence from the start, through the end of the day.

1. Using the daily log on the worksheet, record your activities for a 24-hour period.
2. Include the start and end times for each activity.

If more space is needed, continue keeping the log on the back or on another sheet of paper.

Activity Category	**Total time**
Misc.	
Total Time (should equal 24 hours)	

Pick activity categories that will encompass the entire day. Label those below and add up the total time spent on that particular activity category. Include a miscellaneous category for things that do not fit well into typical categories. Keeping the Activity Log for several days helps managers analyse their time and answer questions like:

— What is the most productive period of time?

— What is the least productive time?

— Did they achieve their goals?

— How could they have done what they were doing more effectively?

Activity logs are valuable tools for scrutinising the way managers use their time. They can also help managers to track changes in their energy, alertness and effectiveness through-out the day. By examining their activity log, they will be able to discover and obviate time-wasting or low-yield jobs. They will also know the times of day at which they are the most effective, so that they can carry out their most important tasks during those times.

Studies reveal that managers do a miniscule of real work per day – 1.5 hours of actual work per day. The rest of the time is spent socialising, taking coffee breaks, eating, engaging in non-productive communication, shuffling papers and other preventable time-wasters.

After completing your Daily Time Log, take a few moments to analyse your results.

This analysis will give you a clear picture on how you spend your time and how you can improve.

1. Did you have a plan for each day with clear priorities in writing?
2. Were you doing the right job at the right time?
   - What did you do that should not have been done at all?
   - Could it have been done more effectively at another time?
   - Could it have been delegated? If so, to whom can it be delegated?
3. What could be done in a better way?
   - Faster
   - More simply
   - In less detail
   - With better results
4. Concerning interruptions:
   - How are you interrupted (phone, visitors, meetings, crises, self, boss, clients)?
   - How often are you interrupted?
   - For how long have you been interrupted?

- — How important were the interruptions?
- — How long does it take to recover—to get back on track?
- — How many interrupted tasks were left unfinished at the end of the day?

5. Concerning contacts/ communications with others:
   - — How important is time spent in accordance with your real priorities?
   - — Who (with the right person) are they?
   - — How often do you spend with them?
   - — How long?
6. To what extent did you reach your goals?

Based on the analysis of Activity Time Log over some period, it is possible for managers to calculate their daily efficiency ratio. Daily efficiency ratio is the amount of time spent by managers on the work divided by the total amount of time they spent in the office.

Efficiency Ratio = (Time Doing "Real Work") / (Time Spent "At Work")

Assuming that managers have done only 15 hours of actual productive time in a week (60 hrs), the Daily Efficiency Ratio of a manager is only 25% of the time.

Goal-Setting

Why is goal-setting so important in time management? From the time management perspective, a person's life is a sequence of big and small choices and decisions. It is those choices that a person really manages, not the flow of time. A key difference between successful and unsuccessful managers is the quality and practicality of the goals they set for themselves. Goals state clearly the measurable and specific results to be accomplished by the managers and the timeframe to attain them.

Goal-setting is the wisdom that comes from practical experience that helps managers direct their conscious and subconscious decisions towards success. The process of setting goals helps managers choose where they want to go in personal and professional life. By being aware of precisely what they want to achieve, they know the efforts required for it.

Goals help in monitoring the day to day activities and ensure the activities are progressing in the right direction. There are two types of goals managers can set for themselves -- rational goals and directional goals. Rational goals are specific, short-time goals focusing on the questions:

— What do I want to accomplish?
— Why am I doing this task?
— Who are all involved in the task?
— What are the expected outcomes of this task?
— When can this task be expected to be completed?

Directional goals (also known as domain planning) are long-term goals with no predictable outcomes, focusing on the question - What do I want to accomplish? To stay focused, managers should aim and visualise these goals. They should identify possible quarters from where they can pool up the support and required resources needed to put together and accomplish those goals.

Time Management Goal Planner

Lifetime Goals (long range)

— 1.
— 2.
— 3.
— 4.

One-year goals (medium range)

— 1.
— 2.
— 3.
— 4.

One-month goals (short range)

— 1.
— 2.
— 3.
— 4.

Pick two top priority goals from each category. Enter them here. These are the goals, you will begin to work on, now.

— 1.

— 2.

— 3.

— 4.

— 5.

— 6.

The above six top priority goals should occupy a manager's time for one month. Next month, they should make a new list. Some goals will remain top priority while others will drop off. The goals will always be accompanied by a list of specific, easy to accomplish steps. They should set aside a certain time each day to work on top priority goals. Emphasis should be on results rather than activity.

What makes a good goal? A good goal is one that when followed, offers a reasonably high probability of success in the defined time-frame. Gene Donohue ("Goal Setting Powerful Written Goals in 7 Easy Steps!") lays down the following 7 goal setting steps for the managers to follow that help in building the road map to good goals.

1. Make sure the goal you are working for is something you really want, not just something that sounds good: When setting goals it is very important for the managers to remember that the goals are compatible with their personal interests and values. Any inherent conflict or incompatibility will cause unwarranted friction and adversely impact accomplishment of the goals.
2. A goal cannot contradict any of your other goals: Non-integrated thinking can also sabotage all the hard work managers put into their goals. Non-integrated thinking can also hamper their everyday thoughts. Managers should continually strive to eliminate contradictory ideas from their thinking.
3. Develop goals in the 6 areas of life: Setting goals in each area of life will ensure a more balanced life as managers begin to examine and change the fundamentals of everyday living. Setting goals in each area of life also helps in eliminating the non-integrated thinking. The six areas of life that need goal-setting include –

- — Family and Home
- — Physical and Health
- — Mental and Educational
- — Financial and Career
- — Spiritual and Ethical
- — Social and Cultural

4. Write down your goals: The difference between a goal and a dream is the written word. Writing down the goals creates the roadmap to success. Although the mere act of writing them down can set the process in motion, it is also extremely important to review the goals frequently. The more focused the managers are on their goals, the more likely they are to accomplish them.
5. Write your goal in the positive instead of the negative: The subconscious mind can not determine right from wrong and it does not judge. It's only function is to carry out its instructions. The more positive instructions one gives it, the more positive results one will get.
6. Write your goal out in complete detail. Writing down goals in details is once again giving the subconscious mind a detailed set of instructions to work on. The more information one gives it, the more clear the final outcome becomes. The more precise the outcome, the more efficient the subconscious mind can become.
7. By all means, make sure your goal is high enough: Keeping in view the time and resources at their disposal, managers should set fairly high but practicable goals. Lower goals are indicators of lower motivational levels on the part of managers. Higher goals are pointers to the zest managers have toward their work.

Apart from the above, traditional goal-setting wisdom teaches that a good goal must be believable, specific and measurable, and have a deadline.

Managers must believe that it is possible for them to achieve the goal or they will not be motivated to try. The goals should also be measurable and specific enough for them to know unambiguously whether they have been completed yet or not. For goals to be meaningful, managers must know the time-frame by when they are to be accomplished.

Reviewing your goals daily is a crucial part of a manager's success and must become part of his/her routine. At the beginning of each day, they must take stock of the list of goals and identify the efforts required on their part, for the day, to accomplish each of the goals by the set deadline. Each night, they should review the goals to ascertain whether the required work has been done or not. This process will set their subconscious and conscious minds working towards the goal. This will also begin to replace any of the negative self-talk they may indulge in and replace it with positive self-talk.

A manager's time can best be directed by using goals. Without goals, they become easily side-tracked and waste time.

Defining Priorities

Prioritising means "taking conscious control of one's choices and deciding to spend more time on the activities and tasks that are important and valuable, and less time on the ones that are not...." The importance of prioritising tasks or activities is best driven home by the popular 'pebbles and jar' parable.

One day, an expert in time management was speaking to a group of managers. As he stood in front of the group of high-powered over-achievers he said, "Okay, time for a quiz" and he pulled out a one-gallon, wide-mouth mason jar and set it on the table in front of him. He also produced about a dozen fist-sized rocks and carefully placed them, one at a time, into the jar. When the jar was filled to the top and no more rocks would fit inside, he asked, "Is this jar full?" Everyone yelled, "Yes."

The time management expert replied, "Really?" He reached under the table and pulled out a bucket of gravel. He dumped some gravel in and shook the jar causing pieces of gravel to work themselves down into the spaces between the big rocks. He then asked the group once more, "Is the jar full?" "Probably not," one of them answered.

"Good!" he replied. He reached under the table and brought out a bucket of sand. He started dumping the sand in the jar and it went into all of the spaces left between the rocks and the gravel. Once more he asked the question, "Is this jar full?" "No!" the audience shouted. Once again he said, "Good." Then he grabbed a pitcher of water and began to pour it in until the jar was filled to the brim. Then he looked at the spectators and asked, "What is the point of this illustration?" One eager beaver raised his hand and said, "The point is, no matter how full your schedule is, if you try really hard you can always fit some more things in it!" "No," the speaker replied, "that's not the point. The truth this illustration teaches us is, "If you don't put the big rocks in first, you'll never get them in at all.What are the 'big rocks' in your life, time with loved ones, your faith, your education, your dreams, a worthy cause, teaching or mentoring others?

Remember to put these Big Rocks in first or you'll never get them in at all. So, tonight, or in the morning, when you are reflecting on this short story, ask yourself this question, "What are the 'big rocks' in my life?" Then, put those in your jar first.

Time management expert Alec Mackenzie in *The Time Trap* narrates an anecdote that underscores the importance of prioritising activities.As the story goes, an efficiency consultant by the name of Ivy Lee was meeting with the president of a large steel mill. The president, one Charles Schwab, was interested to find out how he could increase performance. Lee was telling Schwab how he could provide him with advice to better manage the company. Schwab, however, was not interested because he did not want more knowledge. Instead, he wanted to find out how to get more done within available time, and he was willing to pay anything within reason for such advice. Lee said that he could help him increase his efficiency by at least 50% provided he could have about 20 minutes of his time.

After Schwab consented, Lee gave him a blank piece of paper and told him to write down the six most important things he wanted to accomplish tomorrow. Schwab thought about it and completed the task in about three minutes. Then Lee instructed him to order these things from most important to least important. That, too, took very little time. Now the executive was instructed to keep the list until the following morning, at which time he was asked to look at the first item and to start working on it until it was completed. After that he was told to work on task number two and so on until the end of the day. Lee further advised Schwab not to worry about those tasks that he could not get done, since it didn't matter because they would not have gotten done anyway.

Then Schwab was asked to repeat this process every working day. Lee then told him to try this system as long as he likes. Lee also asked Schwab to have his employees try this system and, if it worked, to send him a check for whatever the idea was worth to him and the company. After several months, Lee received a check for $25,000 and a letter in which Schwab said that this was one of the most profitable ideas that he had ever been taught. It is further reputed that the consistent application of this strategy helped to turn this small steel mill into Bethlehem Steel.

Managers must realise that they cannot simply do task or activity they take up. Given the constraints of time and resources, they have to be selective and consciously choose to spend time on what is most important tc them. They have to keep in mind is that whenever they start an activity or task, they are inevitably ruling out everything else they could have done with that time. When managers have to choose among several tasks, they can use several prioritisation tools.

Covey's Quadrants

Discussed earlier under Time Matrix, Steven Covey describes a high-level prioritisation Time Management Grid in his book *The Seven Habits of Highly Effective People*. In this grid, tasks are categorised by four quadrants:

Urgency

Importantance		
	Quadrant 1 Urgent and Important "Firefighting"	**Quadrant 2** Important but Not Urgent "Quality Time"
	Quadrant 3 Urgent But not Important "Distraction"	**Quadrant 4** Neither Urgent nor Important. "Time wasting"

Figure 2. Time Management Grid

— Quadrant 1 represents things which are both urgent and important - labelled "firefighting". The activities need to be dealt with immediately, and they are important.

- Quadrant 2 represents things which are important, but not urgent - labelled "Quality Time". Although the activities here are important, and contribute to achieving the goals and priorities - they do not have to be done right now. As a result, they can be scheduled when they can be given quality thought to them. A good example would be the preparation of an important talk, or mentoring a key individual. Prayer time, family time and personal relaxation/recreation are also part of Quadrant 2.
- Quadrant 3 represents distractions. They must be dealt with right now, but frankly, are not important. For example, when a person answers an unwanted phone call, -he/she has had to interrupt whatever he/she is doing to answer it.
- The final quadrant, Quadrant 4, represents things which are neither urgent nor important. Some meetings could fall into this category – they have been scheduled in advance, but if they achieve nothing, then they have simply wasted time. Other examples could include driving time and low quality relaxation or family time.

Using the Tool

Managers must strive to maximise Quadrant 2 time. They should allocate time in the diary to carry out these tasks when they are at their best. Doing so can reduce the amount of time taken up by firefighting quadrant 1 activities, since many quadrant 1 activities could

have been quadrant 2 if they had been done earlier. Managers can also seek to reduce time spent in Quadrant 3 by improving the systems and processes for dealing with distractions, and they can eliminate as much as possible of quadrant 4 activities, by either not spending time on these things, or changing the nature of them to make them more productive. For example, driving can be quadrant 4 if the time is unproductive, but there are a number of ways of making this time more productive by learning new skills, planning and so on.

Ken Blanchard's Quadrants

Ken Blanchard - the author of the popular book "The One Minute Manager" and "The On-Time, On-Target Manager" – sets out his quadrants a little differently:

— Have to Do, Want to Do
— Have to Do, Don't Want to Do
— Don't Have to Do, Want to Do
— Don't Have to Do, Don't Want to Do

Most of the managers do not have a problem with Quadrants 1 and 4. If It is Quadrant 1, they will willingly do it. If it is Quadrant 4, they never do it. It is Quadrants 2 and 3 where the conflict is likely to arise and most of the managers are likely to be attracted to Quadrant 3, meaning things that do not have to be done get done.

The Blanchard advice for the managers is to take up tasks in the order of Quadrant 2 and Quadrant 1, and spend little or no time on Quadrant 3 items. To use this model, managers have to chart out to-do list and plan accordingly.

Paired Comparison

The Simple Paired Comparison method uses a simple scoring system for comparing activities. The following example illustrates how this method can be applied:

Here is the list of example tasks or activities to be performed:

1. Call home about dinner plans
2. Fire Venkat
3. Draft budget report
4. Respond to e-mails

Compare the following and put a check mark against the relatively important task of each comparison:

— 1 to 2, 1 to 3, 1 to 4
— 2 to 3, 2 to 4
— 3 to 4

Let's say the result is as follows:

1. Call home about dinner plans XX
2. Fire Venkat XXX
3. Draft budget report X
4. Respond to e-mails

So, the order you would do the tasks in would be 2, 1, 3, 4.

The ABC Method

The ABC method ranks tasks into the following categories:

— 'A' are activities which Absolutely must get done now

— 'B' are those that Better get done soon

— 'C' are those that could wait for now

— 'D' are those that can be Delegated but require follow up

Then it subdivides tasks in these categories into A1, A2, A3, ..., B1, B2, ... and so forth. A lot of people find this prioritisation method helpful.

The Payoff versus Time Method

With this method, the managers have to weigh each task by the payoff they expect from it versus the time it takes to do it. Tasks that have high payoff and that take little time are the ones they would take up first. Correspondingly, tasks that have low payoff and that take a lot of time are ones they would do last or not do them at all.

Whichever method one uses - whether a particular method listed above, a combination of methods, or one of one's own design - a manager should use it not only to rank the order in which they will do things, but also to defer or eliminate items that are not important or of least priority.

Scheduling Activities

After identifying the activities and prioritising them, it is time to create a schedule. When scheduling, it is important to plan a weekly schedule as well as a daily schedule. The weekly schedule is important for the overall success of the activities and tasks, but it is the daily planning that will help one to track one's progress and determine whether or not one is on schedule.

Managers should try using significant project milestones in their weekly planning but for daily planning break each milestone down into the necessary components and plan the completion of those components on a daily basis.

The following points demonstrate why scheduling is so critical to success.

— Scheduling can greatly reduce your stress quotient. Proper scheduling gives one the peace of mind of knowing that one has formulated a feasible plan of action and that one's goals are attainable.

— Scheduling also helps one to be prepared for obstacles because part of the scheduling process is creating a contingency plan for unexpected problems.

— Scheduling serves as a way to evaluate your progress as you work. Planning your daily and weekly activities will clearly illustrate whether or not you are staying on schedule.

When scheduling the activities, ideally managers should follow the below procedure:

— Block out times on the schedule for each of the major activities.

— Start with recurring activities that occur at a fixed time

— Then block out time for activities that they want to do on a regular basis

— Allot ample time for each activity, especially high priority activities.

— Take into account when they are most effective. Morning people might schedule more activities early in the day. Night owls might schedule things later.

Work your way down from the top items. Only when they are completed should you work on the middle priority tasks. Only when everything else is done should you work on the low priority items.

Steps in Using A Time Planner

Outlined below is a step-by-step approach for using a day planner to manage time effectively.

1. *Select a Compatible Time Planner:* A day planner is a device that includes a calendar, space to write "to-do" lists, and space to write telephone numbers, addresses, and other/ reference information. It can be a Franklin Planner (simple paper-and-pencil type), Day Timer, a fancy electronic organiser or time management software

on a computer. If techno-savvy, a manager can pick an electronic organiser. If not, a manager can choose the paper-and-pencil method.

2. *Single, Accessible Place to Keep the Planner*: Having selected a planner, managers should cultivate the habit of keeping it in an exclusively designated and easily accessible place at home and workplace. An ideal place to keep the planner could be near the telephone or on the office desk.
3. *Enter the Basic in the Day Planner*: Managers should consider what vital information might be useful to enter in the Planner - such as insurance policy numbers, computer passwords, telephone numbers, equipment numbers - and arrange the information in alphabetical order.
4. *Carry the Planner at All Times*: Carrying the planner at all times means that the managers have all the vital information they need with them all the time. Ideally the Day Planner should be their integral part and constant companion of managers.
5. *Refer to the Day Planner Regularly:* Managers should make it a habit to refer to the Day Planner thrice a day - at the start of the day to be sure of the things to be done, afternoon to monitor the progress of their activities, and night to take stock of the status of the activities for the day.
6. *Use the Day Planner as a Calendar for Everything:* Appointments, and activi-ties for the day on personal, family and professional fronts should be listed in the planner. It is advisable that activities relating to family and professions are high-lighted using different colours. It is also essential that crucial activities or tasks that need personal attention and close scrutiny are highlighted using different colours to review their progress from time to time.
7. *Use Day Planner as a 'Brain Dump' to Capture Ideas*: Day Planner also doubles up as a Brain-Dump for managers as they can put down the ideas as they surface in the planner. That way it helps to refer to them and weigh their value and feasibility at the appropriate time.
8. *Conduct a Daily Planning Session*: The goal of this session is to plan the upcoming day's activities and develop a plan of attack

and to carry out the same. In addition to listing priorities and reviewing schedules, the planning session is the time to consider exactly how each task will be accomplished. What materials will be needed? What obstacles are likely to be encountered? How can these obstacles be overcome?

9. *Prioritise* 'To-Do' List and Action in Accordance with Priorities: There are many ways to prioritise a "to do" list. One way is to number all of the items on the list in order of decreasing priority. Another way is to classify items into one of three categories: "Essential," "Important," and "Do only if I have extra time." The managers should pick the method that best fits their style, and begin prioritising their daily "to do" list.
10. *Generate a List of Long-Term Goals and Break the Long-Term Goals into Small, Manageable Chunks:* First, generate a list of all long-term goals. These are broad goals to be accomplished over many months and years. Then, take one goal at a time and break it down into small chunks or sub-goals that might be accomplished on a monthly basis. Assign one sub-goal to each month of the year.

At the beginning of the month, conduct a monthly planning session to decide how to accomplish the sub-goal over the course of the month. Assign various tasks to each week of the month. At the beginning of each week, conduct a weekly planning session to decide how to assign aspects of that week's sub-goal to the daily task lists for the entire week.

References

Allen, David (2001). *Getting things done: the Art of Stress-Free Productivity.* New York: Viking.

Fiore, Neil A (2006). *The Now Habit: A Strategic Program for Overcoming Procrastination and Enjoying Guilt- Free Play.* New York: Penguin Group.

Le Blanc, Raymond (2008). *Achieving Objectives Made Easy! Practical goal setting tools & proven time management techniques..* Maarheese: Cranendonck Coaching.

Secunda, Al (1999). *The 15 second principle : short, simple steps to achieving long-term goals.* New York: New York : Berkley Books. pp. 157.

5

Skills for Managing Organisational Conflicts

Organisational conflict is a state of discord caused by the actual or perceived opposition of needs, values and interests between people working together. Conflict takes many forms in organisations. There is the inevitable clash between formal authority and power and those individuals and groups affected. There are disputes over how revenues should be divided, how the work should be done, and how long and hard people should work. There are jurisdictional disagreements among individuals, departments, and between unions and management.

Types of Organisational Conflicts

There are subtler forms of conflict involving rivalries, jealousies, personality clashes, role definitions, and struggles for power and favor. There is also conflict within individuals — between competing needs and demands — to which individuals respond in different ways.

Personal Conflict

Conflict sometimes has a destructive effect on the individuals and groups involved. At other times, however, conflict can increase the capacity of those affected to deal with problems, and therefore it can be used as a motivating force toward innovation and change. Conflict is encountered in two general forms. Personal conflict refers to an individual's inner workings and personality problems.

Many difficulties in this area are beyond the scope of management and more in the province of a professional counselor, but there are some aspects of personal conflict that managers should understand and some they can possibly help remedy. Social conflict refers to interpersonal, intragroup, and intergroup differences.

It was pointed out that there is a basic incompatibility between the authority and structure of formal organisations and the human personality. Human behavior cannot be separated from the culture that surrounds it.

Role Conflict

Another facet of personal conflict has to do with the multiple roles people play in organisations. Behavioral scientists sometimes describe an organisation as a system of position roles. Each member of the organisation belongs to a role set, which is an association of individuals who share interdependent tasks and thus perform formally defined roles, which are further influenced both by the expectations of others in the role set and by one's own personality and expectations. For example, in a common form of classroom organisation, students are expected to learn from the instructor by listening to him, following his directions for study, taking exams, and maintaining appropriate standards of conduct. The instructor is expected to bring students high-quality learning materials, give lectures, write and conduct tests, and set a scholarly example. Another in this role set would be the dean of the school, who sets standards, hires and supervises faculty, maintains a service staff, readers and graders, and so on. The system of roles to which an individual belongs extends outside the organisation as well, and influences his functioning within it.As an example, a man's roles as husband, father, son, and church member are all intertwined with each other and with his set of organisational roles.

As a consequence, there exist opportunities for role conflict as the various roles interact with one another. Other types of role conflict occur when an individual receives inconsistent demands from another person; for example, he is asked' to serve on several time-consuming committees at the same time that he is urged to get out more production in his work unit. Another kind of role strain takes place when the individual finds that he is expected to meet the opposing demands of two or more separate members of the organisation. Such a case would be that of a worker who finds himself pressured by his boss to improve the quality of his work while his work group wants more production in order to receive a higher bonus share.

These and other varieties of role conflict tend to increase an individual's anxiety and frustration. Sometimes they motivate him to do more and better work. Other times they can lead to frustration and reduced efficiency.

Organisational Conflict Theories

Maturity-immaturity Theory

According to Maslow, Argyris, McGregor, Rogers, and other writers of the so-called growth schools, there is a basic tendency in the development of the human personality toward self-fulfillment, or self-actualisation. This implies that as an individual matures, he wants to be given more responsibility, broader horizons, and the opportunity to develop his personal potential. This process is interrupted whenever a person's environment fails to encourage and nurture these desires.

Formal organisations are rational structures that, based on their assumption of emotions, feelings, and irrationality as human weaknesses, try to replace individual control with institutional control. Thus the principle of task specialisation is seen as a device that simplifies tasks for the sake of efficiency. As a consequence, however, it uses only a fraction of a person's capacity and ability. The principle of chain of command centralises authority but makes the individual more dependent on his superiors. The principle of normal span of control. which assigns a maximum of six or seven subordinates to report to the chief executive, reduces the number of individuals reporting to the head of the organisation or to the manager of any subunit. Although this simplifies the job of control for the manager, it also creates more intensive surveillance of the subordinate, and therefore permits him less freedom to control himself.

Under such conditions, subordinates are bound to find themselves in conflict with the formal organisation, and sometimes with each other. They advance up the narrowing hierarchy where jobs get fewer, and "fewer" implies competing with others for the decreasing number of openings. Task specialisation tends to focus the subordinate's attention on his own narrow function and divert him from thinking about the organisation as a whole. This effect increases the need for coordination and leads to a circular process of increasing the dependence on the leader.

They may respond to organisational pressures and threats by defensive reactions such as aggression against their supervisors and co-workers, fixated behavior or apathy, compromise and gamesmanship, or psychological withdrawal and daydreaming. All of these defense mechanisms reduce a person's potential for creative, constructive activity on the job. Finally, employees may organise unions or unsanctioned informal groups whose norms of behavior are opposed to many of the organisation's goals. As a sort of self-fulfilling prophecy, all of these reactions to the constraints of the formal organisation merely serve to reinforce and strengthen them.

The conflict between the formal organisation and the individual will continue to exist wherever managers remain ignorant of its causes or wherever the organisational structure and the leadership style are allowed to become inconsistent with the legitimate needs of the psychologically healthy individual. Everyone recognises the necessity for order and control in organisations. Those of us who enter management, however, must learn to recognise in addition that order and control can be achieved only at the expense of individual freedom.

Subordinates adapt to these conditions in the organisation in several ways. In the extreme, they may find the situation intolerable and leave the organisation. Or they may strive to advance to positions of higher authority, there to adopt the controlling style they are trying to escape.

Conflict within Groups

Conflicts between people in work groups, committees, task forces, and other organisational forms of face-to-face groups are inevitable. As we have mentioned, these conflicts may be destructive as well as constructive.

Conflict arises in groups because of the scarcity of freedom, position, and resources. People who value independence tend to resist the need for interdependence and, to some extent, conformity within a group. People who seek power therefore struggle with others for position or status within the group. Rewards and recognition are often perceived as insufficient and improperly distributed, and members are inclined to compete with each other for these prizes.

In western culture, winning is more acceptable than losing, and competition is more prevalent than cooperation, all of which tends to intensify intragroup conflict. Group meetings are often conducted in a win-lose climate — that is, individual or subgroup interaction is conducted for the purpose of determining a winner and a loser rather than for achieving mutual problem solving.

Effects of Group Conflicts

The win-lose conflict in groups may have some of the following negative effects :

— Divert time and energy from the main issues
— Delay decisions
— Create deadlocks
— Drive unaggressive committee members to the sidelines
— Interfere with listening
— Obstruct exploration of more alternatives
— Decrease or destroy sensitivity
— Cause members to drop out or resign from committees
— Arouse anger that disrupts a meeting
— Interfere with empathy
— Leave losers resentful Incline underdogs to sabotage
— Provoke personal abuse
— Cause defensiveness

Conflict in the group need not lead to negative results, however. The presence of a dissenting member or subgroup often results in more penetration of the group's problem and more creative solutions. This is because disagreement forces the members to think harder in an attempt to cope with what may be valid objections to general group opinion. But the group must know how to deal with differences that may arise.

True interdependence among members leads automatically to conflict resolution in the group. Interdependence recognises that differences will exist and that they can be helpful. Hence, members learn to accept ideas from dissenters (which does not imply agreeing with them), they learn to listen and to value openness, and they learn to share a mutual problem-solving attitude to ensure the exploration of all facets of a problem facing the group.

Intergroup conflict between groups is a sometimes necessary, sometimes destructive, event that occurs at all levels and across all functions in organisations. Intergroup conflict may help generate creative tensions leading to more effective contributions to the organisation's goals, such as competition between sales districts for the highest sales.

Intergroup conflict is destructive when it alienates groups that should be working together, when it results in win-lose competition, and when it leads to compromises that represent less-than-optimum outcomes.

Intergroup conflict occurs in two general forms. *Horizontal strain* involves competition between functions: for example, sales versus production, research and development versus engineering, purchasing versus legal, line versus staff, and so on. *Vertical strain* involves competition between hierarchical levels: for example, union versus management, foremen versus middle management, shop workers versus foremen.

A struggle between a group of employees and management is an example of vertical strain or conflict. A clash between a sales department and production over inventory policy would be an example of horizontal strain.

Certain activities and attitudes are typical in groups involved in a win-lose conflict. Each side closes ranks and prepares itself for battle. Members show increased loyalty and support for their own groups. Minor differences between group members tend to be smoothed over, and deviants are dealt with harshly. The level of morale in the groups increases and infuses everyone with competitive spirit. The power structure becomes better defined, as the "real" leaders come to the surface and members rally around the "best" thinkers and talkers.

In addition, each group tends to distort both its own views and those of the competing group. What is perceived as "good" in one's own position is emphasised, what is "bad" is ignored; the position of the other group is assessed as uniformly "bad," with little "good" to be acknowledged or accepted. Thus, the judgment and objectivity of both groups are impaired. When such groups meet to "discuss" their differences, constructive, rational behavior is severely inhibited.

Each side phrases its questions and answers in a way that strengthens its own position and disparages the other's. Hostility between the two groups increases; mutual understandings are buried in negative stereotypes.

It is easy to see that under the conditions described above, mutual solutions to problems cannot be achieved. As a result, the side having the greater power wins; the other side loses. Or the conflict may go unresolved, and undesirable conditions or circumstances continue. Or the conflict may be settled by a higher authority.

None of these outcomes is a happy one. Disputes settled on the basis of power, such as through a strike or a lockout in a labor-management dispute, are often deeply resented by the loser. Such settlements may be resisted and the winner defeated in underground ways that are difficult to detect and to counter. When this happens, neither side wins; both are losers. If the conflict is left unresolved, as when both sides withdraw from the scene, intergroup cooperation and effectiveness may be seriously impaired to the detriment of the entire organisation. Disputes that are settled by higher authority also may cause resentment and what is called "lose-lose" consequences. Such settlements are invariably made on the basis of incomplete information —without data that the conflict itself obscures — and therefore are poor substitutes for mutually reasoned solutions. Again, both sides have lost. A specific approach to resolving intergroup conflict is outlined in the next chapter on organisation development.

Thus, conflict affecting organisations can occur in individuals, between individuals, and between groups. Conflicts within work groups are often caused by struggles over control, status, and scarce resources. Conflicts between groups in organisations have similar origins. The constructive resolution of such conflicts can most often be achieved through a rational process of problem solving, coupled with a willingness to explore issues and alternatives and to listen to each other.

Conflict is not always destructive, it may be a motivator. When it is destructive, however, managers need to understand and do something about it. A rational process for dealing with the conflict should be programmed. Such a process should include a planned action response on the part of the manager or the organisation, rather than relying on a simple reaction or a change that occurs without specific action by management.

Conflict Resolution Methods

Counseling

When personal conflict leads to frustration and loss of efficiency, counseling may prove to be a helpful antidote. Although few organisations can afford the luxury of having professional counselors on the staff, given some training, managers may be able to perform this function. Nondirective counseling, or "listening with understanding", is little more than being a good listener — something every manager should be.

Sometimes the simple process of being able to vent one's feelings — that is, to express them to a concerned and understanding listener, is enough to relieve frustration and make it possible for the frustrated individual to advance to a problem-solving frame of mind, better able to cope with a personal difficulty that is affecting his work adversely. The nondirective approach is one effective way for managers to deal with frustrated subordinates and co-workers.

There are other more direct and more diagnostic ways that might be used in appropriate circumstances. The great strength of the nondirective approach (nondirective counseling is based on the client-centered therapy of Carl Rogers), however, lies in its simplicity, its effectiveness, and the fact that it deliberately avoids the manager-counselor's diagnosing and interpreting emotional problems, which would call for special psychological training. No one has ever been harmed by being listened to sympathetically and understandingly. On the contrary, this approach has helped many people to cope with problems that were interfering with their effectiveness on the job.

Strategies for Managing Group Conflicts

- *Avoidance*—a management strategy which includes nonattention or creating a total separation of the combatants or a partial separation that allows limited interaction·
- *Smoothing*—technique which stresses the achievement of harmony between disputants
- *Dominance or Power Intervention*—the imposition of a solution by higher management, other than the level at which the conflict exists
- *Compromise*—strategy that seeks a resolution which satisfies at least part of the each party's position·
- *Confrontation*—strategy featuring a thorough and frank discussion of the sources and types of conflict and achieving a resolution that is in the best interest of the group, but that may be at the expense of one or all of the conflicting parties ·

A trained conflict resolver can begin with an economical intervention, such as getting group members to clarify and reaffirm shared goals. If necessary, he or she moves through a systematic series of interventions, such as testing the members' ability and willingness to compromise; resorting to confrontation, enforced counseling, and/or termination as last resorts.

Change and Conflicts

Management is presumed to be guided by a vision of the future. The manager reflects in his decision-making activities the values of the organisation as they have developed through time, from the original founder-owner to the present top-management personnel. In navigating a path between the values of the organisation and its objectives and goals, management has expectations concerning the organisation's effectiveness and efficiency and frequently initiates changes within the organisation. On other occasions, changes in the external environment — market demand, technology, or the political, social, or economic environment — require making appropriate changes in the activities of the organisation. The organisation faces these demands for change through the men and women who make up its membership, since organisational change ultimately depends on the willingness of employees and others to change their attitudes, behavior, their degree of knowledge and skill, or a combination of these.

Personality change

In many contexts, the manager appears to be asking an employee to change his personality to conform to new requirements. This was the challenge that faced Freud as he used psychoanalysis in treating his patients, who had varying degrees of neurosis. The relationship between the psychoanalyst and his patient is one in which the individual seeking help is asked over a period of time to reach into his memory, and through free associations to communicate with the psychoanalyst about past incidents and events. The patient is peeling off layer after layer of experience stretching over a lifetime, with the support, understanding, and guidance of the psychoanalyst.

As the patient unfolds his life story, he may reach a particular incident or event that may be a root cause of his problem in living a "normal" life. If such an event in his past took place in preverbal infancy or before, he may never be able to recall it. Nevertheless, the psychoanalytic relationship itself, because it involves a high degree of trust and confidence and an opportunity to admit to a sympathetic and understanding listener hidden anxieties and fears, may provide the therapeutic experience that is needed for the patient to decide that he has solved his problem.

Though there are various theories of psychotherapy in addition to traditional Freudian psychoanalysis, the processes of therapy are often quite similar. In any case, changing an individual's personality is rarely possible in the short run. After all, it presumes changing the meaning that an individual has assigned to his life experiences. The Neo-Freudian point of view, however, assumes that an individual is amenable to personality change until he dies, though any change must become increasingly difficult as the individual adds layer upon layer of experience as he moves along life's path. Changing the core of an individual's personality within a "reasonable" time may offer little hope of success.

LIFE CYCLE OF A CONFLICT

On a general level, conflict prevention and conflict management are broad terms for methods and mechanisms used to avoid, minimise, and manage conflicts between different parties. Conflict prevention is a set of instruments used to prevent or solve disputes before they have developed into active conflicts. Conflict management is a theoretical concept focusing on the limitation, mitigation, and/or containment of a conflict without necessary solving it. Conflict resolution has traditionally referred to measures attempting to resolve the underlying incompatibilities of a conflict, including attempts to get the parties to mutually accept each others' existence. It is important to note here that the traditional separation of conflict prevention, management and resolution not only treat them as different concepts, but also as separate processes.

After presenting a working definition of conflict, a theoretical model of the conflict lifecycle will be provided. This model is thereafter used to elaborate upon different forms of conflict cycles, including addressing the problem with a conflict consisting of a large number of conflictual issues, or sub-conflicts.

The perception of threat, or actual occurrence of conflict, is necessary for the initiation of conflict prevention or management measures, and hence it is essential to address the concept of conflict before exploring how to prevent and manage such occurrences.

The first step is to understand what a conflict is made up by exactly. The starting point for this is the traditional definitions of conflicts, according to which a conflict is the result of opposing interests involving scarce resources, goal divergence and frustration. Then addresses more recent perceptions of the conflict concept. We suggest that conflicts should not be defined simply in terms of violence (behaviour) or hostility (attitudes), but also include incompatibility or "differences in issue position" (*Positiondifferenzen*) Such a definition is designed to include conflicts outside the traditional military sphere and is based on behavioural dimensions.

According to Mitchell, the conflict structure consists of three parts: attitudes, behaviour and situations that interact and create conflicts between actors. Mitchell's conflict structure simplifies the complex reality in an understandable way. (Model 1) The model was created for political and military conflicts, but is also applicable to the changes in perception of conflicts that the international community has experienced - economic, environmental and human security have became fundamental aspects of international and regional interaction.

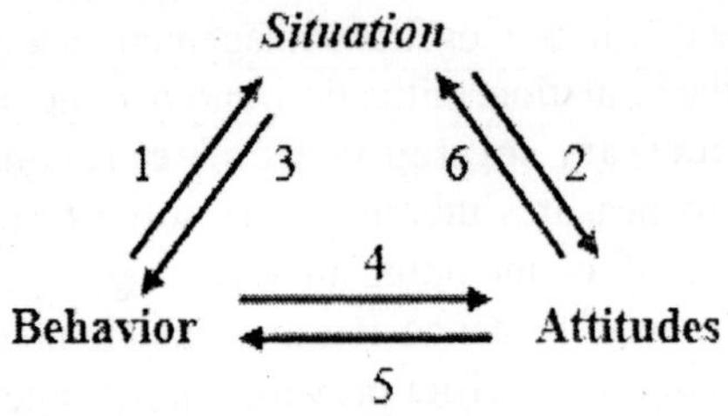

1. The situation impacts the behavior (failure to reach targeted goals, especially important goals, creates frustration and increases the willingness to reach these goals).
2. The situation impacts attitudes (incompatible goals increase the suspicion and distrust between the actors).
3. Behavior impacts the situation (success can introduce new questions in the conflict as demands increases).
4. Behavior impacts the attitudes (destruction increases hatred, success can impact the group solidarity and the notion of "us").
5. Attitudes impact the behavior (expectations such as "our traditional enemies will attack again" will impact the defensive planning and preventive actions).
6. Attitudes impact the situation (the longer the conflict continues the more questions will be introduced).

Model 1. Mitchell's Conflict Model

Mitchell's model is able to incorporate this. However, this model is complicated by the fact that conflicts often occur in mixed-motive relationships where the involved parties both have cooperative and competitive goals and Mitchell's model seems to have neglected this pluralistic/multifaceted/more complex dimension to the relationship. The competitive element creates conflict and the cooperative element creates incentives to negotiate an agreement. There are, however, studies that confirm that conflicts tend to occur even when the involved parties have highly compatible goals. This can be explained by including frustration, obstruction, and interference in the definition. The theoretical framework presented here has been adjusted to leave room for an interpretation of conflict which includes tensions, misunderstandings, political and economic interests, and historical animosity.

A conflict has generally been defined as a situation in which two or more parties strive to acquire the same scarce resources at the same time. Scholars generally agree that there needs to be more than one part to have a conflict, and that the time factor is important. What does cause concern is the term *scarce resource*. The central point in this argument is scarcity, but resources need also be included in the discussion. Peter Wallensteen has pointed out that resources are not only economic in nature, and that the terminology might miss conflicts involving economic orientation, human security, environment, historical issues, etc. Such conflicts are not necessarily about resources, and when they are, these resources are, more importantly, not necessarily scarce. A conflict is, moreover, in many cases based on perceptions, rather than on attitudes or behaviour as it has generally been defined.

When discussing the concept of conflict, perception should be included as a central concept since the conflicts and the opponent's intentions often are defined according to subjective perceptions. There could be an abundance of space for agreement in a conflict, but if the parties perceive the conflict as being impossible to resolve or the opponent to be untrustworthy this might not help in resolving the conflict. The normative disputes (often subjectively defined) are also left out of the rational definitions. These disputes involve religion, values and beliefs and do not always have a military outcome. In conclusion, we suggest the following definition of conflict: *perceived differences in issue positions between two or more parties at the same moment in time.*

A conflict is not a static situation, but a dynamic one – the intensity level changes over a conflicts' life cycle. An understanding of the conflict cycle is essential for an understanding of how, where and when to apply different strategies and measures of conflict prevention and management. Over time, numerous suggestions and models of conflict patterns have been put forward. Among these models and suggestions, a number of patterns stand out. Conflicts tend to be described as cyclical in regard to their intensity levels, i.e. escalating from (relative) stability and peace into crisis and war, thereafter deescalating into relative peace. Most scholars also agree that these cycles are reoccurring. This proposition is strongly supported by empirical research on conflict patterns. Here, it should also be noted that many scholars add stable, sometimes called durable, peace as an additional phase in which the conflict is considered resolved – i.e. the reoccurring pattern of the conflict has been stopped. Also, most models divide both the escalation and de-escalation of the conflict cycle into phases. It can also be noted that in many cases the conflict model has taken the form of a U, or an upside-down U.

The division into phases, and the cyclical perception of conflict, has also become the starting point for research on conflict prevention, management and resolution. In principle, conflict prevention, conflict management and conflict resolution are regarded as applicable in different phases of a conflict. In sum, conflict prevention measures are designed for the early phases, before a conflict has become manifest (open). Management measures are applied in later phases when a conflict is manifest, but before violence has occurred. Conflict resolution could, on the other hand, be applied in the de-escalation phase after a violent conflict has occurred. As illustrated below, the division into phases is a much simplified description of reality. Also, there are disagreements both within the academic and the policy community, as well as between the two as to how these measures should be understood and applied.

The model of the life-cycle of conflicts presented here includes both the conflict process itself and possible prevention, management and resolution measures. (Model 2) This conflict cycle is presented in the form of an upside-down U-curve, illustrating a conflict cycle in its most simplified form, i.e. the rise from stable peace to war and the de-escalation to stable peace. The model presented below is an ideal model of the conflict cycle, an analytical construction developed to simplify analysis. This model is simplified and is not always in line with the empirical reality.

The curve is divided into five levels of conflict intensity (stable peace, unstable peace, open conflict, crisis, and war) in a total of nine chronological phases. *Stable peace* is a situation where tension

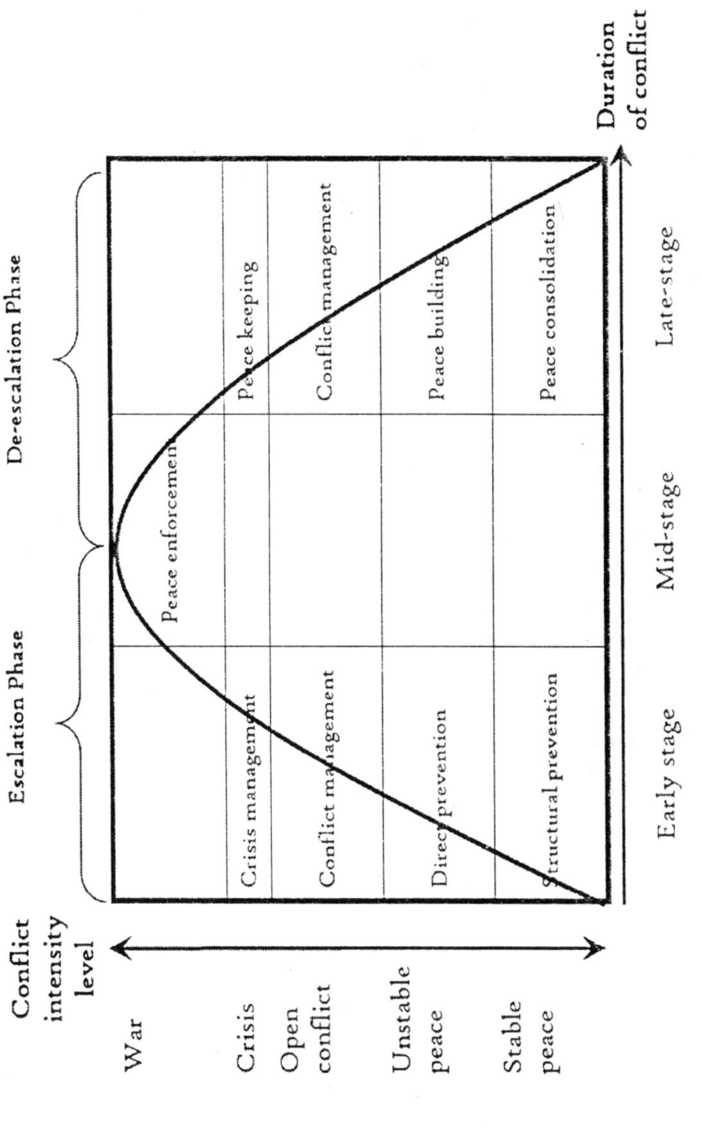

Model 2: The Conflict Cycle

between the parties is low and there exists different forms of connections and cooperation between them, often including economic and environmental cooperation, as well as cooperation within other non-sensitive issue-areas. During a period of *unstable peace,* tension has increased. This is a situation where, albeit the existing negative peace, the tension between the parties is so high that peace no longer seems guaranteed. An *open conflict* is when the conflict is defined and the parties have taken measures to deal with it, even if militarised options are not adopted. In the *crisis phase*, the risk of war is imminent and militarised options are the preferable or likely option. There may be sporadic violence between the parties at this stage, but there is no regular open violence. In the *war phase*, on the other hand, there is widespread and intense violence. In the de-escalation phase the pattern is reversed, moving from war to crisis, through open conflict and unstable peace to finally reach a situation of stable peace.

Just as the phases of the conflict cycle are important, the connection between conflict prevention and conflict- and crisis managing needs to be developed further. The easiest way to separate between the concepts is by focusing on the time factor. Starting with conflict prevention, it is by definition applied *before* the conflict has become open and violent, i.e. to prevent a conflict from emerging in the first place (or to prevent a conflict from re-escalating in a post-conflict phase). Conflict prevention measures are effective at the levels of stable- and unstable peace before a conflict has become manifest. Here, it is important to differentiate between structural- and direct preventive measures.

The former are most applicable in the stable peace phase and consist of structural measures that often aim at specific groups or issues such as economic development, political participation or cultural autonomy. The benefits of applying structural measures at an early stage is simply that the acceptance of preventive measures tends to be higher at low levels of inter-party suspicion and hence more far-reaching and institutional measures can be implemented. If structural preventive measures are implemented at an early stage, including both the building of institutions and development of trust and (longer-term) cooperation, they decrease the perceived need to, and hence risk of, escalating a potential conflict issue into the level of unstable peace. The more pronounced a conflict becomes the more specific measures it requires. At the same time, structural measures are losing importance as a probable strategy.

In the unstable peace phase, the direct preventive measures are directed at issues with a shorter term goal in mind, i.e. to reduce tension and create trust between the actors. Simultaneously, the window of opportunity for longer-term initiatives, such as the building of institutions, fades away slowly and the conflict becomes more issue specific and more costly in financial and political terms. Direct preventive measures can, for example, be formal or informal workshops dealing with the possible conflict issues. They can also aim at creating openness in certain fields such as the military, reducing military spending, or achieving cooperation in rescue operations. Other examples include sanctions, coercive diplomacy, the dispatch of special envoys, and problem-solving workshops. It should be noted that the border between structural and direct prevention is unclear and that aspects of the two are often overlapping.

Conflict management and crisis management do, on the other hand, involve tactics that are enforced when violent conflict is deemed likely (conflict management) or imminent (crisis management), but before a situation escalates into war. Conflict management can be enforced, as soon as the conflict has been identified by the actors, as an effort to reduce tension and prevent further escalation. Direct measures, such as reduction of military forces, third party intervention, informal and formal communication or general CBMs, can be designed to handle the conflict and reverse destructive behaviour into constructive. The measures are often bilateral as questions many times are sensitive and not seen as threatening at this stage. However, multilateral forums, such as the UN, are increasingly being used.

Crisis management is employed in the short time frame before a war is to erupt, when the conflict escalates rapidly and the time for management measures is limited. This period is characterised by a scarcity of time and other resources to address the conflict, as well as inadequate information. Crisis management entails more drastic measures than conflict management and aims at containing the outbreak of militarised conflicts with all available means. Examples of such measures include third party intervention by actors such as NATO or the UN. Some analysts also view preventive strikes as possible conflict- and crisis management measures.

During the stage of war, neither prevention nor management is possible. Military means are used as the primary tool, even if political, economic and social tools are used simultaneously to decrease the opponent's willingness and/or capability to fight. At this stage, the actors either have to fight things out until reaching a so-called hurting stalemate where both parties realise the need to end the conflict, or peace has to be enforced by external actors. At this stage there are of course many different measures that could be utilised, but few of these are peaceful. One example of a measure is to prevent military conflicts from spreading to other states or regions. It should be noted that there often is a great reluctance to allow external intervention before war tiredness and a hurting stalemate has been reached.

If the militarisation of a conflict is temporarily controlled, either through a peace treaty or a cease fire, it may be possible to reverse the positions of the actors and make them adopt more constructive behaviour. Initially, the focus is on separating the actors and preventing further mistakably or deliberate escalation (peace keeping). This stage is comparable to the crisis stage in the escalation phase and often involves third party actors that assist with peacekeeping and/or monitoring. When the more imminent threats of re-escalation have been dealt with, further opportunities exist for less short-term and direct measures, and the conflicts move into the conflict management phase. There is still a risk for escalation, but no imminent threat of war. When the conflict has deescalated further, a phase of peace building follows, which gives room for more long-term measures. Finally, if the peace building efforts meet with success, the conflict moves to the peace consolidation phase where the aim is to make actors more cooperative and create an inclusive peace for all involved parties. In other words, the de-escalation phase shares many similarities with the escalation phase.

The later stages of peace building and peace reconciliation are often financially costly and require enormous political and economic commitment from the international community as well as the involved actors. This is not to mention the economic and social costs that affect the population at large, but especially the poorer sections of society. Thus, the conviction that resolution and other mechanisms applied to deal with conflicts have to be introduced after the conflict is militarised is humanitarian as well as financially unsound. In general, the measures used in the de-escalation phase are often much more financially and politically demanding than pro-active measures in the escalation phase. Furthermore, measures taken after a war often have to involve third parties, like the UN or stronger military actors that can guarantee security for all actors involved, which is not needed to the same extent in the escalation phase. This takes a lot of political compromises and intense negotiations in an environment that lacks trust. Without exception, trust is lacking after a militarised conflict and trust between the involved parties is tremendously difficult, although not impossible, to rebuild. In the real world, there are often no, or limited, trust until the peace consolidation phase has been initiated.

Conflict Prevention

Conflict prevention means different things to different people and there is no single definition that is agreed upon. During the Cold War, many practitioners and academics viewed preventive action as synonymous with pre-emptive strikes. After the Cold War, this has changed, and preventive measures have come to receive a new meaning and the emphasis has shifted to the peaceful prevention of disputes. With regard to the development of the concept of conflict prevention, Anders Bjurner has pointed out that conflict prevention is a fairly new sub-culture of security and foreign policy studies. This is in a sense true, but one should note that it is a sub-culture with a long history. Indeed, the idea of prevention was central during the congress of Vienna in 1815 (A.D.) and in the writings of Sun Tzu. Conflict prevention was never mentioned as a concept but in practice there was a practical concern to prevent conflicts and deter the reoccurrence of conflicts.

Conflict prevention is often divided into two categories: direct prevention and structural prevention. Direct conflict prevention refers to measures that are aimed at preventing short-term, often imminent, escalation of a potential conflict. Structural prevention focuses on more long term measures that address the underlying causes of a potential conflict along with potentially escalating and triggering factors. Economic development assistance or increased political participation are examples of structural prevention, while the dispatch of a mediator or the withdrawal of military forces are examples of direct prevention. The distinction between structural and direct prevention is important, especially in the policy field although many measures such as military disarmament can have both structural and direct effects.

The next concept that needs to be defined is conflict prevention. Despite the wide array of writings on conflict prevention, there is a lack of consensus regarding its definition. Thus there is a wide range of definitions, ranging from more narrow ones focusing on limited ways of prevention such as Michael Lund's definition of preventive diplomacy, to broad ones such as David Carment and Albrecht Schnabel's definition of conflict prevention.

Michael Lund defines preventive diplomacy as "actions taken in vulnerable places and times to avoid the threat or use of armed force and related forms of coercion by states or groups to settle the political disputes that can arise from destabilising effects of economic, social, political, and international change." Boutros Boutros-Ghali has defined preventive diplomacy as "the use of diplomatic techniques to prevent disputes arising, prevent them from escalating into armed conflict ... and prevent the armed conflict from spreading." These definitions are limited to diplomatic measures and exclude non-diplomatic measures such as economic development or military measures.

It needs to be noted that preventive diplomacy is a problematic term. As has been noted above the term focuses on diplomatic efforts of conflict prevention during the early stages of a conflict, while conflict prevention defines a wider set of preventive measures of which diplomacy merely is one aspect. However, some even argue that in order to be considered diplomacy, or even an effective tool, preventive diplomacy needs to be official. More recent publications on conflict prevention do not always make this division between preventive diplomacy and conflict prevention, but at the same time many keep the old separation. This sometimes creates a communication problem when actors believe that they understand each other, whereas they in fact are talking about different types of preventive measures. Many believe that they are limiting themselves to the official efforts, while others consider the same discussion as entailing additional non-official strategies.

Among the more inclusive definitions is David Carment and Albrecht Schnabel's definition of conflict prevention as "a medium and long-term proactive operational or structural strategy undertaken by a variety of actors, intended to identify and create the enabling conditions for a stable and more predictable international security environment." Another broader definition is provided by Gabriel Munuera, who defines conflict prevention as the application of non-constraining measures that are primarily diplomatic in nature. Non-constraining measures are those that are not coercive and depend on the goodwill of the parties involved. Michael Lund has also suggested a wider definition:

> "any structural or intercessory means to keep intrastate or interstate tension and disputes from escalating into significant violence and use of armed forces, to strengthen the capabilities of potential parties to violent conflict for resolving such disputes peacefully, and to progressively reduce the underlying problems that produce these issues and disputes".

This definition takes into consideration any measures that prevent violent conflicts and strengthen the capacity of concerned actors to act structurally to reduce the possibility of conflict.

It is currently being discussed whether a more narrow definition is needed to make conflict prevention researchable, or whether a broader definition is preferable since it allows for a broadening of the operational alternatives and an expansion outside the box. The Swedish Foreign Ministry has, for example, emphasised the importance of a broad definition of conflict prevention. It promotes a definition that takes a holistic view on conflict prevention and human security and includes both individuals and states. The argument for the inclusion of both individuals and states is that a focus solely on political disputes would be to narrow of a definition to incorporate all possible threats to stability and peace. This broader definition is a reaction against earlier failures to see security threats. It could be said that the international community has been slow, or in some cases, inactive in its response to new security threats. It has also been slow to adapt to the non-conventional manner in which these threats materialise and the levels they are materialising on, i.e. transnational and non-governmental levels.

The broader approach acknowledges the importance of economic and social development, as well as security, military, and judicial measures. These aspects form an integral part of conflict prevention and have contributed to the growing effectiveness of prevention measures. The importance of conflict prevention has also been emphasised by the World Bank.

The World Bank views conflict prevention together with post-conflict reconstruction as critical to the bank's mission of poverty reduction, thereby acknowledging the vicious circles in many of the world's poorest states, where poverty causes conflict and conflict causes poverty. This new more inclusive approach is increasingly accepted by policy-makers and has introduced new security threats onto the agenda.

Finally, the idea of a cultural of prevention needs to be mentioned as it is central to thinking about conflict prevention in the 21st century. This idea indicates a regional or global understanding of the need and methods of prevention and is being promoted by the UN Secretary General Kofi Annan who has been trying to move his organisation away from a culture of reaction to one of prevention. Also the Organisation for Economic Co-operation and Development (OECD) has emphasised the need for a culture of prevention, both in development cooperation and foreign policy. In its DAC guidelines, the OECD urges the international community to apply a conflict prevention dimension to all its actions.

According to the OECD, a culture of prevention could be accomplished if the international community was better able to "analyse the causes and dynamics of conflict and peace in order to understand how their actions will affect the "structural stability" of a society or country". Furthermore, it urges the international community to be more aware of "the political aspects of any activity and understand how its aims, design, and implementation may interact with the political and economic dynamics in that society, including their effect on poverty" The idea of a culture of prevention has also been discussed by prominent scholars and practitioners in a recent volume on conflict prevention which was published in memory of the late Swedish Foreign Minister Anna Lind. Nevertheless, the concept has been less than successful in practice, despite its rhetoric power in the international community.

Conflict Management and Resolution

Fred Tanner has defined conflict management as the limitation, mitigation and/or containment of a conflict without necessarily solving it. Peter Wallensteen and Niklas Swanström have added to this definition and argue that conflict management should imply a change, from destructive to constructive, in the mode of interaction. William I. Zartman has argued that conflict management refers to eliminating violent and violence-related actions and leaving the conflict to be dealt with on the political level. Zartman's argument has been somewhat criticised as NGOs, academic institutions and half-formal (track-two) structures have emerged as important actors and now influence the conflict management process.

Wallensteen has also claimed that conflict management typically focuses on the armed aspects of a conflict. Swanström, on the other hand, has argued that an armed conflict not necessarily is needed for conflict management to be applied. Swanström's argument is that as soon a structural problem is defined or a direct conflict is manifest, without being militarised, it can and should be addressed by the active parties and the international community. As soon as a conflict has been militarised, the momentum has been lost and the political and economic cost to solve or manage the conflict escalates quickly. It is far easier to change the mode of interaction from destructive to constructive in an early rather than late phase. In this process confidence-building measures (CBMs) are crucial as they serve to strengthen the conflict management process by increasing trust between the actors. This is true both in the case of formal and informal conflict management. It should indeed be noted that the best result often are achieved by combining informal and formal conflict management. The importance of using both formal and informal mechanisms can for example be seen in the negotiations regarding the Korean Peninsula, negotiations which would not have taken place without the use of both formal and informal measures and mechanisms.

The process of conflict management is the foundation for more effective conflict resolution. A distinction between conflict management and conflict resolution is, however, needed as a starting point as the concepts often are confused or integrated in an inappropriate manner. Conflict resolution refers to the resolution of the underlying incompatibilities in a conflict and mutual acceptance of each party's existence, while conflict management refers to measures that limit, mitigate and/or contain a conflict without necessary solving it.

William I. Zartman has pointed out that both the conflict resolution aspect (negotiation) and the conflict management aspect is needed to arrive at a positive result. He argues that they are both ends of the same continuum. One end aims at resolving the current conflict so that business or peace can move on while the other aims at resolving the deeper underlying conflict over time.

Conflict resolution can be both formal and informal. It can either aim at resolving or terminating conflicts in an open and predictable process in accordance with legal principles or focus on

> "efforts to increase cooperation among the parties to a conflict and deepen their relationship by addressing the conditions that led to the dispute, fostering positive attitudes and allaying distrust through reconciliation initiatives, and building or strengthening the institutions and processes through which the parties interact".

The final aim of resolving the conflict is however shared by both perspectives regardless of process.

A number of scholars, especially from non-Western societies, have argued that conflict management is a successful tool for resolving conflicts over a longer time period, and that it creates the foundation for effective conflict resolution. This is contrasted to a more Western argument that the importance of conflict management lies in its ability to solve short-term conflicts. Both of these views are entirely accurate, and compatible, and there might just be a cultural difference in our focus. Both of these views can, and should, be incorporated in a theoretical framework for conflict management and resolution, since they entail no inherent contradiction. They are in fact often applied in different stages of a conflict and address fundamentally different issues. Nevertheless, a number of Western scholars claim that the difference is one of long-term versus short-term perspectives and that it is a question of either resolving the underlying problem or the current problem. Kwok Leung and Dean Tjosvold, and other scholars focusing on Asia, have taken the opposing view and argue that it is more about relationships and that blind justice could terminate long-term relationships.

However, in reality, the integration of two fundamentally opposing cultures of conflict management and resolution into one organisation has resulted in apparent cases of stalemate. When comparing two or more cultural settings, the difference in perception is an interesting factor when dealing with mechanisms for handling conflicts. In sum, conflict management and conflict resolution are different concepts, but at the same time they are closely interrelated. They are two mechanisms at different sides of a continuum, used to deal with the same conflicts but at different stages of these conflicts.

Conflict management and conflict prevention has, in a similar way, been argued to be different sides of the same coin. It has also been argued that conflict management is required in order to enable the initiation of preventive measures aiming at resolving the dispute. Zartman argues that the difference merely exists in theory and that both concepts are intertwined in the practical implementation. Preventive measures are designed to resolve, contain and manage conflicts so that they do not erupt into violent conflicts. This makes conflict management an important part of conflict prevention. It is important to point out that conflict management can be introduced at all levels of a conflict spiral and that it is widely used in crisis management and war situations.

At the operational level of conflict prevention, Michael Lund argues that preventive measures are especially effective at the level of unstable peace, which is a "situation where tension and suspicion among parties run high but violence is either absent or only sporadic". This is arguably not always the case since some preventive measures are best operationalised at an earlier stage, preferable during stable peace where there is a minimum of suspicion between potential adversaries. The reason for this is simply that the acceptance of preventive measures is higher when no suspicion disturbs the situation. If institutions, trust and cooperation is built at an early stage, it is less likely that the conflict reaches the stage of unstable peace.

It is clear that many states and regional organisations see little or no point in working with conflict prevention since there are no military conflicts. The old saying "why fix it when it is not broken" becomes a sad reality. This is the same as saying "why buy insurance if you are not sick". The simple answer is that when you need the insurance, it is too late to get it. It is not argued that all potential conflicts can be prevented, only that early prevention will decrease the amount of conflicts that will escalate to unstable peace or war, thereby preventing human suffering and saving economic capital. This argument has, over time, become more accepted among international organisations. They have gradually moved towards emphasising the importance of pro-active and structural measures to prevent conflicts, especially in their development policies.

This tendency can not least be seen in the emphasis on the development of a culture of prevention. However, in practice the implementation is still problematic as it tends to be difficult to legitimise huge costs to prevent potential conflicts that have not yet reached a critical level. It is simply easier to successfully argue for spending more money once an open conflict has started, despite the waste of political and economic resources, not to mention the social and humanitarian suffering.

Integrated Approach to Conflict Prevention

The separation of the three concepts, even when approached as different sides of the same coin or as a certain continuum, creates a problem with existing theory. In theory, it has been regarded necessary to make a distinction between the resolution, management and prevention of conflicts, as a way of simplifying reality to enable the construction of a theoretical model. However, this separation is not only artificial, but also incoherent as different scholars use their own definition of the respective concepts. A more coherent definition of prevention and management is thus needed, a definition that can be integrated with other mechanisms for handling conflicts.

In addition, a theory that differentiates between conflict prevention, conflict management and conflict resolution also risks being counterproductive when applied to a reality in which these concepts in fact are indistinguishable. In practice these measures can be seen as working side by side at different levels and within different issues in a larger conflict. It is thus possible, as argued earlier, to resolve certain issues in a conflict, while at the same time managing or preventing other issues from taking a violent form. This does not imply that the conflict has been resolved, or even that tension has been reduced since new issues can be brought into the conflict at any time.

Due to the complexity of the conflict cycle there is a dire need of a holistic approach to conflict prevention, management and resolution, and the tool box needs to be open for alternative thinking. Disseminating a conflict into several subgroups and core issues increases the possibility to act even in conflicts that seem difficult to act in. Prevention, management, and resolution measures need to be applied in a coordinated and integrated fashion that leaves nothing open to minimise lost opportunities to act.

The problems that the separation of these concepts entail need to be addressed in future research. As opposed to the existing theoretical frameworks, an integrated theoretical approach would have the potential to minimise conflicts, both in number and intensity. Policy-makers and military staff is often put off by the non-operationality of many of the models that are presented and regard the concepts as mere academic exercises. This can, in many cases, be traced back to a practical realisation that the differences between the concepts are small and that they often go hand in hand. Arguably, this last point is, on its own, a good enough reason to explore the possibility of an integrated framework.

References

Alfred W Clark (1976). *Experimenting with organisational life: the action research approach*. New York: Plenum Press.

Chris Argyris (1957). *Personality and organisation; the conflict between system and the individual*. New York: Harper & Row. pp. 47–54.

Daniel Katz; Robert Louis Kahn (1966). *The social psychology of organisations*. New York: Wiley. pp. 18–33.

Henry P Knowles; Börje O Saxberg (1971). *Personality and leadership behavior*. Reading, Mass.: Addison-Wesley Pub. Co.

John E Jones; J William Pfeiffer (1973). *The 1973 annual handbook for group facilitators*. San Diego, Calif.: University Associates. pp. 106–109.

Kenneth Kaye (1994). *Workplace Wars and How to End Them: Turning Personal Conflict into Productive Teamwork*. New York: AMACOM.

Patrick J. Montana (2008). *Management*. New York: Barron's Educational Series. p. 265.

Richard Arvid Johnson (1976). *Management, systems, and society : an introduction*. Pacific Palisades, Calif.: Goodyear Pub. Co.. pp. 148–142.

Theodore M Mills (1967). *The Sociology of Small Groups*. Englewood Cliffs, N.J.: Prentice-Hall. pp. 14–17

6

Skill and Competence Management

Management is an unpredictable process. Making the right decision is difficult; even effective managers often make mistakes, but the most effective managers are the ones, like Nardelli, who learn from their mistakes and continually strive to find ways to help their companies increase their competitive advantage and performance.

Organisations are collections of people who work together and co-ordinate their actions to achieve a wide variety *of goals,* or desired future outcomes. Second, as managers, they are the people responsible for supervising the use of an organisation's human and other resources to achieve its goals. Management, then, is the planning, organising, leading, and controlling of human and other resources to achieve organisational goals efficiently and effectively. An organisation's *resources* include assets such as people and their skills, know-how, and knowledge; machinery; raw materials; computers and information technology; and financial capital.

One of the most important goals that organisations and their members try to achieve is to provide some kind of good or service that customers desire. The principal goal of CEO Bob Nardelli is to manage The Home Depot so that the stores stock the kinds of home improvement products customers want and sales associates provide customers with excellent advice and quality service. The principal goal of doctors, nurses, and hospital administrators is to increase their hospital's ability to make sick people well. Likewise, the principal goal of each McDonald's restaurant manager is to produce burgers, fries, and shakes that people want to pay for and eat.

Organisational performance is a measure of how efficiently and effectively managers use resources to satisfy customers and achieve organisational goals. Organisational performance increases in direct proportion to increases in efficiency and effectiveness.

Efficiency is a measure of how well or how productively resources are used to achieve a goal. Organisations are efficient when managers minimise the amount of input resources (such as labor, raw materials, and component parts) or the amount of time needed to produce a given output of goods or services. For example, McDonald's developed a more efficient fat fryer that not only reduces the amount of oil used in cooking by 30 percent but also speeds up the cooking of french fries. Bob Nardelli instructed Home Depot's store managers to reduce the range of products sold in their stores to reduce costs, while better meeting the needs of the customers. A manager's responsibility is to ensure that an organisation and its members perform as efficiently as possible all the activities needed to provide goods and services to customers.

Effectiveness is a measure of the appropriateness of the goals that managers have selected for the organisation to pursue and of the degree to which the organisation achieves those goals. Organisations are effective when managers choose appropriate goals and then achieve them. Some years ago, for example, managers at McDonald's decided on the goal of providing breakfast service to attract more customers. The choice of this goal has proved very smart, for sales of breakfast food now account for more than 30 percent of McDonald's revenues. Nardelli's goal is to ensure a constant flow of state-of-the-art home improvement products into his stores. High-performing organisations are simultaneously efficient and effective. Effective managers are those who choose the right organisational goals to pursue and have the skills to utilise resources efficiently.

Importance of Management Studies

Today,, more students are competing for places in business courses than ever before; the number of people wishing to pursue Master of Business Administration (MBA) degrees—today's passport to an advanced management position—either on campus or from online universities is at an all-time high. Why is the study of management currently so popular? First, in any society or culture resources are valuable and scarce, so the more efficient and effective use that organisations can make of those resources, the greater the relative well-being and prosperity of people in that society. Because managers are the people who decide how to use many of a society's most valuable resources-its skilled employees, raw materials like oil and land, computers and information systems, and financial assets—they directly impact the well-being of a society and the people in it. Understanding what managers do and how they do it is of central importance to understanding how a society works and how it creates wealth.

Second, although most people are not managers, and many may never intend to become managers, almost all of us encounter managers because most people have jobs and bosses. Moreover, many people today are working in groups and teams and have to deal with co-workers. Studying management helps people to deal with their bosses and their co-workers. It reveals how to understand other people at work and make decisions and take actions that win the attention and support of the boss. Management also teaches people not yet in positions of authority how to lead co-workers, solve conflicts between them, and increase team performance.

Third, in any society, people are in competition for a very important resource— a well-paying job and an interesting and satisfying career—and understanding management is one important path toward obtaining such a position. In general, jobs become more interesting the more complex or responsible they are. Any person who desires a motivating job that changes over time might therefore do well to develop management skills and become promotable. A person who has been working for several years and then returns to school for an MBA can usually, after earning the degree, find a more interesting, satisfying job and one that pays significantly more than the previous job.

MANAGERIAL FUNCTIONS

The job of management is to help an organisation make the best use of its resources to achieve its goals. How do managers accomplish this objective? They do so by performing four essential managerial functions: *planning, organising, leading,* and *controlling* (Figure 1).

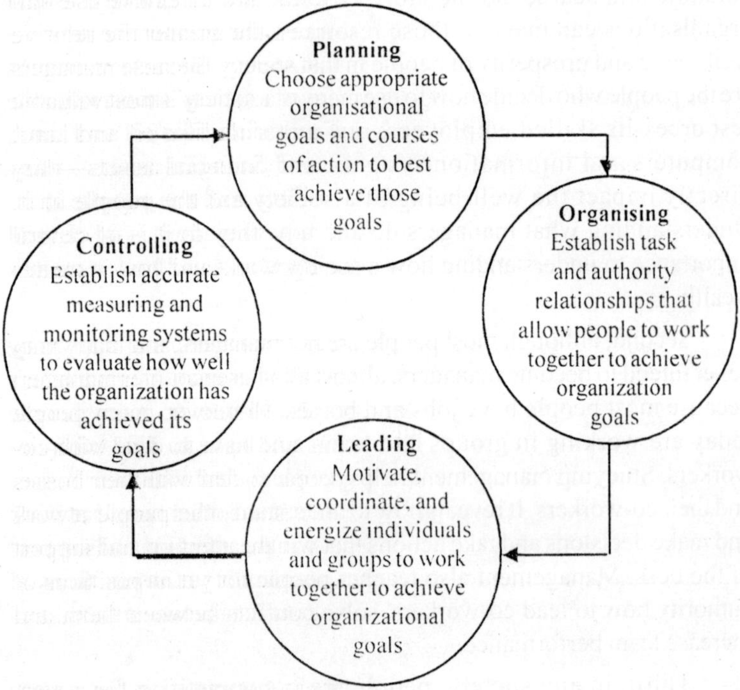

Figure 1. Four Functions of Management

The arrows linking these functions in Figure 1 suggest the sequence in which managers typically perform the functions. French manager Henri Fayol first outlined the nature of these managerial activities around the turn of the twentieth century in *General and Industrial Management,* a book that remains the classic statement of what managers must do to create a high-performing organisation. Managers at all levels and in all departments—whether in small or large organisations, for-profit or not-for-profit organisations, or organisations that operate in one country or throughout the world—are responsible for performing these four functions, which we look at next. How well managers perform these functions determines how efficient and effective their organisations are.

Planning

Planning is a process that managers use to identify and select appropriate goals and courses of action. Three steps in the planning process are (1) deciding which goals the organisation will pursue, (2) deciding what courses of action to adopt to attain those goals, and (3) deciding how to allocate organisational resources to attain those goals. How well managers plan determines how effective and efficient the organisation is—its performance level.

As an example of planning in action, consider the situation confronting Michael Dell, CEO of Dell Computer, the most profitable PC maker and Apple's main competitor. In 1984, the 19-year-old Dell saw an opportunity to enter the PC market by assembling PCs and then selling them directly to customers. Dell began to plan how to put his idea into practice. First, he decided that his goal was to sell an inexpensive PC, to undercut the prices of companies like Compaq and Apple. Second, he had to decide on a course of action to achieve this goal. He decided to sell directly to customers by telephone and to bypass expensive computer stores that sold Compaq and Apple PCs. He also had to decide how to obtain low-cost components and how to tell potential customers about his products. Third, he had to decide how to allocate his limited funds (he only had $5,000) to buy labor and other resources. He chose to hire three people and work with them around a table to assemble his PCs.

Thus, to put his vision of making and selling PCs into practice, Dell had to plan, and as his organisation grew, his plans changed and became progressively more complex. Dell and his managers are continually planning how to help the company maintain its position as the biggest and highest-performing PC maker. In 2003, Dell announced it would begin to sell printers and personal digital assistants (PDAs); this brought it into direct competition with Hewlett-Packard (HP), the leading printer maker, and Palm One, the maker of the Palm Pilot. In 2003, Dell also brought out its own Internet music player, the Digital Jukebox, to compete against Apple's iPod, and in 2005 it announced it would sell a new line of low-priced servers and storage devices to compete with those offered by HP and Sun.

As Dell's actions suggest, the outcome of planning is a strategy, a cluster of decisions concerning what organisational goals to pursue, what actions to take, and how to use resources to achieve goals. The decisions that were the outcome of Michael Dell's planning formed a *low-cost strategy.* A low-cost strategy is a way of obtaining customers by making decisions that allow the organisation to produce its goods or services cheaply so that prices can be kept low. Dell has been constantly refining this strategy and exploring new strategies to reduce costs. Dell has become the most profitable PC maker as a result of its low-cost strategy, and it is hoping to repeat its success in the music player business. By contrast, Apple Computers current strategy is to deliver new, exciting, and different computer and digital products, such as the iPod, to its customers—a strategy known as *differentiation.* The mini iPod and photo iPod were developed for people on the go, for example; they have unique, easy-to-use controls and come in a variety of bright contemporary colours.

Planning is a difficult activity because normally what goals an organisation should pursue and how best to pursue them—which strategies to adopt—is not immediately clear. Managers take risks when they commit organisational resources to pursue a particular strategy. Either success or failure is a possible outcome of the planning process. Dell succeeded spectacularly, but many other PC makers either went out of business (such as Packard Bell and Digital) or lost huge sums of money (like IBM and AT&T) trying to compete in this industry.

Organising

Organising is a process that managers use to establish a structure of working relationships that allow organisational members to interact and cooperate to achieve organisational goals. Organising involves grouping people into departments according to the kinds of job-specific tasks they perform. In organising, managers also lay out the lines of authority and responsibility between different individuals and groups, and they decide how best to coordinate organisational resources, particularly human resources.

The outcome of organising is the creation of an organisational structure, a formal system of task and reporting relationships that coordinates and motivates members so that they work together to achieve organisational goals. Organisational structure determines how an organisation's resources can be best used to create goods and services. As Dell Computer grew, for example, Michael Dell faced the issue of how to structure the organisation. Early on he was hiring 100 new employees a week and deciding how to design his managerial hierarchy to best motivate and coordinate managers' activities. As his organisation grew, he and his managers created progressively more complex kinds of organisational structures to help it achieve its goals.

Leading

In leading managers not only articulate a clear vision for organisational members to follow but also energise and enable organisational members so that they understand the part they play in achieving organisational goals. Leadership depends on the use of power, influence, vision, persuasion, and communication skills to coordinate the behaviours of individuals and groups so that their activities and efforts are in harmony and to encourage employees to perform at a high level. The outcome of leadership is a high level of motivation and commitment among organisational members. Employees at Dell Computer, for example, responded well to Michael Dell's hands-on leadership style, which has resulted in a hardworking, committed workforce. Similarly, Home Depot's store managers now recognise how important it was that Bob Nardelli centralised purchasing to reduce costs.

Controlling

In controlling, managers evaluate how well an organisation is achieving its goals and take action to maintain or improve performance. For example, managers monitor the performance of individuals, departments, and the organisation as a whole to see whether they are meeting desired performance standards. Michael Dell learned early in his career how important this is. If standards are not being met, managers take action to improve performance.

The outcome of the control process is the ability to measure performance accurately and regulate organisational efficiency and effectiveness. To exercise control, managers must decide which goals to measure—perhaps goals pertaining to productivity, quality, or responsiveness to customers—and then they must design information and control systems that will provide the data they need to assess performance. The controlling function also allows managers to evaluate how well they themselves are performing the other three functions of management—planning, organising, and leading—and to take corrective action.

Michael Dell had difficulty establishing effective control systems because his company was growing so rapidly and he lacked experienced managers. In 1988 Dell's costs soared because no controls were in place to monitor inventory, which had built up rapidly. In 1993 financial problems arose because of ill-advised foreign currency transactions. In 1994 Dell's new line of laptop computers crashed because poor quality control resulted in defective products, some of which caught fire. To solve these and other control problems, Dell hired experienced managers to put the right control systems in place. As a result, by 1998 Dell was able to make computers for about 10 percent less than its competitors, creating a major source of competitive advantage.

The four managerial functions—planning, organising, leading, and controlling-are essential to a manager's job. At all levels in a managerial hierarchy, and across all departments in an organisation, effective management means making decisions and managing these four activities successfully.

Types of Managers

To perform efficiently and effectively, organisations employ three types of managers—first-line managers, middle managers, and top managers—arranged in a hierarchy. Typically, first-line managers report to middle managers, and middle managers report to top managers. Managers at each level have different but related responsibilities for utilising organisational resources to increase efficiency and effectiveness. These three types of managers are grouped into departments (or functions) according to their specific job responsibilities. A department, such as manufacturing, accounting, or engineering, is a group of people who work together and possess similar skills or use the same kind of knowledge, tools, or techniques to perform their jobs. Within each department are all three levels of management. Next, we examine the reasons why organisations use a hierarchy of managers and group them into departments. We then examine some recent changes taking place in managerial hierarchies.

Levels of Management

Organisations normally have three levels of management: first-line managers, middle managers, and top managers.

First-Line Managers

At the base of the managerial hierarchy are first-line managers, often called supervisors. They are responsible for the daily supervision of the nonmanagerial employees who perform many of the specific activities necessary to produce goods and services. First-line managers work in all departments or functions of an organisation.

Examples of first-line managers include the supervisor of a work team in the manufacturing department of a car plant, the head nurse in the obstetrics department of a hospital, and the chief mechanic overseeing a crew of mechanics in the service function of a new-car dealership. At Dell Computer, first-line managers include the supervisors responsible for controlling the quality of Dell computers or the level of customer service provided by Dell's telephone salespeople. When Michael Dell started his company, he personally controlled the computer assembly process and thus performed as a first-line manager or supervisor.

Middle Managers

Supervising the first-line managers are middle managers, responsible for finding the best way to organise human and other resources to achieve organisational goals. To increase efficiency, middle managers find ways to help first-line managers and nonmanagerial employees better utilise resources to reduce manufacturing costs or improve customer service. To increase effectiveness, middle managers evaluate whether the goals that the organisation is pursuing are appropriate and suggest to top managers ways in which goals should be changed. Very often, the suggestions that middle managers make to top managers can dramatically increase organisational performance. A major part of the middle manager's job is developing and fine-tuning skills and know-how, such as manufacturing or marketing expertise, that allow the organisation to be efficient and effective. Middle managers make thousands of specific decisions about the production of goods and services: Which first-line supervisors should be chosen for this particular project? Where can we find the highest-quality resources? How should employees be organised to allow them to make the best use of resources?

Behind a first-class sales force look for the middle managers responsible for training, motivating, and rewarding the salespeople. Behind a committed staff of high school teachers look for the principal who energises them to find ways to obtain the resources they need to do outstanding and innovative jobs in the classroom.

Top Managers

In contrast to middle managers, top managers are responsible for the performance of all departments. They have cross-departmental responsibility. Top managers establish organisational goals, such as which goods and services the company should produce; they decide how the different departments should interact; and they monitor how well middle managers in each department utilise resources to achieve goals. Top managers are ultimately responsible for the success or failure of an organisation, and their performance (like that of Bob Nardelli and Patricia Russo) is continually scrutinised by people inside and outside the organisation, such as other employees and investors.

The *chief executive officer (CEO)* is a company's most senior and important manager, the one to whom all other top managers report. Today, the term *chief operating officer (COO)* is often used to refer to the top manager who is being groomed to take over as CEO when the current CEO retires or leaves the company. Together, the CEO and COO are responsible for developing good working relationships among the top managers of various departments (manufacturing and marketing, for example); usually top managers have the title "vice president." A central concern of the CEO is the creation of a smoothly functioning top-management team, a group composed of the CEO, the COO, and the department heads most responsible for helping achieve organisational goals.

The relative importance of planning, organising, leading, and controlling—the four managerial functions—to any particular manager depends on the manager's position in the managerial hierarchy The amount of time that managers spend planning and organising resources to maintain and improve organisational performance increases as they ascend the hierarchy. Top managers devote most of their time to planning and organising, the functions so crucial to determining an organisation's long-term performance. The lower that managers' positions are in the hierarchy, the more time the managers spend leading and controlling first-line managers or nonmanagerial employees.

Areas of Managers

Because so much of a manager's responsibility is to acquire and develop critical resources, managers are typically members of specific departments. Managers inside a department possess job-specific skills and are known as, for example, marketing managers or manufacturing managers. First-line, middle, and top managers, who differ from one another by virtue of their job-specific responsibilities, are found in each of an organisation's major departments. Inside each department, the managerial hierarchy also emerges.

At Dell Computer, for example, Michael Dell hired experts to take charge of the marketing, sales, and manufacturing departments and to develop work procedures to help first-line managers control the company's explosive sales growth.

The head of manufacturing quickly found that he had no time to supervise computer assembly, so he recruited manufacturing middle managers from other companies to assume this responsibility.

Changes in Managerial Hierarchies

The tasks and responsibilities of managers at different levels have been changing dramatically in recent years. Two major factors that have led to these changes are global competition and advances in new information technology (IT) and in e-commerce. Stiff competition for resources from organisations both at home and abroad has put increased pressure on all managers to improve efficiency, effectiveness, and organisational performance. Increasingly, top managers are encouraging lower-level managers to look beyond the goals of their own departments and take a cross-departmental view to find new opportunities to improve organisational performance, as Michael Dell and Bob Nardelli have done. New information technologies give managers at all levels access to more and better information and improve their ability to plan, organise, lead, and control; this has also revolutionised the way the managerial hierarchy works.

Restructuring and Outsourcing

To take advantage of IT and e-commerce and their ability to reduce operating costs, CEOs and top-management teams have been restructuring organisations and outsourcing specific organisational activities to reduce the number of employees on the payroll.

Restructuring involves the use of information technology to downsize an organisation or shrink its operations by eliminating the jobs of large numbers of top, middle, or first-line managers and nonmanagerial employees. For example, IT allows fewer employees to perform a given task because it increases each person's ability to process information and make decisions more quickly and accurately. U.S. companies are spending over $50 billion a year on advanced IT that improves efficiency and effectiveness.

Restructuring, however, can produce some powerful negative outcomes. IT can reduce the morale of the remaining employees, who are worried about their own job security. And top managers of many downsised organisations are realising that they downsised too far. because employees complain they are overworked and because more customers complain about poor-quality service.

Outsourcing involves contracting with another company, usually in a low-cost country abroad, to have it perform an activity the organisation previously performed itself, such as manufacturing or marketing. Outsourcing promotes efficiency by reducing costs and by allowing an organisation to make better use of its remaining resources. The need to respond to low-cost global competition has speeded outsourcing dramatically in the 1930s Three million U.S. jobs in the manufacturing sector have been lost since 2000 as companies moved their operations to countries such as China, Taiwan, and Malaysia. Tens of thousands of high-paying jobs in IT have moved to countries like India and Russia, where programmers work for one-third the salary of those in the United States.

Large for-profit organisations today typically employ 10 to 20 percent fewer employees than they did 10 years ago because of restructuring and outsourcing. General Motors, IBM, AT&T, HP, Dell, and Du Pont are among the thousands of organisations that have streamlined their operations to increase efficiency and effectiveness. The argument is that the managers and employees who have lost their jobs will find employment in new and growing U.S. organisations where their skills and experience will be better utilised. For example, the millions of manufacturing jobs that have been lost overseas will soon be replaced by higher-paying U.S. jobs in the service sector that are made possible because of the growth in global trade.

Empowerment and Self-Managed Teams

Another major change in management has taken place at the level of first-line managers, who typically supervise the employees engaged in producing goods and services. By taking advantage of advanced IT, many companies have taken two steps to reduce costs and improve quality. One is the empowerment of their workforces by using powerful new software programs to expand employees' knowledge, tasks, and responsibilities. The other is the creation of self-managed teams—groups of employees given responsibility for supervising their own activities and for monitoring the quality of the goods and services they provide.

Such teams input the results of their activities into computers, and through IT middle managers have immediate access to what is happening. As a result of IT, members of self-managed teams assume many of the responsibilities and duties previously performed by first-line managers. What is the role of the first-line manager in this new IT work context? First-line managers act as coaches or mentors whose job is not to tell employees what to do but to provide advice and guidance and help teams find new ways to perform their tasks more efficiently Empire's use of IT to change the tasks and responsibilities of its sales force illustrates many important ways in which IT can affect the management process.

John Deere, the well-known manufacturer of tractors, also took steps to empower its employees to raise performance. Deere's managers realised that the employees who assemble its vehicles, with their detailed knowledge about how Deere products work, could become persuasive salespeople. So groups of these employees are now given training in sales techniques and sent to visit Deere customers to explain to them how to operate and service the organisation's new products. While speaking with customers, these newly empowered "salespeople" are able to collect information that helps Deere develop new products that appeal to customers. The new sales jobs are temporary. Employees go on assignment but then return to the production line, where they use their new knowledge to find ways to improve efficiency and quality.

Its moves to empower employees have been so successful that Deere negotiated a new agreement with its workers designed to promote empowerment. The agreement specifies that pay increases will be based on workers' learning new skills and completing college courses in areas such as computer programming that will help the company increase efficiency and quality. And the satisfaction that workers feel as they use their new skills and develop new capabilities will increase their commitment to the company and thus help it succeed.

Information Technology and Managerial Skills

Infromation Technology (IT) is having many important effects on the way managers perform their four functions. IT is also having major effects on the way managers perform their roles and on the skills they develop to perform those roles effectively. A managerial role is a set of specific tasks that a manager is expected to perform because of the position he or she holds in an organisation. One well-known model of managerial role was developed by Henry Mintzberg, who detailed 10 specific roles set of specific tasks that that effective managers undertake. Although Mintzberg's roles overlap with Fayol's model, they are useful because they focus on what managers do in a typical hour, day, or week in an organisation as they go about the actual job of managing. Below, we discuss these roles and the skills managers need to develop to perform effectively in a time when advanced IT and e-commerce are changing the way managers behave.

Managerial Roles

Henry Mintzberg reduced to 10 roles the thousands of specific tasks that managers need to perform as they plan, organise, lead, and control organisational resources. Managers assume each of these roles to influence the behaviour of individuals and groups inside and outside the organisation. People inside the organisation include other managers and employees. People outside the organisation include shareholders, customers, suppliers, the local community in which an organisation is located, and any local or government agency that has an interest in the organisation and what it does. Managers often perform many of these roles from minute to minute while engaged in the more general functions of planning, organising, leading, and controlling. IT is changing how they do so.

Decisional roles

Decisional roles are closely associated with the methods managers use to plan strategy and utilise resources. IT helps a manager in the role of *entrepreneur* by providing more and better information to use in deciding which projects or programs to initiate and in investing resources to increase organisational performance. As a *disturbance handler,* a manager can get realtime information through IT to manage the unexpected event or crisis that threatens the organisation and to implement solutions quickly. As a *resource allocator,* a manager using human resource software systems from companies such as Oracle and SAP has easy access to the detailed information needed to decide how best to use people and other resources to increase organisational performance. While engaged in that role, the manager must also be a *negotiator,* reaching agreements with other managers or groups claiming the first right to resources or with the organisation and outside groups such as suppliers or customers. The emergence of electronic markets and business-to-business (B2B) networks that link organisations to thousands of suppliers is but one example of the many ways IT helps managers perform the negotiator role.

Informational roles

Informational roles are closely associated with the tasks necessary to obtain and transmit information and so have obviously been dramatically impacted by IT. Acting as a *disseminator,* a manager can use IT to quickly and effectively transmit information to employees to influence their work attitudes and behaviour. Wal-Mart, for example, has nationwide videoconferencing linking top managers to each individual store and uses the Internet to provide up-to-date training programs to its employees. IT also provides managers with much greater ability to act as a *spokesperson* and promote the organisation so that people inside and outside the organisation respond positively to it.

Interpersonal roles

Managers assume interpersonal roles to provide direction and supervision for both employees and the organisation as a whole. IT can make managers much more visible throughout the organisation. As *a figurehead,* the person who symbolises an organisation or a department, a CEO can use the Internet to inform employees and other interested parties, such as shareholders, about what the organisation's mission is and what it is seeking to achieve. At all levels managers can use email and the Internet to act as figureheads and role models who establish appropriate ways to behave in the organisation. For example, anybody in Microsoft is allowed to directly email CEO Bill Gates if he or she thinks it necessary. For similar reasons IT allows managers to perform better as *leaders* because they have more and better-quality information available for training, counselling, and monitoring subordinates to help them reach their full potential. Finally, as a *liaison,* a manager can use IT to improve his or her ability to link and co-ordinate the activities of people and groups both inside and outside the organisation.

Terri Patsos Stanley, the manager of a small short-term rental business, has used IT to help her better perform many of these roles. Patsos Stanley pioneered the concept of providing business travellers with high-quality apartments as an alternative to staying in more expensive and often less convenient hotels in the Boston area. Her company, Boston Short-Term Rentals, grew rapidly because of her drive to keep costs down and customers happy. To achieve these goals, Patsos Stanley had to learn all the different managerial roles.

As the president of a rapidly growing company, Patsos Stanley is continually required to make decisions. In the role of *entrepreneur*, she searched for opportunities to increase revenues by increasing the number of apartments that she manages. One solution she adopted was to use the Internet and develop a strong presence on the World Wide Web to attract customers. As a *disturbance handler*, she deals with unexpected problems such as plumbing breakdowns in the middle of the night; therefore, all staff members are connected by electronic paging and personal messaging devices to speed response to customer problems. As a *resource allocator*, she decides how much money to spend to refurbish and upgrade the apartments to maintain their luxury appeal. She maintains close contact with the apartment owners through the Internet—she sends digital images of the apartments over the Web, for example. As a *negotiator*, she contracts with other organisations such as cleaning or painting services to obtain the most economical services her business requires—once again, the information available through the Internet makes this more efficient.

With more than 200 apartments to oversee, Boston Short-Term Rentals' information management is a vital activity, and Patsos Stanley's role as *monitor* is important. The sophisticated computer system she developed allows her to evaluate the performance of her business by occupancy rates, customer complaints, and other indicators of the quality of her service. The system facilitates her ability to respond quickly to problems as they arise. In her ongoing role as *disseminator*, she uses IT to update her staff with information about changes in visitor arrivals and departures, but as a *spokesperson* she is always on the phone to persuade visitors who may be somewhat hesitant about staying in an apartment that they know nothing about as opposed to staying with a hotel chain that has a well-recognised name.

In fact, Patsos Stanley learned the importance of an extremely hands-on approach to managing her company. She and her employees personally greet the new arrivals and perform the activities that porters, the concierge, and frontdesk staff do in the typical hotel. In interpersonal terms, Patsos Stanley is the *figurehead* who provides the personal touch her guests expect; she is the person they can contact if problems arise. With her small staff of carpenters, electricians, interior decorators, and maintenance workers, she acts as a *leader*, energising them to provide the quick service that guests expect. She is also a *liaison,* able to link her guests to organisations that provide services they may need, such as dry cleaning, catering, or hairdressing.

Patsos Stanley enjoys the variety of her work and relishes the pleasure of meeting the senior managers, actors, and overseas visitors who stay in the apartments. The owner/manager of any small business such as Boston Short-Term Rentals continually performs all these managerial roles.

Managerial Skills for Strategy Building

Both education and experience enable managers to recognise and develop the personal skills they need to put organisational resources to their best use. Michael Dell realised from the start that he lacked sufficient experience and technical expertise in marketing, finance, and planning to guide his company alone. Thus, he recruited experienced managers from other information technology companies, such as IBM and HP, to help him build his company. Research has shown that education and experience help managers acquire three principal types of skills: *conceptual, human,* and *technical.* As you might expect, the level of these skills that managers need depends on their level in the managerial hierarchy. Typically planning and organising require higher levels of conceptual skills, while leading and controlling require more human and technical skills.

Conceptual Skills

Conceptual skills are demonstrated in the ability to analyse and diagnose a situation and to distinguish between cause and effect. Top managers must possess a high level of conceptual skills because their primary responsibilities are planning and organising. By all accounts, Bob Nardelli was appointed as CEO of Home Depot because of his ability to identify new opportunities and mobilise managers and other resources to take advantage of those opportunities.

Formal education and training are very important in helping managers develop conceptual skills. Business training at the undergraduate and graduate (MBA) levels provides many of the conceptual tools (theories and techniques in marketing, finance, and other areas) that managers need to perform their roles effectively. The study of management helps develop the skills that allow managers to understand the big picture confronting an organisation. The ability to focus on the big picture lets managers see beyond the situation immediately at hand and consider choices while keeping in mind the organisation's long-term goals.

Today, continuing management education and training, including training in advanced IT, are an integral step in building managerial skills because new theories and techniques are constantly being developed to improve organisational effectiveness, such as B2B networks. A quick scan through a magazine such as *BusinessWeek* or *Fortune* reveals a host of seminars on topics such as advanced marketing, finance, leadership, and human resources management that are offered to managers at many levels in the organisation, from the most senior corporate executives to middle managers. Microsoft, IBM, Motorola, and many other organisations designate a portion of each manager's personal budget to be used at the manager's discretion to attend management development programs.

In addition, organisations may wish to develop a particular manager's abilities in a specific skill area—perhaps to learn an advanced component of departmental skills, such as international bond trading, or to learn the skills necessary to implement a new IT system. The organisation thus pays for managers to attend specialised programs to develop these skills. Indeed, one signal that a manager is performing well is an organisation's willingness to invest in that manager's skill development. Similarly, many nonmanagerial employees who are performing at a high level (because they have studied management) are often sent to intensive management training programs to develop their management skills and to prepare them for promotion to first-level management positions.

Human Skills

Human skills include the ability to understand, alter, lead, and control the behaviour of other individuals and groups. The ability to communicate, to coordinate, and to motivate people, and to mold individuals into a cohesive team, distinguishes effective from ineffective managers. By all accounts, Bob Nardelli, Michael Dell, Patricia Russo, and Terri Patsos Stanley all possess a high level of these human skills.

Like conceptual skills, human skills can be learned through education and training, as well as be developed through experience. Organisations increasingly utilise advanced programs in leadership skills and team leadership as they seek to capitalise on the advantages of self-managed teams. To manage personal interactions effectively, each person in an organisation needs to learn how to empathise with other people—to understand their viewpoints and the problems they face. One way to help managers understand their personal strengths and weaknesses is to have their superiors, peers, and subordinates provide feedback about their performance in the roles identified by Mintzberg. Thorough and direct feedback allows managers to develop their human skills.

Technical Skills

Technical skills are the job-specific knowledge and techniques required to perform an organisational role. Examples include a managers specific manufacturing, accounting, marketing, and, increasingly, IT skills. Managers need a range of technical skills to be effective. The array of technical skills managers need depends on their positions in their organisations. The manager

Effective managers need all three kinds of skills—conceptual, human, and technical. The absence of even one managerial skill can lead to failure. One of the biggest problems that people who start small businesses confront is their lack of appropriate conceptual and human skills. Someone who has the technical skills to start a new business does not necessarily know how to manage the venture successfully. Similarly, one of the biggest problems that scientists or engineers who switch careers from research to management confront is their lack of effective human skills. Management skills, roles, and functions are closely related, and wise managers or prospective managers are constantly in search of the latest educational contributions to help them develop the conceptual, human, and technical skills they need to function in today's changing and increasingly competitive global environment.

Today, the term competencies is often used to refer to the specific set of skills, abilities, and experiences that gives one manager the ability to perform at a higher level than another manager in a particular organisational setting. Developing such competencies through education and training has become a major priority for both aspiring managers and the organisations they work for. As we discussed earlier, many people are enrolling in advanced management courses, but many companies, such as General Electric (GE) and IBM, have established their own colleges to train and develop their employees and managers at all levels.

Every year, for example, GE puts thousands of its employees through management programs designed to identify the employees who the company believes have superior competencies and whom it can develop to become its future top managers. In many organisations promotion is closely tied to a manager's ability to acquire the competencies that a particular company believes are important. At 3M, for example, the ability to successfully lead a new product development team is viewed as a vital requirement for promotion; at IBM the ability to attract and retain clients is viewed as a vital competency its consultants must possess.

Management in a Global Environment

Because the world has been changing more rapidly than ever before, managers and other employees throughout an organisation must perform at higher and higher levels. In the last 20 years, competition between organisations competing domestically (in the same country) an d globally (in countries abroad) has increased dramatically. The rise of global organisations, organisations that operate and compete in more than one country, have put severe pressure on many other organisations to improve their performance and to identify better ways to use their resources. The successes of the German chemical companies Schering and Hoechst, Italian furniture manufacturer Natuzzi, Korean electronics companies Samsung and LG, Brazilian plane maker Embraer, and Europe's Airbus Industries are putting pressure on organisations in other countries to raise their level of performance to compete successfully with these global companies.

Even in the not-for-profit sector, global competition is spurring change. Schools, universities, police forces, and government agencies are reexamining their operations because of looking at the way things are done in other countries. For example, many curriculum and teaching changes in the United States have resulted from the study of methods that Japanese and European school systems use. Similarly, European and Asian hospital systems have learned much from the U.S. system—which may be the most effective, though not the most efficient, in the world.

Today, managers who make no attempt to learn and adapt to changes in the global environment find themselves reacting rather than innovating, and their organisations often become uncompetitive and fail. Four major challenges stand out for managers in today's world: building a competitive advantage, maintaining ethical standards, managing a diverse workforce, and utilising new information systems and technologies.

What are the most important lessons for managers and organisations to learn if they are to reach and remain at the top of the competitive environment of business? The answer relates to the use of organisational resources to build a competitive advantage. Competitive advantage is the ability of one organisation to outperform other organisations because it produces desired goods or services more efficiently and effectively than its competitors. The four building blocks of competitive advantage are superior *efficiency; quality; speed, flexibility,* and *innovation; and responsiveness to customers.*

Increasing Efficiency

Organisations increase their efficiency when they reduce the quantity of resources (such as people and raw materials) they use to produce goods or services. In today's competitive environment, organisations constantly are seeking new ways to use their resources to improve efficiency. Many organisations are training their workforces in the new skills and techniques needed to operate heavily computerised assembly plants. Similarly, cross-training gives employees the range of skills they need to perform many different tasks, and to organise employees in new ways, such as in self-managed teams, allowing them to make good use of their skills. These are important steps in the effort to improve productivity. Japanese and German companies invest far more in training employees than do American or Italian companies (Fig. 2).

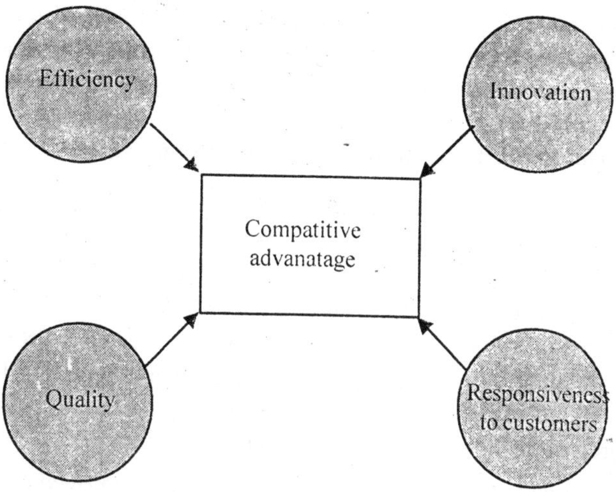

Figure 2. Building Blocks of Competitive Advantage

Managers must improve efficiency if their organisations are to compete successfully with companies operating in Mexico, Malaysia, and other countries where employees are paid comparatively low wages. New methods must be devised either to increase efficiency or to gain some other competitive advantage—higher-quality goods, for example—if outsourcing and the loss of jobs to low-cost countries are to be prevented.

Increasing Quality

The challenge from global organisations such as Korean electronics manufacturers, Mexican agricultural producers, and European marketing and financial firms also has increased pressure on companies to improve the skills and abilities of their workforces in order to improve the quality of their goods and services. One major thrust to improving quality has been to introduce the quality-enhancing techniques known as *total quality management (TQM)*. Employees involved in TQM are often organised into quality control teams and are responsible for continually finding new and better ways to perform their jobs; they also must monitor and evaluate the quality of the goods they produce. TQM is based on a significant new philosophy of managing behaviour in organisations; we thoroughly discuss this approach and ways of managing TQM successfully.

Increasing Speed, Flexibility, and Innovation

Today, companies can win or lose the competitive race depending on their speed—how fast they can bring new products to market—or their flexibility—how easily they can change or alter the way they perform their activities to respond to the actions of their competitors. Companies that have speed and flexibility are agile competitors: Their managers have superior planning and organising abilities; they can think ahead, decide what to do, and then speedily mobilise their resources to respond to a changing environment.

Innovation, the process of creating new or improved goods and services that customers want or developing better ways to produce or provide goods and services, poses a special challenge. Managers must create an organisational setting in which people are encouraged to be innovative. Typically, innovation takes place in small groups or teams; management decentralises control of work activities to team members and creates an organisational culture that rewards risk taking. Understanding and managing innovation and creating a work setting that encourages risk taking are among the most difficult managerial tasks.

Increasing Responsiveness

Organisations compete for customers with their products and services, so training employees to be responsive to customers' needs is vital for all organisations, but particularly for service organisations. Retail stores, banks, and hospitals, for example, depend entirely on their employees to perform behaviours that result in high-quality service at a reasonable cost. As many countries move toward a more service-based economy, managing behaviour in service organisations is becoming increasingly important. Many organisations are empowering their customer service employees and giving them the authority to take the lead in providing high-quality customer service. As noted previously, the empowering of nonmanagerial employees changes the role of first-line managers and often leads to the more efficient use of organisational resources.

Achieving a competitive advantage requires that managers use all their skills and expertise to develop resources and improve efficiency, quality, innovation, and responsiveness to customers. We revisit this theme often as we examine the ways managers plan strategies, organise resources and activities, and lead and control people and groups to effectively use human and other resources to achieve organisational goals.

Maintaining Ethical Standards

While mobilising organisational resources, managers at all levels are under considerable pressure to increase the level at which their organisations perform. For example, top managers receive pressure from shareholders to increase the performance of the entire organisation to boost the stock price, improve profits, or raise dividends. In turn, top managers may then pressure middle managers to find new ways to use organisational resources to increase efficiency or quality and thus attract new customers and earn more revenues.

Pressure to increase performance can be healthy for an organisation because it causes managers to question the way the organisation is working and it encourages them to find new and better ways to plan, organise, lead, and control. However, too much pressure to perform can be harmful. It may induce managers to behave unethically in dealings with individuals and groups both inside and outside the organisation. For example, a purchasing manager for a large retail chain might buy inferior clothing as a cost-cutting measure; or to secure a large foreign contract, a sales manager in a large defense company might offer bribes to foreign officials. In 2004, the four top executives of Lucent's Korean division were fired after it was revealed they used bribery to obtain lucrative contracts for Lucent in that country. The issue of social responsibility concerns the obligations that a company should have toward people and groups such as customers or the communities in which they operate. An example of companies that act in a socially irresponsible and unethical way is described in the following "Ethics in Action."

Managing the Workforce

Another challenge for managers is to recognise the need to treat human resources in a fair and equitable manner. Today, the age, gender, race, ethnicity, religion, sexual preference, and socioeconomic makeup of the workforce present new challenges for managers. Managers must establish employment procedures and practices that are legal, are fair, and do not discriminate against any organisational members.

In the past, white male employees dominated the ranks of management. Today increasing numbers of organisations are realising that to motivate effectively and take advantage of the talents of a diverse workforce, they must make promotion opportunities available to all employees, including women and minorities. Managers must also recognise the performance-enhancing possibilities of a diverse workforce, such as the ability to take advantage of the skills and experiences of different kinds of people. The following "Focus on Diversity" feature looks at how one company took advantage of diversity to enhance its competitive advantage.

The bank, like many other organisations, also discovered that diversity can lead to competitive advantage because diverse employees approach the same issue—for example, how to attract customers—in very different ways. The bank found that creating diverse teams of employees helped improve the quality of decision making inside the organisation. Furthermore, the bank's reputation of being a good place for minorities to work attracted highly skilled and motivated minority job candidates. Managers who value their diverse employees not only invest in developing these employees' skills and capabilities but also link rewards to their performance. They are the managers who best succeed in promoting performance over the long run.

Skill Management and Personnel Development

In an economy where the only certainty is uncertainty, the one sure source of lasting competitive advantage is knowledge." wrote Ikujiro Nonaka in his frequently quoted article, published in the Harvard Business Review, which paved the way for the discipline of knowledge management. Although the importance of this intangible asset has been recognised for some time now, the vision of Ikujiro Nonaka maintains its relevance in today's environment.

In the following 12 years more research strongly showed that the knowledge and the competence of the firm members are substantial success factors in the world-wide competition. This applies also to Putzmeister, Inc. with its headquarters in Aichtal/Germany. This "Hidden Champion" in the field of construction machinery produces concrete pumps and mortar machines for the world market. Like many other Swabian machine-builders it is a medium-sized Company operating in a small market niche and therefore, gathered enormous specific knowledge about its market segments over the last decades. To maintain the high skill and knowledge level, a strategically designed Personnel and Organisational Development are essential. For this purpose the Personnel management of the Company started a pilot project to introduce a Skill Management System as part of an Integrated Personnel Development (IPD).

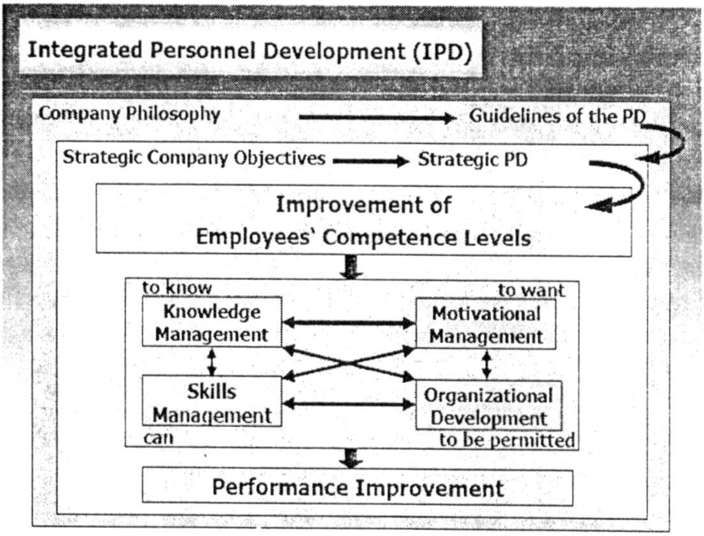

Figure 3. Integrated Personnel Development (IPD)

Competence management on a corporate level wants not only to improve the competence of its employees, but to improve their performance. Performance is measured by the achievement of personal and corporate objectives, which are set according to the company's strategy and philosopy. To enable the employee to perform better the company needs more than just Classroom Training. Therefore, the Integrated Personnel Development (IPD) combines knowledge (I know how to) with skills (I can), motivation (I want to) and permission by the organisation (I am permitted to) and puts the according Management instruments in relation to each other. The hypothesis is: To improve employees' competence levels all of the four instruments are needed to achieve the final goal which is optimal performance of the employee.

As an example, a company wants to improve their image as a service-oriented company with knowledgeable workers. All the call-center agents are now trained to perform according to the expected image in the four fields of Competence Management. First, they need knowledge about the company's knowledge. Second, they need the skill to use the databases at their workplace. Third, they must be motivated to serve their customers according to the plan and fourth, be permitted to provide the information needed. Otherwise, the performance will not be satisfactory. The following example shows how Putzmeister Inc. tried to achieve an integrated Competence Development.

In the fifth decade of its existence, Putzmeister, Inc. is challenged by specific knowledge problems. First, the knowledge of the long-serving specialists has to be transferred to the younger employees. Secondly, the globalisation forces the Company to link its foreign subsidiaries into the IPD System shown above.

Thus, new methods are needed to identify and document the unique knowledge of the Company. Employees need easy access to this knowledge and have, as well, the visibility of his or her own colleague's knowledge by "Company Yellow Pages".

The Skill Management System (SMS) is an essential part of the Knowledge Organisation at Putzmeister, Inc. The project to prepare the SMS was launched in the middle of 2001 by the Human Resources department. The objective was to build up the foundation for an integrated skill management process by developing a central database, which shows the skill levels of the employees and the requirements of the job profiles. As both the skill and the job profiles are designed in the same way, matching of the two profiles is possible and allows the design of individual training programs, which are carried out by the PM Academy. The Yellow Pages Project, as mentioned above, can then be derived from the SMS.

Developing a Skill Management System

Skill management is defined as the management of the qualifications, experiences and knowledge of the employees. The objective is to allocate the appropriate skills at the correct place, at the right time, at optimal costs. The information of a skill database can be used in many ways:

1. *In Knowledge Management Concepts:* Skill management databases are designed to match skill profiles with job profiles, or allow searches for a special skill profile needed. This feature is used especially in project staffing. If the skill profiles are linked with personal data, the database can also be used for a "Yellow Pages System".
2. *Recruiting:* The required skill profile for a certain post can be used in the assessment of the applicants to determine whose skill profile matches best with the requirements. The job profile can also be offered to internal and external applicants for Self-Assessment.
3. *Computer-aided Personnel Development Process:* Managers and employees are able to find out the appropriate training measures with the skill management system.

The starting point of all considerations is the separation of job and person. The questions are, what does a job require and what does the person deliver. The "cans" and the "cannots" are compared and the gaps then are analysed through so-called "Gap Analysis". The identified gaps should then be discussed between the employee and the manager in the annual personal evaluation meeting. This conversation is the core element of the skill development process. Having discussed the gap analysis results, the employee and the manager should agree upon appropriate development measures for the upcoming year.

The process of developing a skill management system seems very simple. However, it poses many critical questions: How does one define skills and how should the profiles be arranged? How can the required skills for a function be identified? How can all the data be kept current? Who evaluates the skill levels of the employee? Who should be allowed to view the skill profiles of an employee? How can acceptance be built up for such a system? and so on. To receive answers to those questions before a broad roll-out of a skill management system, the personnel managers at Putzmeister, Inc. decided to go for a scientifically supported pilot project. This project should develop an outline for a realistic model for the implementation of a skill management process. The project also outlines all the specific requirements for a skill management software solution.

After one-to-one meetings with all managers, the project team started with three pilot departments. First, the three groups, i.e. the managers and the employees together, went into workshops and compiled the requirement skills for the chosen job profile. The profiles and the skill management process were then programmed under MS-Access to provide the necessary features for a Self-Assessment. Afterwards, the participating managers would evaluate the skill levels of their departments' pilot function, i.e. they considered for each skill the level desired in the particular job.

The advantage of the self-assessment lays in the increased motivation of the participants. An assessment by the manager usually creates more conflicts. The manager will assess the employee indirect way when the discuss the results of the matching in the yearly development talks. If both profile sides of the database are filled, the program runs the gap analysis. This analysis has to be given in print to both the employee and the manager some time before the yearly development talks. For showing deficits suitable personnel development measures for the coming year should be found and agreed upon by the employee and the manager. If the gap analysis shows higher skill levels than required the employee could be considered as a potential candidate for job enlargement, job rotation or even for a certain career plan. Another feature of this Skill management system is the opportunity for the employee to compare his own skill profile with every possible job profile within the Company. So he is able to recognise his career possibilities and knows about the skills and knowledge necessary for it.

References

Andersen Consulting Company (2000) *Skills Needed for the E-Business Environment*. Andersen Consulting.

Bass, Bernard (1990) *Handbook of Leadership: Theory, Research, and Managerial Applications*. (3rd Edition) New York: Macmillan.

Boyatzis, Richard E. (1982) *The Competent Manager*. New York: Wiley.

Cox, Taylor H. and Ruby L. Beal (1997) *Developing Competency to Manage Diversity*. San Francisco: Barrett-Koehler.

Paul S. Adler. (1986). New Technologies, New Skills. *California Management Review* 9–28.

Quinn, Robert E. (1988) *Beyond Rational Management*. San Francisco: Jossey-Bass.

Rigby, Darrell (1998) *Management Tools and Techniques*. Boston: Bain and Company.

Vance, Charles M. (1993) *Mastering Management Education*. Newbury Park, CA: Sage.

Whetten, David A., & Cameron, Kim S. (1983) "Management skill training; A needed addition to the management curriculum." *Organisational Behavior Teaching Journal*, 8: 10-15.

7

Developing Skilled Labour Force

Todays employers demand more skills than they did in the past. Several factors have contributed to the rising demand for skills in the labor market: technological and organisational change, trade, deregulation of key industries, and the decline of unions. Three types of empirical evidence support the hypothesis that the demand for skills has risen: estimates of the returns to skill, time series data on the content of a representative sample of jobs, and evidence from case studies of individual firms or industries.

There is an increasing demand of skilled labour. This is on account of globalisation, changes in technology as well as work processes. Production has been getting globalised and financial markets the world over, are becoming integrated. Information Technology has been primarily instrumental in increasing the speed of communications and reducing its costs. Globalisation, in turn, has led to intensified competition, technological diffusion and adoption of new forms of organisation. As a result of the heightened competition and economic change, developing nations are facing a tough challenge in maintaining the employability of large segments of their labour force. Simultaneously, competition and economic change also provide an opportunity for economic growth and employment expansion. To take advantage of these opportunities, the level and quality of skills that a nation possesses are critical. Moreover, rapid technology changes and transition to a more open economy entails social costs. These can be restricted only through equally rapid upgradation of the capabilities of the workforce.

Against this backdrop, countries like India, which have opened their economy in the last decade, need to invest in the skill development, training and education of their workforce. As technological change, shorter product cycles and new forms of work organisation alter the environment, training systems come under pressure. To counter these pressures on training, incentives for training systems need to be considered. These will help the country's industry to adapt successfully to ongoing economic change.

Skills of Indian Labour Force

At present, labour is used as an input in the various sectors of the economy to produce a visible output viz. the finished product or the service. It may be mentioned that these sectors of the economy also produce surplus workforce, which may be arising out of various reasons like:

a) Companies turning sick
b) Closure of companies
c) Recession leading to reduced workforce
d) Process automation
e) Shift of labour from Manufacturing sector to Services sector
f) Mergers and Acquisitions
g) Obsolescence of skill sets e.g. typing

The surplus workforce that arises in the system therefore needs to be retrained for better employability. While retraining is one aspect, there is also the need for skill development and training for improving quality, cost and delivery of product/service. Training institutions thus, have to serve as the means for meeting the needs of skill development, training, retraining and education of the workforce.

Segmentation of Labour

The entire labour force can be segmented in a 4X2 matrix with the Degree of organisation of labour on the x-axis and the Type of sector of economy on the y-axis. As can be observed from Table 1, there has been a gradual shift of workers from the agricultural sector to the informal sector, as the percentage of people in the organised sector has more or less remained constant at around 7%. Substantial employment growth is taking place in the small and unorganised sector i.e. in tiny and small enterprises. Based on the figures mentioned in Table 1 the informal sector has grown at 1.06% per annum over the period 1997-2000.

Table 1. Distribution of Workers by Major Sector of Economic Activity

(Numbers in millions)

Year (%)	*Agriculture (%)*	*Non-Agriculture*		*Total (%)*
		Organised (%)	*Informal (%)*	
1972-73	175	18.8	42.5	236.3
	74	8	18	100
1977-78	195	21.2	54.5	270.7
	72	8	20	100
1982-83	206.2	24.1	72.5	302.8
	68	8	24	100
1987-88	206.4	25.7	89.9	322
	64	8	28	100
1990-91	218.4	26.7	96.8	341.9
	64	8	28	100
1993-94	242.5	27.4	104.6	374.5
	65	7	28	100
1996-97	243.8	28.2	110.1	382.1
	64	7	29	100
1999-2000	237.6	28.1	131.3	397
	60	7	33	100

A numerical overview of the strength of the Indian labour force in the organised and unorganised sector is given in Figure 1.

The distribution of employment in different segments of the informal sector is given in Figure 2. Approximately 67% of the workers are employed in the establishments either as workers, or as entrepreneurs. It may be mentioned that as data on skill levels is not readily available, it is difficult to quantify the level of skills in the labour force. However, a snapshot of the education levels of the Indian labour force in 1999-2000 reveals a dismal picture with about 44.0% of all workers being illiterate. It may be observed from the table that 51.3% of the total rural area workers is illiterate while only 21.5% of the urban area workers is illiterate.

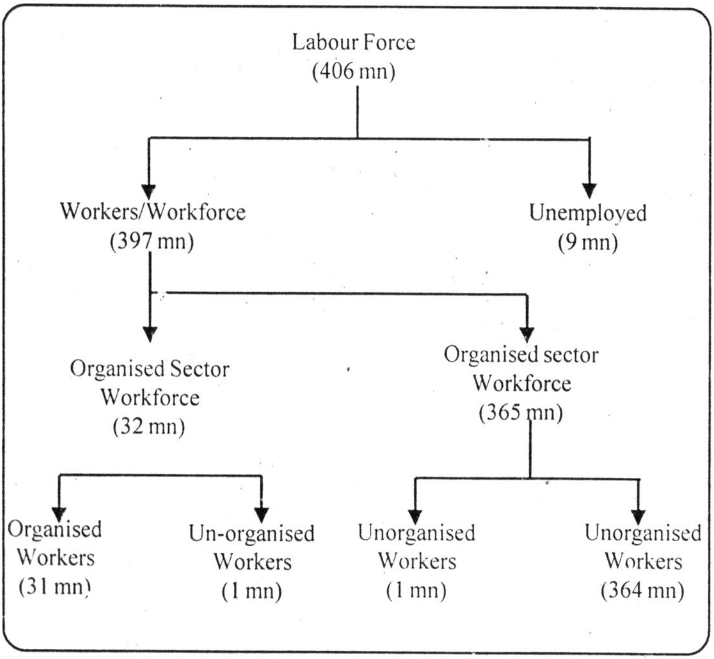

Figure 1. Distribution of the Labour Force

These figures indicate the deficiencies in the general education level of the labour force. The overall trend of enrolment in middle classes and higher secondary classes has been growing over the years and it can be inferred from the increasing trend that the new entrants to the labour force will be significantly better educated than the present.

Further, the category "middle school and above" includes all those who have had some middle school education even though they may have dropped out of the school before completing middle school. The provisional drop out rate at middle school levels was quite high at 42% in the year 1998-99. As per a rough estimate from the 52nd round (1995-96) survey of the National Sample Survey Organisation

(NSSO), only 20% of the population in the age group of 14-16 years actually completes secondary school the present.

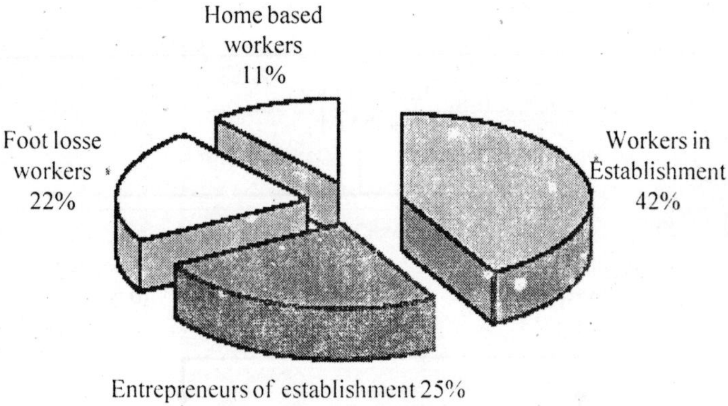

Figure 2. Distribution of Employment in the Informal sector

Table 2. Composition of Workers of Age 15 Years and Above by Level of Education 1999-2000

(All figures in percentage)

	Not Literate	*Literate & Schooling upto primary level*	*With schooling upto middle & higher level*	*Total*	*Share in workforce*
Rural Areas					
Male	39.6	27.3	33.1	100	49.7
Female	74	15.5	10.5	100	25.8
Person	51.3	23.3	25.4	100	75.5
Urban Areas					
Male	16	22	62	100	19.7
Female	43.9	17.6	38.5	100	4.8
Person	21.5	21.1	57.4	100	24.5
All Areas					
Male	32.9	25.8	41.3	100	69.5
Female	69.3	15.8	14.9	100	30.5
Person	44	22.7	33.3	100	100

While general education is required for most jobs, possession of "marketable skills" (or specific skills) is a must for the labour force for obtaining employment. The NSSO Survey on Employment & Unemployment (1993-94) gives information on the possession of 30 specific marketable skills, by persons in the labour force and the results are summarised in the Table 3. In the rural areas, only 10.1% of the male workers, and 6.3% of the female workers possessed specific marketable skills and in the urban areas, 19.6% of males and 11.2% of females possessed marketable skills.

Table 3. Percentage Distribution of Persons by Possession of Marketable Skill; 1993-94

(All figures in percentage)

Possessing	*Rural*		*Urban*	
	Male	*Female*	*Male*	*Female*
No Skill	89.9	93.7	80.4	80.4
Some Skill	10.1	6.3	19.6	11.2
Total	100	100	100	100
Sample Persons	(183464)	(172835)	(109067)	(99283)

As per the report of the Task force on Employment Opportunities set up by the Planning Commission, about 12.3 million persons are expected to enter the labour force per year, aggregating 86.2 million persons between the year 2000 and year 2007 (Table 4).

Table 4. Entrants to Labour Force Between 2000-2012

(million persons)

Entrants to Labour Force	2000 to 2007 7 years	2007 to 2012 5 years
Rural Areas	52.40	40.30
Urban Areas	33.80	28.10
All India	86.20	68.40

After allowing for underutilisation of seats in training institutions and some overlaps, the percentage of those entering the labour force with some degree of formal training is about 12% gross of the new entrants (about 1.5 million per year) into the labour force. It is estimated that a significant number of new entrants will be absorbed in various types of unskilled labour in agricultural and non-agricultural occupations, while the rest will enter the market with some skills.

It may be mentioned that only 5% of the Indian labour force in the age category 20-24 years, has obtained vocational training. The corresponding figure in other industrialised nations is much higher, lying between 60% and 80%, except for Italy, which is 44%. The corresponding percentage for Korea is very high at 96%. Even if India is benchmarked against developing nations, the Indian figure of 5%, is far behind Mexico at 28%, Botswana at 22% and Peru at 17%.

METHODS OF SKILL ACQUISITION

At present, persons entering the labour workforce acquire skills from a variety of methods as given below.

a) *Hereditary skills acquired:* In The Family. In traditional family based crafts e.g. pottery, carpet weaving, etc. the younger members of the family learn the art of the craft from senior members in the family. This is also the most common method for acquiring contemporary skills viz. tailoring, repair work etc.

b) *Induction training:* In most organisations, immediately after an employee joins the organisation, he or she is sent for an induction which involves rotation through various departments and familiarisation with the normal practices of the department and method of work.

c) *On the job training:* This is the most popular method in the informal sector, wherein workers join as unskilled or semiskilled workers and learn specific skills in the course of their employment. Larger industrial units also impart on the job training in a more structured manner through in-house training facilities

d) *Vocational training in specialised institutions:* Vocational skills are also acquired through formal vocational training in specialised institutions. There are 4274 Industrial Training Institutes (ITIs) in India, which impart training in 43 engineering and 24 non- engineering trades. Of these 1654 are in the government sector and the remaining 2620 institutes are in the private sector. The total seating capacity in these ITIs is 6.28 lakhs. Further, there are 6 Advanced Training Institutes (ATI) which are managed by the Central Government that provide training for instructors in ITIs and ATIs for Electronics and Process Instrumentation offering long and short courses for training of skilled personnel at technician level in the fields of industrial, medical and consumer electronics and process instrumentation. There are also proprietary institutes organised as businesses, which provide training of various types in areas such as computer applications, readymade garments and hardware maintenance

e) *Formal Apprenticeship:* Historically, apprenticeship was the principal means of training semiskilled workers. At its simplest, it is by far the predominant mode of acquisition of trades, crafts and occupations. The most famous is the German "dual system" where apprenticeship is combined with school - based education. The Indian Apprenticeship Act, 1961, requires employers in notified industries to engage apprentices in specified ratios in relation to the workforce. Apprentices get trained for periods ranging from 6 months to 4 years and at the end of the period they are trade-tested by the National Council for Vocational Training. The Apprenticeship Act thus serves two purposes: A) to regulate the programme of training apprentices in industry so as to conform to the prescribed syllabi, period of training etc. and B) to fully utilise the facilities available in industry for imparting practical training with a view to meeting the requirement of skilled workers.

f) *Vocational training linked to development programmes:* These are specifically designed to provide training in the informal sector e.g. the schemes for the training of women by the Department of Women & Child Development, Skill development programmes by the Khadi and Village Industries Commission (KVIC), Training programmes of the Department of Small Scale Industry (SSI) etc.

Table 5. Annual Training Capacity of Various Training Providers

Department/ Institution	*Figures in lakhs*
DGE&T, State Government etc.	
- Industrial Establishments	2.27
- Seats in it is	6.28
Dept. of sec. and Higher Education	
- Polytechnics	2.20
- Arts and crafts	2.20
- Vocational stream	5.00
- Community polytechnics	3.07
- Vocational Courses under National Open School	0.20
Dept. of Women and Child labour	
- Support to Training & Employment programmes for women (STEP)	0.10
Dept. of SSI & Rural industry	
-EDP	0.16
Dept. of Rural development	
- SGSY	2.14
Dept. of urban employment and poverty alleviation	
- SJSRY	2.00
Ministry of textiles	N.A.
Ministry of Information technology	0.35
Ministry of Tourism	
- Hotel Management	0.024
Total capacity	25.99

VOCATIONAL TRAINING

Vocational training could be:

a) Institutional pre-employment training

b) In-plant Training

c) Apprenticeship Training

d) Post employment /In-service/Job Related training

e) Advanced / Specialist training

The Indian Trade Apprenticeship Act 1961 was implemented to cover training of trade apprentices. The responsibility of implementation of the Act is with the Central Apprenticeship Advisor/ Director of Apprenticeship Training in Directorate General of Employment & Training, Ministry of Labour. The Act was amended in 1973 to cover Graduate & Diploma holders in Engineering and Technology as Graduate and Technician Apprentices. In 1987 the Act was amended again to cover training of students passing out of the 10+ vocational streams, as Technical Vocational Apprentice. As on June 30, 2000, only 1.65 lakh seats were utilised out of a total of 2.27 lakh seats for apprenticeship training in central or state/ private sector enterprises combined.

The lacunae in the present trade apprenticeship training can be summarised as follows:

a) Inadequate coverage of skill requirements
b) Mismatch in demand and supply relation
c) Lack of flexibility in the engagement of Trade Apprentices within the same Trade Group
d) Lengthyand clumsy administrative procedures of record keeping and filling up of return
e) Lack of incentives to encourage industries to modernise their training facilities
f) Inadequate and poor quality of training facilities as well as training staff
g) Small establishments unable to engage apprentices

Challenges of Labour

Having discussed the needs and the current status of the Indian workforce, we can summarise the seven key existing and future challenges for Indian labour.

a) *Challenge of globalisation:* The Indian economy has opened up in the last decade. India has also become a member of the World Food Organisation (WTO). In order to remain competitive, the organised sector has commenced outsourcing. The use of casual and contractual labour has increased for meeting varying production levels. Globalisation has also thrown up a challenge in the form of exposure to new technologies and products, which are perceived as a threat to the traditional areas, particularly in the unorganised sector. The lessons from this exposure need to be assimilated by the workforce.

Challenge of Labour Competitiveness vis-à-vis China and Other Nations: India has been facing competition from China and other South East Asian nations in various sectors including toys, electricals and handlooms. The workforce of these nations is disciplined and cheaper as compared to the Indian workforce. With China becoming a member of the WTO at the November WTO meeting at Doha, Qatar, the challenge to the Indian workforce to remain competitive has increased manifold.

In India the quality of skilled labour is good. But the proportion of skilled labour in the total labour force of the country is too small. With the result, though the country ranked first among the Newly Industrialised Countries, in terms of quality of skilled labour, with regard to their ready availability it ranked 7 out of 10.

b) *Challenge of Redeployment of Surplus Manpower from Agriculture and Manufacturing to Services & Trade (within self-employed and wage earners):* Due to a variety of reasons, there is surplus manpower arising from the organised sector. These persons need to be retrained and made employable. The shift may largely require attitudinal orientation and skill based training.

c) *Challenge of Recognising Labour as Human Capital rather than as a Cost:* Two views can be taken of human resources, one being that they are a cost and the other being that they are an investment. The first view translates into attempts to keep wages low and to spend as little as possible on training and human resource development. The second view treats people as a source of competitive advantage. It leads organisations to invest in skill development.

The industry therefore needs to recognise labour as Human Capital and invest in training. The labour too must make their effort to gain clear acknowledgement from industry and society of their competence, commitment and contribution. Global competitiveness as a nation is a joint task and can be achieved only through the sense of common endeavour between employers and the employed. Short-term programmes to upgrade the skills and output quality of the labour force may be devised by industry associations, which include cross-functional skills.

d) *Challenge of Continuous Employability of Labour:* With rapid changes in technology, markets and environment, skill obsolescence is growing. Employment is contingent on employability. Employability is contingent partly on skills and largely on attitude. The best insurance against job loss is to effectively nurture and nourish a culture of multi-skills in place of mono-skills. This provides career resilience and career self-reliance.

   In certain sectors of economic activity in India, labour does not get employment throughout the year, and there are idle periods. The challenge is to ensure they are continuously employable throughout the year and also over their working life. Higher levels of workers' education will allow possibilities of their pursuing more than one occupation during the year, as per seasonal demand. Multi-skilled labour can be utilised for various work

e) *Challenge of enlarging and utilising effectively the infrastructure for education and training:* While the existing infrastructure for imparting vocational training and education needs remedial attention, these facilities also urgently need to be expanded. Only then can they meet the increased challenges before them to equip and orient large numbers of the workforce with the latest techniques and operational skills.

f) *Challenge of absorption of new technologies by labour using education and training:* The Indian workforce has been faced with new production concepts like Computer aided design (CAD), Computer aided manufacturing (CAM), Robotics, Just-in-time (JIT) and Flexible Manufacturing Systems (FMS), which require increased knowledge to be imparted to them. Likewise, in the white-collar segment, MS-Office, Desktop Publishing, Accounting Software etc. have become ubiquitous and vocational institutes must include them in their curriculum. Some of the skill sets tend to become insufficient by themselves for employment e.g. typing.

Standards of Excellence

Based on the above challenges, the knowledge, skill and attitudinal requirements of the labour force are expected to attain the following standards of excellence:

Table 6. Standards of Excellence

Standard\s of excellence	*Knowledge requirements (what the job holder must know and understand)*	*Skill requirements (what the jobholder mustbe able to do and demonstrate)*	*Attitudinal requirements (how the jobholders mustconductthem selveswith others)*
Service	Optimisation ofthe equipment usage for the benefit of end users	Customise services tosuitindividual andend users	High level of team work, ability toconstantly learn new skills
Product	Requirements of the market place including niches	Ability toprototype product fast	Focus on the market placeand customers
Market	Market dynamics of changing user tastes	Shortest timeto marketproduct/ service	Speed isof theessence
People	High level of specialised domain knowledge	Ability to work with one's own hands	Positive attitude and national pride
Control	Should know source of new knowledge and set it online	Should be able to change skills fast	Passion to excel and handle one's emotions

New Approach to Vocational Training

Training Systems

Training targeted at achieving global competitiveness can be successful only through a sense of shared purpose between employers and the employed. The Study group examined the training systems of various countries, which are found to be broadly of three types – "co-operative," "enterprise based" and "state-driven." These have been summarised in Table 7 In the co-operative system there is no single institution responsible for the planning and delivery of the training system. Instead, the employers' organisation and trade unions cooperate strongly for producing the desired result. Germany is one of the successful examples of this system.

Table 7. Training Systems

System	*Countries*	*Main Feature*
"Co-operative"	Austria, Germany, Switzerland, many countries in Latin America	Pressures to undertake training resulting from strong co-operation amongst employers' organisations, the state and trade unions
"Enterprise-based" - Low labour turnover	Japan	Low labour mobility, life time employment for many staff, 'long-termism' arising from absence of stock market pressure. Wage system based on seniority and enterprise-based trade unions
Voluntarist	United Kingdom, United States	Few institutional pressures on firms to provide training
"State- driven" - Demand-led	Hong Kong, Malaysia Republic of Korea, Singapore, Taiwan, China	State plays a leading role in coordinating the demand for and supply of skills. Operates in an open and competitive economic environment
Supply-led	Economies in transition; many developing countries, especially in Asia & Africa	Government takes on a prime responsibility for formal sector training in training institutes. Little or no pressure on employers to train

In the "enterprise based system," as prevalent in Japan, the educational system provides a foundation of basic skills, which is then built upon by employers through intensive off-and on-the-job training. While vocational and technical schools provide some initial training, the bulk of skills development is provided and financed primarily by employers. Employees with few industry-specific skills on entry are shaped by the system into a highly skilled workforce that is very adaptable to change.

In the "state-driven system" of the demand-led type, which is prevalent in the East and South East Asian economies, the education and training systems of these economies have to respond to rapid changes in the demand for skills. In this, the governments have played a key role, especially in meeting the demand for higher-level skills. In Singapore, the Skills Development Fund has financed a vast expansion of continuous training for all types of workers and has been an effective instrument of skill upgradation. In the "state-driven system" of the supply-led type, which was operational in many of the centrally planned economies of Eastern Europe and the erstwhile USSR, the training system was sustained through government financing. It puts little or no pressure on employers to train and instead the government takes on the prime responsibility of running training institutes.

There are different training systems prevalent abroad. It would be suitable for India to adopt a system that gets participation from government, industry and trade unions, as and when required. The study group appointed by us has recommended a new modular approach to vocational training, which will aid multi-skilling, impart skills attuned to the needs of the labour market, and in consonance with the latest technology.

Multi-Skilling

New approaches towards vocational training have become imperative because of the expectations of the industry from the employee. Firstly too narrow a specialisation or inflexible training arrangement restricts the scope for trained persons to improve upon their competencies while working as employees. Secondly, the existing informal system of skill development does not meet the career aspirations of the workers in terms of retraining and upgradation of skills. Thirdly, there is a mismatch between the supply of skills through the formal system of education and training and the demand of skills by the industry.

There is also a distinct shift in the skills from old craftsmanship and physical dexterity of individual trades to mental/ intellectual skills which call for logical/ abstract thinking and willingness/ability to learn new things quickly, as the technological changes are expected to be continuous in future. Multifunction skill is also another requirement of the future. To display versatility and absorb these higher skills, a worker needs to have an open mind, proper attitudes and be quickly adaptable to any change in working conditions or operational areas.

The primary objectives of the new approach towards vocational training will be as given below.

a) Development of proper work culture/work attitude as well as knowledge of diverse technical fields rather than of single skill learning.

b) Multi-skilling which will help in increasing the employability. This is also important from the perspective that within the working lifetime of an individual, he or she may have to cope with increasing demands of technology on the one hand, and changing skills on the other.

c) Training should provide flexible pathways to individuals for moving between training and employment sectors.

d) The final training phase must be conducted in a real work environment or in an environment which is as close to the real as possible, so that the trainees apply all their skill in performing the relevant tasks at the threshold entry level of performance which is acceptable to the employer.

e) Certification of trades/skills should be done by an authorised agency or licensed competent performer who is external to the training institute.

In order to meet the objectives required in the new approach, the Study Group has recommended a modular approach to training. Such an approach will cater to the diverse vocational needs and workplace requirements. It will also offer flexibility to individuals to move through the levels of education and training.

Some of the key para- meters to be considered while developing a new approach are given below.

a) Effectiveness of training should be measured in terms of quality. The proposed approach can set specified minimum standards of quality for satisfying the qualification needs for skilled manpower in various sectors of the economy.

b) Training to be imparted in small result-oriented modules to develop proper work attitudes all through - emphasis on discipline, cleanliness, orderliness & accuracy.

c) To impart inputs to develop the ownership concept and to create a safe and pleasant working environment, by adopting the '5S' concept- to reduce the rate of accidents and loss of man-hours due to damage, with a goal of zero accidents.

d) Team to learn to identify and eliminate non-value adding activities and all kinds of waste.

e) Develop training Module on TPM – Total Productive Self initiated Maintenance - involving total participation to achieve overall equipment effectiveness.

f) Training should focus on teaching Cause - Effect Analysis with inputs on mechanism of a machine or equipment to understand the effect of its malfunctioning and effect of improper tooling / defective processes on quality of product.

g) Motivate the trainees to evaluate themselves and their own work with accuracy and to assume responsibility for faultless operation with a Goal of zero rejection/first time OK – Self Inspection & Self Certification.

h) Inputs on KAIZEN- to achieve significant continuous improvement in performance through elimination of all waste. Trainees to be motivated to take up small KAIZEN events and encouraged throughout.

i) Train to learn Team Work:

— Trainee to be assigned individual exercises and to be guided by the instructor to plan, execute and evaluate performance.

— Trainee to be taught to assume responsibility of planning, execution and evaluation of his own task. Ability to think for oneself. Shift from Dependence to Independence.

— Trainees to be exposed to Team Work by assigning small projects to a group of trainees. Required to plan, execute and evaluate the task assigned collectively.

j) *Market driven approach:* The courses would have to be supported by a system of certification (currently the certification system for vocational trades does not enjoy acceptability from the users. The students carrying certificates are being re-tested/ retrained in the same trade.). Certification system has been discussed separately in later paragraphs.

Modular Approach

The proposed training approach (Manufacturing Sector) is denoted graphically in Figure 3. A relevant example from the services sector (Paramedical) is denoted in Figure 4. A detailed note on the proposed training relating to the figure is given below.

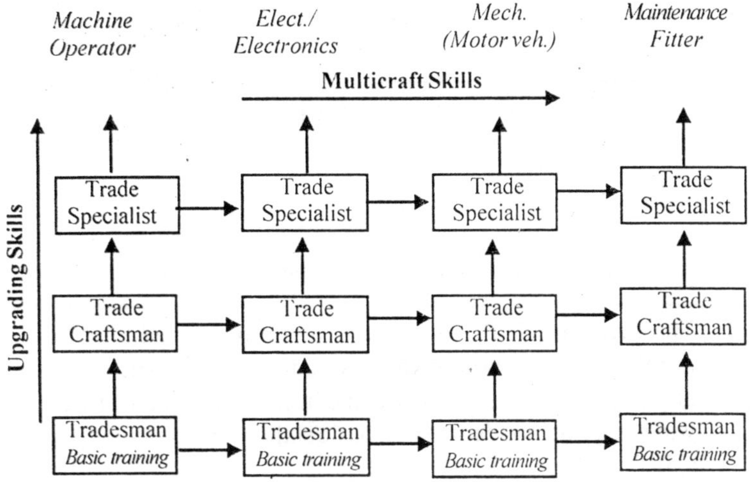

PL = Proficiency level

Figure 3. Proposed Training Approach (Manufacturing sector)

a) PL_1, PL_2, PL_3 etc. are proposed Modules with increasing proficiency levels for a particular group of trades such as, say Machine Shop. Each module will be a cluster of sub-modules, which are designed as a learning element. Each sub-module will represent the smallest possible segment of a required body of knowledge and skill for which measurable learning objective can be defined. These sub-modules will have a learning objective, a list of exercises to be performed, tools and equipment, standards of performance expected and a mechanism for continuous checking of progress and definite period.

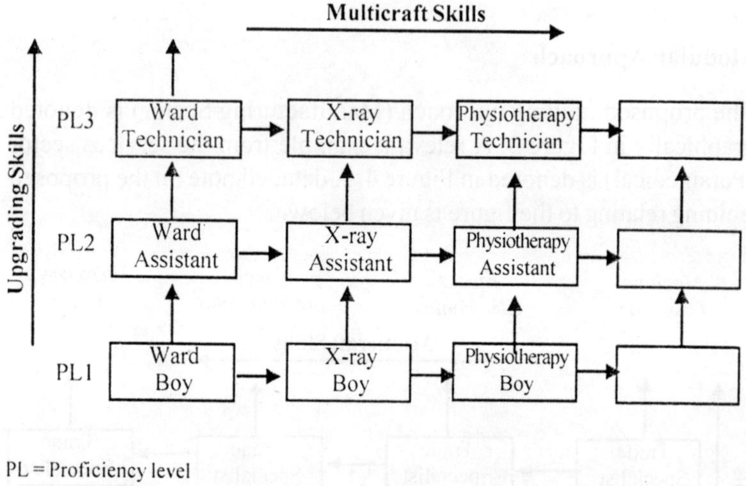

Figure 4. Proposed Training Approach (Paramedical)

b) The first Module PL1 would be for a broad based foundation training and common to various trades from a particular trade group. Through this a trainee could be prepared for undertaking a wide range of jobs demanding basic skills rather than too specific skills.

c) An apprentice after completing first module will be tested to confirm the acquisition of a defined competency/proficiency level – All India Trade Test may be conducted at this stage under the aegis of National Council for Vocational Training (NCVT) to certify the acquisition of 1st level of proficiency. This first certification by National Council for Vocational Training (NCVT) would qualify the trainee for employment.

d) The trainee, after completing the first module will have a choice to undertake a higher proficiency module, which will give him vertical mobility. This will be up gradation of his skill in the selected trade area. It is further proposed that examinations at higher 'P' levels may be conducted by respective States under the aegis of State Council for Vocational Training (SCVT). The trainee may also have a choice to undergo training across other trade areas. This will provide him horizontal/ lateral mobility i.e. an apprentice from machining skill group undertaking 1st module from Electrical group. By undergoing such courses the trainee becomes more versatile/ multi-skilled.

e) Thus, a trainee with modular approach can pick up either high skills (skill promotion) or greater variety of skills (versatility–mobility across trades). An apprentice of a course will be required to fulfil certain qualifying norms such as certain number of years of shop floor experience etc. for undergoing training at higher proficiency level or across the trades.

f) Figure 5 indicates the modular approach towards cross-functional training. A trainee from the 'Production' area may be able to move to 'Maintenance' or 'Inspection' group, by selecting and undertaking appropriate modular training on fulfilling the necessary qualifying norms and at appropriate time. This cross-functional training would help a person to move up into Supervisory or Technician positions.

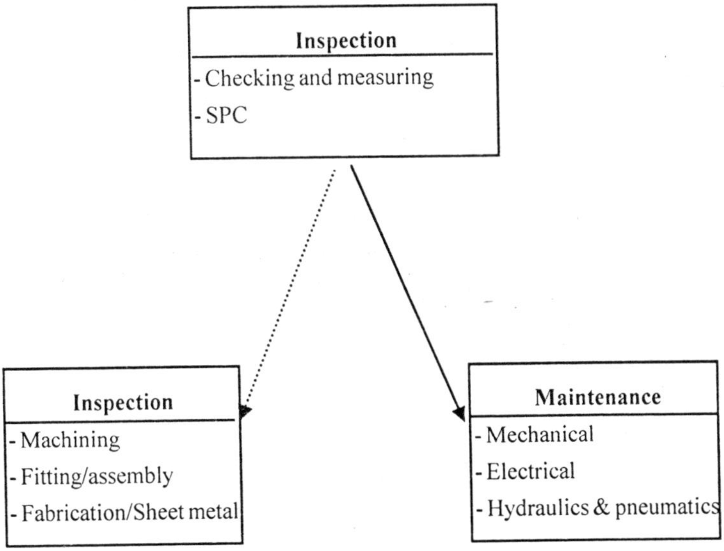

Figure5. Modular Approach to Cross-Functional Training

g) Thus there is an inherent motivational dimension incorporated in modular training approach and the ongoing modular programmes may enhance the career prospect of the individuals.

h) The concept of continuing Vocational Training will be possible with this module system and then it will become an accepted part of career growth and development.

i) Once the modular concept is accepted the structure modules could be designed. The existing facility available at ITIs could be rearranged/realigned to make these modules available to the trainees. Establishments having basic training facilities also could take up this new system of modular training. Individuals on their own can take up these modules if employed even after working hours. Facilities at ITIs could be made available on part-time basis for employed persons. Industries may also sponsor the workmen to undergo training in appropriate modules considering their own skill requirements of future at ITIs or they may impart training according to modular plan in their own premises and allow workmen to appear for final examinations and certification.

j) Rotational programme for various trade groups to ensure the optimum utilisation of facilities. It has been observed that the present Apprenticeship Training Programme recommends a set of machines / equipment for each trade. To cite an example Lathe, Milling, Grinding, Drilling machines are prescribed for each of the trades like Turner, Machinist, Grinder, Fitter, Tool & Die Maker, and Millwright Mechanic etc. It is seen that a cluster of such machines are made available in the respective trade training areas at ITIs. These machines remain idle once the respective skills are imparted. This could be avoided by a rotation plan, which makes training cost effective.

Modular Approach to the Service Sector

The modular approach mentioned above is also applicable to the services sector. As an illustration, the approach for the paramedical field is shown at Figure 5. The broad level occupations and the course content (as illustration) are mentioned subsequently.

a) Few Occupations under Para-Medical field are:

i) Ward Technician

ii) Operation Theatre Technician

iii) X-ray Technician

iv) Ophthalmic Technician

v) Medical Lab. Technician

vi) Life Support Care (ICU) Technician

vii) Occupational Health Centre Technician

viii) Dressers / First Aiders

ix) Physiotherapy technician

x) Dental technician

For the occupation of Ward Technician, the basic module for the Ward Boy at Proficiency Level PL_1 can be as follows (given as illustration only):

b) Course Contents covering both Theory and Practice – Hands on experience in Hospital / Laboratories / Clinics / Physiotherapy Centres.

i) Study/ understanding of the 'Human Body.."' Different parts and their functions

ii) Understanding of common anatomical terms

iii) Surface Anatomy

iv) Study of function of different organs (Basic Physiology)

v) Human health and disease

vi) Acquaintance with Medical Terms used in 'Clinical Practice'

vii) Aseptic precautions/ Sterilisation of Instruments, Dressings, Linen

viii) Patients handling / Communication with patients & relatives

ix) Basic 'Biochemistry'

x) Training in day to day working like measuring body temperature, administering injection, dressing, bandaging etc.

xi) Housekeeping and sanitation in hospitals / Labs etc.

xii) Preparation of beds

xiii) Safety precautions while handling patients, instruments

xiv. Basic 'First-aid' treatment

xv) General Lab Management and Ethics

c) On completion of the entire training course in one of the occupations, the trainee may have wage employment or self-employment as illustrated below (for the occupation of medical laboratory technician):

Table 8. Occupation : Medical Laboratory Technician

Wage Employment	*Self Employment*
– Technician / Lab. Technician in	. Diagnostic Laboratory
– Blood Bank	. Sale of Readymade treatment kits / medicine
– Public Health Lab	. Distributor for Lab chemicals
– Pharmaceutical Labs / industrial or Occupational Health Centres	. Distributor for lab wares, equipment / spare parts.
– Taluka. District Hospitals	
– Private Hospitals, Nursing homes & diagnostic Labs	
– Primary Health Centres	
– Dental / Pharmacy Colleges	
– Micro biology / Biochemistry / Pathology Dept. of Medical Colleges & Hospitals etc.	
– Physiotherapy clinics	
– Municipal Dispensaries	

Training Modules for Self Employment

While developing modules based on proficiency levels PL_1, PL_2 etc., one sub-module, covering necessary inputs useful for the trainee to engage themselves in self-employment on completion of training, could be designed wherever possible, depending upon the trade group areas. Separate training modules suitable for only self-employment could otherwise be designed keeping the modular approach in mind.

The institutes may develop small sections with appropriate training facilities in the selected self-employment areas. To illustrate this point a sub-module on "Plumbing Skills" may form part of the main module of Assembly Fitter or Maintenance Fitter. Initially, a trainee will learn all plumbing skills in the well developed/equipped section and then practice on live jobs. The Institute may provide on the job training by exposing the trainee to real life situations. For example, the trainee can be put on the job by the institute, if the institute has an annual repair contract with the Bungalow Owners or Housing Societies in the neighbouring residential areas. Institutes thus, would continuously get repair jobs in plumbing; the customer would get prompt service and trainees would get the opportunity of real life experiences and on the job training. With this approach towards training for self-employment the institute would be able to earn 'Revenues.' The institute may, at its discretion, pay a small portion of the earning to the trainee to motivate them to perform well. Trainees will also learn how to communicate with the customer and develop self– confidence in doing repair jobs independently. They can also be trained to keep accounts, spare part inventory and to take proper care of tools and equipment. Such modules would certainly help in developing and consolidating the necessary skills of entrepreneurship.

Many such modules covering the service sector like "Repairs of Electrical Domestic Appliance" or "House Wiring" or Motor Winding, which form a part of main module of "Mechanic Electrical and Electronics," could be designed to promote self-employment. The modular approach to vocational training is applicable to the labour force both in the organised and the unorganised sectors. As has been indicated in the illustrative examples pertaining to manufacturing (machinist) and service (paramedical – ward boy) sub sectors, this system is applicable for horizontal, vertical and diagonal upgradation of skills. This system results in creating a multi-skilled workforce as well as in increasing the employability of the workforce.

Competency-based Training System

In order to meet the new challenges facing the Indian workforce, the Study Group has recommended setting up of a competency based continuing training system covering all sectors of the economy. The training system will have a well-defined certification system for the competencies acquired during the program. It will help in providing learning, training, retraining, assessment and accreditation opportunities, with desired academic flexibility to those who wish to achieve higher skill standards and performance at the work place. This means that the trainees are free to leave the training and join work as and when they feel that they have received adequate amount of training. After some time, they can again join in for training if the situation demands or they feel a need to upgrade or shift laterally.

The purpose of competency based training (CBT) is to develop a competent workforce which will consist of individuals who can consistently perform work activities to the standards required in employment over a range of contexts or conditions.

CBT differs from the traditional training on the basis of which the training cycle is operated. In CBT, the basis of training design is explicit, standards of performance are measurable and reflect the actual expectations of performance in a work role.

The key features of this approach are:

a) Competencies to be demonstrated are derived from the job function/ roles of different categories of employees

b) The methodology for assessing the performance is based upon achieving specified competencies and is made public in advance

c) The rate of progress through the training programme is determined by demonstration of competency rather than time required for completion

d) The learning programme is individualised as far as possible, through the use of instructional modules for each competency, which offer different instructional alternatives

e) Some of the competencies like leadership, team work will be developed in group situations during the contact sessions.

Model for Competency based Training

A model for Competency based training for developing required competencies is given as Figure 6. It consists of 4 core areas:

a) Identification of Competency Requirements

b) Preparation of Modules for Instruction

c) Programme Implementation and Evaluation

The first step in the development of this CBT method is the identification of the target group for which the CBT programme is being designed. The target group is that category of the people, which has to undertake a specific vocation (occupation) after the stipulated programme of study. Their occupation (when technical education is considered) could be at various levels such as craftsmen/ technicians/ engineers etc. Every occupation consists of a number of jobs (roles) that are to be performed.

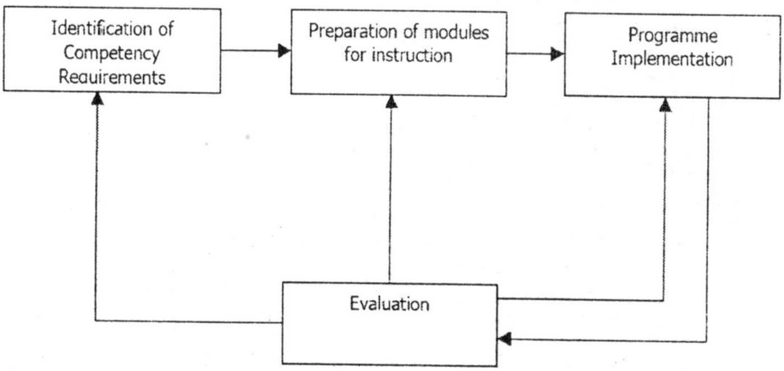

Figures 6. Model for Competency Based Training (CBT)

Identification of competencies is done by analysing the job functions, receiving feedback from allumini employers and trainers looking into personal growth needs and assessing the future requirements of the occupation. Identification of competencies will also provide us with a list of attitudes, which are desirable for performing the job proficiently. Desirable attitudes represent those qualities relating to the readiness and willingness in the employee to use cognitiveand practical skills in the work situation (without much hesitation, ability to work as a team member, to take leadership, to be sensitive to the environment) and those qualities, which deal with feelings, emotions and interests.

The next step is to identify who should be deciding the group of competencies to be included for a particular level of job/role. A systematic and scientific process calls for a group consisting of all the stakeholders such as representatives from the industry and educational institution that will undertake this work. Alternatively, Needs Assessment Boards (NABs) comprising the stakeholders can be established. Their function will be focused on assessing, compiling and standardising competencies required for selected occupations, on a continuous basis, for both the near and the far future of the labour force of unorganised sector.

Preparation of Modules for Instruction

After identification of competencies, skills and enabling objectives for a given training programme, development of instructional modules will start. The instructional process is through modules and the module will have the following characteristics:

a) The focus is on a competency consisting of distinctive identifiable skill/ skills.

b) Modules are individualised to allow the learner to work at his own place.

c) It would blend theory and practice, reading, reflecting and acting.

d) It would include an objective assessment procedure to the extent possible, whether self-monitoring or requiring partner/ observer or both.

It would be reality oriented involving the learners in real or simulated situations fairly directly and immediately.

Programme Implementation

The three critical factors on which the success of the implementation of competency-based training depends are given below.

a) *Feedback on programme:* A CBT programme will function effectively if appropriate strategies are put into place which will gather information leading to modifications in the programme. Such strategies could include normal feedback channels from learners, their employers and the faculty involved in implementation. Yet another strategy could be research into the job performance of employees before and after attending the CBT programme. It may also be possible to explore a mixture of such strategies to provide reliable data on which decisions could be based.

b) *Resource Mobilisation and Delivery*: The modular approach with its emphasis on individualised instruction demands a great deal of updated learning materials. Hence, there should be planned generation of resources such as filmstrips, slides, video CDs, apart from the usual print material. Provision has to be made for competency testing at different stages, as the concept of an end or terminal examination is no more valid. Further, considering the need to provide basic occupational competencies to a large number of learners in a short time, it may be possible to identify a select group of competencies to be included in the first phase of the CBT programme, which may be about one to two months duration or more, depending on the needs of the clients. In subsequent phases, optional competencies could be offered. An achievement of about 75% of the competencies offered could lead to career advancement.

c) *Commitment:* Another key factor for the successful implementation of the CBT programme is the commitment of the institutions and the individuals responsible. Such commitment could be ensured by involving the entire faculty at each stage of development and implementation and by adopting a group strategy.

Evaluation

The evaluation in the CBT model means evaluation of learners and evaluation of programme effectiveness.

a) *Evaluation of Learners*: Competency assessment is carried out through post test(s), for each competency. A learner who demonstrates performance of the competency up to a predetermined proficiency level is declared successful (pass).

   Separate tests may be designed for evaluating the knowledge component, skill component and attitude assessment. The knowledge component can be assessed by a written test using objective and short answer questions. It is not necessary that every competency will have a component of knowledge assessment.

This will depend upon specific requirements of the competency. The skill component may consist of assessment of cognitive skills and/or psychomotor skills depending upon the requirement of the competency. This assessment can be either in a simulated situation and/or real life situation. For the attitude assessment, no standard questionnaires are suggested. However, the instructor will assess this component by responses got through the questions/ exercises from each learner during the classroom/ field exercises and formal and informal interactions.

b) *Evaluation of Programme Effectiveness :* The success of the CBT method depends partly on obtaining the feedback and using it to modify the programme. A programme can be modified from time to time to refine the module objectives, improve the learning experience for the trainees, and upgrade the learning materials it uses. The programme evaluation should also attempt to address the criteria for performance assessment and objective attainment.

The competency based training system is applicable to the labour force both in the organised and the unorganised sectors. As has been indicated in the illustrative example pertaining to plumber attendant, this system can be effectively used to develop competencies in any job/vocation in all sectors of economy, such as manufacturing, service, trade and agriculture.

Competency based Certification System

Many developed and developing nations the world over, have evolved a standard of certification of competencies at different levels. Applicable normally to formal education and training programmes, it can be extended to courses or modules in informal training programmes, as and when required.

In India there is a large network of ITIs, Vocational Schools, Institutions, Export Promotion Councils, Commodity Boards, KVIC/ KVIBS, KVKs, Community Polytechnics, Extension Centres of Agriculture/ Horticulture, Universities, NGOs, Professional Bodies & Associations, Chambers of Commerce and Industries, Confederation of Industries at district, state, regional and national levels etc., conducting a large variety of formal and non-formal training programmes. These sectors include: Agriculture and allied activities,

Mining & Quarrying, Manufacturing, Electricity, Gas & Water Supply, Construction, Trade, Hotels, Tourism, Transport and Communication, Financial, Real Estate and Business Services, Community & Social Services and Personal Services.

In order to make the infrastructure more productive and efficient, a national level certification for different trades/skills is recommended. An independent professional body needs to implement competency standards in all vocational trades. Active user involvement in defining quality standards and ensuring that these are duly implemented can be done only by involvement of user associations or individual experts from user sectors.

Independent regulatory Authority

An independent regulatory authority be constituted by the Government, whose functions shall, among other things, include setting standards for skills required for a particular competency, standards for programme implementation and standards for accreditation of institutions imparting training programmes for skill development and retraining. Such an authority needs to have statutory powers in the formulation of policies (including the mechanism of fees and funding), action plans and programmes for providing a continuing, coordinated and fully integrated skill development programme. A case in example is the National Council for Vocational Qualifications (NCVQ), which was created in 1986 in the United Kingdom (UK). The NCVQ, in turn, accredited over 150 industry associations to develop standards for their industries. Supplementation of the NCVQ in UK gained momentum, though slowly, and by 1998 about 2.2 million NCVQ certificates were awarded. The NCVQ is now known as Qualification and Curriculum Authority (QCA). It enters into contracts with the National Training Organisation (NTO) to develop standards and provide training.

The independent National Authority will have the following functions:

a) Formulation of policies, action plans and programmes for providing a continuing, coordinated and fully integrated skill development programme

b) To set sector-wise standards for skill acquisition, development and training programmes

c) To work out plans for more participation and involvement of industry in vocational education

d) To allocate resources amongst programmes and schemes

e) To monitor and review various vocational education programmes and make changes based on the feedback

f) Accreditation of training institutions/ organisations

The National Authority can also seek support of another agency, which will solely focus on qualification and curriculum development. This institution may be made responsible for accreditation of training providers and setting up of sector-wise skill standards on which the curriculum gets developed. It may be mentioned that the training providers/institutions which will be accredited for providing certification will be required to get their systems and processes revalidated after a prescribed period of time.

Certification System

A person who has gained relevant knowledge and skills, formally or informally in a designated occupation can undertake an Evaluation Test for certification and recognition of his/her qualification (of competencies). This means that certification of trainees/learners is competency based. Accredited persons and institutions, can conduct the tests at specified intervals. As the training is modular, credits will be assigned after completion of each module depending on the performance at the test. The agency for qualification and curriculum development will also prescribe minimum credits essential for job positions belonging to categories of technical workforce and would include compulsory accumulation of a minimum number of credits related to one's job.

The credits will be valid for a pre-defined period, thereby necessitating revalidation of the competency. In case a person already possesses competencies, gained hereditary, formally or informally, through distance learning systems such as internet, self-learning modules, previous work in a work place or training in an organisation, he/she can appear for the test with the accredited person (assessor) or organisation for testing and certification of the level of prior learning. This would help a person in assessing competencies in a particular field and also in deciding the modules to be offered for obtaining a particular qualification. Accreditation of prior learning can be done through the formal or informal education and training method. It could be obtained by an individual in an institutional setting or a course undertaken at an industry training centre or 'on-the-job.'

It is also desirable that certification of competencies be done with actual involvement of the user organisations like employers, industry and other user systems. A conscious effort must be made to involve the trade unions to contribute effectively in this endeavour.

A case in example is of TAFE, Australia where a competency-based certificate is issued in a modular manner upon completion of a unit of up to 40 hours of training in a week. Such units can be accumulated over time and can be used for certification based on modules completed.

Entry Qualifications and Re-certification of Instructors

In order that the training is effective at the grass root level, it is essential that the trainers are highly skilled and they also are subject to re-certification of their skills after a set period of time. There is a need to strike a balance between the skill level of the trainer and his/her pedagogical abilities. If the trainer is not a master craftsman, it might turn out that the focus is more on the theoretical aspects and the practical part gets less attention. Also, the trainers/ instructors are to be re-trained in a planned manner for keeping up to date with the changes taking place both in their skill development field as well as the methods of training for skill development. The industry itself can prove to be an appropriate source from where training talent can be recruited for a full time role as skill developers.

Thus, competency based certification system is applicable to the labour force both in the organised and the unorganised sectors. It is not only the trainees who have to be certified, but also the trainers under this system. It will also enable persons, who have acquired skills hereditarily, by experience on the job without formal education or by acquiring skills through self learning, Internet as well as other methods, to get certification. They can use this certification to enhance their earnings as well as employability.

Assessment of Training Needs

For the implementation of Competency Based Training across all sectors of the economy, it is imperative that the competencies for various occupations are established. This also requires imparting attitudinal training requisite for the occupation for which the learner is being trained. Competency Assessment Board should be established at the National Level.

This will focus on assessing, compiling and standardising competencies required for selected occupations on a continuous basis. The competencies will be identified by interactions with the industry associations, detailed regular surveys aimed at projecting the nature and characteristics of the unorganised sector activities and its workers. It will also focus on curriculum development including attitudinal training requirement for the various occupations.

The competencies will be identified by interactions with the industry associations, by utilising the services of various specific institutions, and through detailed regular surveys. The aim of these surveys will be to project the nature and characteristics of the unorganised sector – its activities and its workers. They will contribute information that is relevant for structuring the curricula of Competency Based Training programmes.

Self-employed Training in the Unorganised Sector

A large part of the employment is being generated in the services sector and, there too, mostly in the self-employed sector. The self-employed sector requires additional skills in the area of accounting and marketing which cannot be imparted through structured formal training. It is felt that 'mentors' in actual business conditions will help in the development of skills. The Bhartiya Yuva Shakti Trust, which is a Confederation of Indian Industry (CII) initiative established in 1991, is one of the relevant models in this context. The Trust fosters entrepreneurial activity by providing seed capital loans and practical business advice through mentors. About 1700 people have been employed in 500 ventures between 1991-2000 spread over rural and urban areas. However, it is worth noting that the loan recovery rate is 94%, indicating strong economic viability.

Training of Rural Labour

In order to undertake development of rural areas in the true sense, the country would be required to establish training institutions at the doorsteps of the rural masses. It would be appropriate to establish Block Level vocational educational institutions in a phased manner in each block, so that the country can economise on the creation of a large infrastructure for such institutions. These institutions are to be set up with the financial support of Government, Non Resident Indians, corporate sector, NGOs. These institutions should aim at two important levels: (a) spread of literacy and (b) spread of vocational education with a view to creating marketable skills and continuous employability of rural labour.

Role of trade Unions, NGOs and Other Interest Groups

The objective of achieving a skilled workforce is possible only when all the stakeholders act as partners in training. Trade unions at the national, regional, industry and plant level should all have a say in the running of workers' education programmes.

The Non Governmental Organisations (NGOs) provide an effective interface between the organised sector and the unorganised sector. NGOs provide the most conducive means for providing training at the small and micro level. The workers in the unorganised sector require training linked to specific production activities. The NGOs play a vital role in achieving this objective. The Government's decision to support voluntary organisations from the VIIth Plan period onwards was based on the realisation that voluntary organisations not only provide a new modal approach to the rural development but also secure the involvement of families living below the poverty line in the developmental efforts.

The role of the NGOs assumes more importance in view of the fact that India is a vast country with immense occupational and cultural diversity. With a vast population of Indians living in the rural areas being illiterate, training by formal means becomes difficult. The NGOs are also equipped for capacity building as they can introduce innovation and experimentation since they are unencumbered by Government Rules and Regulations.

Our Study Group conducted two workshops especially in the Unorganised Sector on Skill Development, Training and Workers' Education, to share the experiences of the participants in providing skill development and education in the unorganised sector.

Forecasting of Marketable Skills

For better matching of demand and supply of marketable skills, a labour market intelligence system needs to be set up. This system will forecast the demand of various marketable skills at the national level and at the district level through the existing government machinery, but in consultation with the industry associations, entrepreneurs, experts, NGOs etc. on a continuous basis. This system would take into consideration existing and emerging business opportunities in India and abroad. It will also be applicable for forecasting of marketable skills in both the organised and unorganised sectors.

Strengthening of ITI

At present, there is insufficient capacity in the areas of skill development and training. Hence, there is a pressing need to enlarge the training infrastructure as well, so as to effectively and productively utilise the existing infrastructure. While infrastructure is available in the form of 4274 Industrial Training Institutes (ITI), there are a number of problems with the ITIs. They need to restructure and reorient their courses at a much faster rate so as to respond effectively to current and future needs of the labour market. Further, the Industry-Institute interaction continues to be weak. So far, inputs from the industry into ITIs are merely of advisory nature, which are not very effective. It is necessary to see that advisory inputs are supplemented with managerial inputs.

ITIs need to:

(a) Run market-driven courses

(b) Review, and if necessary, revise curriculum every 5 years to keep it contemporary

(c) Give refresher training on new technologies and tools to teachers at ITIs

(d) Discontinue obsolete (not required by market) courses

Further, to ensure effective involvement of industry in the training process, we recommend that some ITIs may be selected, on a pilot basis, for development into Institutes of Excellence. They should be managed jointly with the industry. In this regard, institutionalisation of Industry-Institute interaction and empowerment of training institutions would be important.

It may be mentioned that in 1997, a study was made in eleven ITIs in North India with the participation of senior officers from Directorate General Employment & Training (DGE&T), State Directorates, Confederation of Indian Industry (CII) and local industry representatives. In January 1998, CII organised a workshop on 'Industry-Institute Interface for the years 2000 and beyond. One of the major recommendations of this workshop was to set up an Institute Managing Committee (IMC) with the participation of local industry for at least one ITI in each State. It was also proposed that a Steering Committee at the State level, be constituted, which would decide the powers to be devolved to the IMCs. The suggested composition of the IMC with roles and responsibilities is mentioned.

New Training Delivery Systems

In order to expand training capacity as well as to provide training anytime and anywhere, new delivery mechanisms such as computer based training, web-based training, distance learning etc. can be adopted which would offer flexibility in timings, pace of learning, and customisation of content to serve the varying needs of the different target groups.

Integrating Vocational Education at School Level

In view of the large number of individuals entering the workforce, vocational education should be integrated at the school level. This will also help in standardisation of training courses. It is relevant to consider, in this context, whether vocational training should be added onto the general school system or whether it should be imparted through separate schools. However, school students should be allowed entry into courses on some trades such as masonry, after the 8th standard (due to low skill level requirement).

Incentives for the Creation of Training Facilities

In order that skill development and training get the due focus, it is felt that fiscal incentives should be extended to industry and other providers of training. They can be given incentives by the government in the form of providing land at concessional rates, a part-funding of the capital cost, tax benefits on the amount spent by them for training and skill development, awards, teachers' training, provision of training material etc. The same can also be extended by way of tax concessions on the amount spent on training and skill development.

We also recommend that the entire expense in training should be treated as a revenue expense and all capital expenditure on training and infrastructure should be eligible for an accelerated depreciation equal to 1.5 times the amount spent during the same financial year. The investment in training and infrastructure is made to encourage the culture of training and to improve the skills and attitude of performance.

Skill Development Fund

As per the World Bank report on Skills Development, well-designed levy-grant schemes can induce firms to train. Several East Asian economies have effectively used direct reimbursement of approved training expenses, funded out of payroll levies, to encourage firms to train their employees. Successful schemessuch as those in Singapore, Malaysia and Taiwan are flexible, demand driven, and often accompanied by an information campaign and a programme of technical assistance to smaller firms. The introduction of such a scheme in Taiwan led to dramatic increases in the volume of training, which continued even after the program was terminated in the 1970s. The Study Group set up by us has thoroughly reviewed such programmes, which are prevalent in Singapore and Malaysia, besides the system prevalent in other countries.

In order to provide for:

(a) Retraining of workers rendered surplus/obsolete by layoffs, retrenchment and Voluntary Retirement Schemes/Early Separation Schemes, and

(b) Training of labour in the unorganised sector, We recommend the establishment of a Skill Development Fund (SDF), in the manner in which it has been established in Singapore.

The key features of the SDFare as below.

(a) The fund will be contributed by organisations which are eligible to contribute Provident Fund either through the Provident Fund office or through their own trust.

(b) The amount of contribution to be paid by such organisations will be 2.0% of the provident fund contribution by the employer. In addition, the employee will also contribute 1.0% of his/her provident fund contribution. The government will also contribute every month, two times the amount collected from the employer and employees to this Fund. A proposed source of the government's contribution is by way of amount received from disinvestments in public sector units.

(c) For the purpose of collection of the contribution, we propose it be routed and administered through the Regional Provident Fund (PF) Office (as per the system prevalent in Singapore), so as to avoid extra administrative burden. The PF office will receive the contribution along with the Provident Fund and deposit the same into a separate account within a week of the receipt.

(d) The respective individuals/ organisations making this contribution to the SDF will be given tax concession for an amount equal to the amount contributed to the SDF.

(e) At all points of time, 25% of the total amount in the SDF will be invested in a corpus with high safety and reasonable return. The balance amount in the SDF will be used for purposes that have been mentioned in preceding paragraphs.

(f) The collections to this SDF shall continue for a period of 10 years. It is expected that by that time the SDF corpus would be self-sustaining. Thereafter, contributions to the SDF may be discontinued. However, this is subject to review based on the requirements of the labour situation at that point of time.

(g) The utilisation of the amount so collected in the SDF, should be monitored by persons of eminence and reputed industry associations in association with the Central and State Governments.

Further, for granting the amounts to be paid by the Fund as an incentive to the organisations, certain norms may be required to be set. The organisations fulfilling the norms make an application, giving details of the training efforts being put by them. After evaluation of the quality of training efforts and the quality of trainees turned out, a committee may prescribe the grants. Guidelines for committee formation and identifying norms can be explored further in consultation with experts.

The grants offered to organisations by the Skill Development Fund as an incentive for promoting skills would also help in developing a training culture among employers as well as employees and ultimately, we believe it would help to build a worldclass workforce for the nation. The fund would also encourage industries to further strengthen their training infrastructure and commitment towards training. Efforts could be directed towards identifying high-end skills, critical for economic growth and encouraging employers to invest in such skills. This will help in increasing the reach of training, to promote skill deepening and in enhancing the employability of the workforce.

Importance of Skill Training

The emerging economic scenario has brought great changes not only to the ways of working and transacting business but also to the management of households, upbringing of children, cultural activities, leisure and social relationships. The success of all technical training will depend not only on the acquisition of work skills but also on the values and attitudes imparted by general education. Education and training also have other objectives in addition to vocational ones, because they open up access to culture, to knowledge and to political and social life and are essential factors in the development of the individual and the values that guide the life of the individual and social groups. If the training of workers is purely technical, they are unable to adjust to new values, new concepts of the nature of work, new ways of interacting with their peers, colleagues and with work itself. This brings out the fact that workers' education has to continue, and needs to upgrade itself, to meet the expectations of the target groups in order to achieve their goals.

Thus, a comprehensive programme of education of workers has to be established with the following key objectives:

a) To instil a sense of belonging in the workers vis a vis their work and organisation, through a better understanding of their work and the work organisation; to inculcate amongst workers a positive sense of dedication and hard work so as to achieve higher productivity and improvement in the quality of products

b) To improve the bargaining power of the workers, through understanding of their rights and environment, and through organising and collective bargaining

c) To assist the worker in identifying skills he/she needs to pick up in order to improve value in the job market, and to provide the avenues for acquiring the skills

d) To encourage the workers to look at alternatives in organisation of their work, like worker cooperatives, in order to improve their collective bargaining power and their quality of work. Specialised programmes may also be conducted for creating interest in self-employment, or in the acquisition of skill upgradation in the situation of job loss.

Scope of the Education Process

The education programme should not be a mechanical approach of skill development towards a changing job market. It also needs to look at the vital question of allowing the workers to understand the environment and processes of which they are a part. They should be enabled to have a say in the way in which the processes affect them, through programmes that improve their individual and collective bargaining abilities.

It is in the context that the education process should specifically focus on an understanding of the economy, industry and the business organisation of which the worker is a part. The scope should include understanding the business and work processes along the supply chain. It should include the potential for workers to keep abreast with changes in technology and work processes in the industry of which they are a part.

The education programme should also look at issues of alternative forms of organisation as ways of improving the involvement and control of workers over their work. These include forms of self-organisation, including producer and consumer cooperatives and the Gandhian value of Trusteeship. These alternatives are particularly significant in the context of current business strategies of dispersal and contractualisation of work.

The programmes should also discuss organisation of workers, and the history of collective bargaining. The new working class should be able to trace its lineage back to older worker class traditions, in order to grow organically and retain a collective identity. This collective identity is essential for developing a sense of worth, and for retaining some control over their work life.

Organisation of the Education Programme

As is evident, such a programme cannot be confined to the classroom. There has to be a context of continuous education. The education process should allow continuous interaction and consultation between various participants in the labour movement. It should encompass the process of tripartite negotiations and collective bargaining between management, government and labour.

Ownership of the Programme

The involvement of workers and workers' organisations in the design, conduct and control of such a training programme is essential to its success. As such, their prominent role in the ownership of the programme is necessary. Trade unions at the national, regional, industry and plant level should all have a say in the running of the programme.

The Role of the Central Board of Workers Education

Since its inception in 1958, the Central Board of Workers' Education (CBWE) has done significant work in injecting an understanding and enthusiasm among workers for the success of industrial growth, production and productivity and harmonious industrial relations.

The CBWE is a tripartite body, which is headed by a part-time non-official Chairman nominated by the Government of India. The Director, CBWE is the Principal Executive Officer who is assisted by one additional Director, 3 Deputy Directors, a Financial Advisor and other supporting staff. The Headquarters of the Board is at Nagpur and has a network of 4 Zonal Directorates, 49 Regional Directorates, 10 Sub-Regional Directorates spread throughout the length and breadth of the country, and an apex training institute viz. Indian Institute of Workers' Education at Mumbai.

Initially, the focus of the programme of the Board was on industrial workers i.e. on workers of the organised sector. As an outcome of the recommendations of the Estimates Committee of Parliament in 1971, the Workers Education Review Committee in 1975 and the Ratification of ILO convention No. 141 concerning organisation of rural workers and their role in economic and social development in the year 1977, CBWE launched programmes for workers of the unorganised and rural sectors during 1977-78. Presently, the Board organises 20 to 25 types of programmes for the workers in the organised, unorganised and rural sectors.

The Study Group has set up by us has identified certain areas where the CBWE can play a vital role which are given below.

a) The CBWE can play an important role in creating awareness on specified skill training required for the development of the industry and availability of such training facilities. The Board may further coordinate such training programmes by bringing together workers, managements and nearby training institutes

b) Though the CBWE organises training of trainer programmes, so far as the conduct of classes in the unit level by the trainers is concerned, the performance has not been satisfactory. A suitable mechanism needs to be devised for regular training programmes through the trainers trained by the CBWE. The Board can play the role of a nodal agency to enforce training programmes through the trainers and also to monitor the same so as to achieve larger coverage of the target groups.

c) The CBWE, through its wide network, may organise specialised training courses for the retrenched workers/workers who have taken VRS so as to help them in proper investment of money, which can ensure a regular income. These training programmes may also help in creating awareness regarding areas of skill development and related issues.

d) The CBWE should become more focused and should organise specialised, need based programmes for the various target groups in the unorganised and rural sectors.

   These programmes can also help workers identify opportunities and areas for self-employment

e) The Co-operative is yet another sector in which there is ample scope for training by the CBWE. There is a lot of demand from this sector for the training programmes of the CBWE. The Board, may therefore give suitable training programmes to the workers in the co-operative sector.

f) As the Panchayati Raj plays a crucial role in the Indian system of governance providing for effective local administration, the functionaries of the Panchayati Raj institutions may be trained on a regular basis by the CBWE in subjects of importance from the point of view of changing scenario.

g) There is a need for more follow-up programmes i.e. to conduct more refresher courses, to repeat the training programmes for the same target groups by the Board as these alone can have a better impact and will sustain the effect.

h) The Board may also involve nongovernmental organisations, academic institutes etc. in conducting various training programmes. This is necessary for a larger coverage, as the Board, with the existing strength, cannot reach the entire workforce.

Leadership Development Programme

In an era of transformation, the trade union movement faces its own urgent need for adjustment, for the modernisation of its own stock of technical knowledge and operational skills, for the rethinking of policies and priorities, and for reflecting of leaders capable of forming and implementing the strategies needed to ensure that the best long term interests of workers are safeguarded. The problems of social and economic development can be surmounted only with the full, knowledgeable and responsible participation of organised labour.

A systematic re-education and training of workers based on their developmental needs and national interest demands a high place on the agenda. It is important that unions themselves take the initiative in studying these problems and that they focus attention on the long-term interests of workers. The training programmes organised by the CBWE for trade unions must be redesigned to focus on the above areas.

Involvement of State Governments

At present, the Workers Education Programmes are carried out with the grants-in-aid made available by the Central Government. As the majority of workers being trained belong to the States, and as their contribution by way of improvement in skills, work culture, personality development, leadership qualities, awareness of responsibilities goes in a big way to the State's development, the State governments must also participate in the Workers Education programmes. State Governments may be approached for contribution to the scheme either by giving grants or providing infrastructure and other facilities.

References

Bresnahan, Timothy F., Erik Brynjolfsson, and Lorin M. Hitt. (1998). *How Do Information Technology and Work Place Organisation Affect Labor Demand? Firm-Level Evidence*. Unpublished manuscript.

Beede, David N. and Kan H. Young. (1996). *Patterns of Advanced Technology Adoption and Manufacturing Performance: Employment Growth, Labor Productivity, and Employee Earnings*. U.S. Department of Commerce, Washington, DC.

Cappelli, Peter. (1993). "Are Skill Requirements Rising? Evidence From Production and Clerical Jobs." *Industrial and Labor Relations Review* 46, no. 3: 515-30.

Holzer, Harry J. (1996). "Employer Skill Needs and Labor Market Outcomes by Race and Gender." *Discussion Paper No. 1087-96*, Institute for

Howell, David R. and Edward Wolff. (1991)."Trends in the Growth and Distribution of Skills in the US Workplace, 1960-1985." *Industrial and Labor Relations Review* 44, no. 3: 486-502.

Levenson, Alec R., Elaine Reardon, and Stefanie Schmidt. (1999). *Welfare Jobs and Basic Skills: The Employment Prospects of Wefare Recipients in the Most Populous U.S. Counties,* National Center for Adult Learning and Literacy, Report #10. Cambridge, MA.

Wood, Adrian. (1995). "How Trade Hurt Unskilled Workers." *The Journal of Economic Perspectives* 9, no. 3: 57-80.

9

Skill Training and Organisational Learning

Modern conditions of dynamic competition, sophisticated information technology, knowledge economy, market globalisation, has changed the relation to importance of human resources in organisation. These conditions actualise the human capital as the strategic resource of every organisation. Differences between the organisations exist exactly due to the differences between human capital, i.e. the organisations human resources, ways of their management and development. In a more and more global, complex and turbulent environment, knowledge is the only reliable source of competitive advantage. Traditional factors of manufacturing as the soil, labour and capital did not disappear, but their significance is not primary anymore. Knowledge is viewed as the key of realisation of a competitive advantage. And therefore the question of where the corporative knowledge is located, how to release it and develop to achieve organisational goals has become very important. Since the organisational knowledge is largely located inside the human mind, i.e. the head of employees, as carriers of knowledge and activities, human resources are becoming the key factor of business success.

Organisational development is always conditioned by human knowledge and skills. That is why, contemporary organisations pay more and more attention to the development of their employees. Thus, employee education and training are becoming an optimal answer to complex business challenges, and the management of human resources is taking central role in modern management. Through the process of employee training and development, the management of human resources provides constant knowledge innovation, creates conditions for mutual knowledge and experience exchange and proactive behaviour, in this way contributing to competitive advantage and satisfaction of all participants in business procedures.

As a consequence of these procedures a learning organisation has formed. Learning organisation is organisation that promotes learning of all of its members and it transforms permanently. Individuals and societies that do not have enough knowledge are in inferior position, compared to societies and organisations that have it and even permanently acquire new knowledge. That is the reason why we say that success is not among the educated but among those that are learning permanently, and everything changes except knowledge acquirement, which is constant. The fore mentioned statements in the best way show the direction in which learning organisations move.

Employee Training and Development

Understanding the phenomenon of employee training and development requires understanding of all the changes that take place as a result of learning. As the generator of new knowledge, employee training and development is placed within a broader strategic context of human resources management, i.e. global organisational management, as a planned staff education and development, both individual and group, with the goal to benefit both the organisation and employees. To preserve its obtained positions and increase competitive advantage, the organisation needs to be able to create new knowledge, and not only to rely solely on utilisation of the existing. Thus, the continues employee training and deployment has a significant role in the development of individual and organisational performance. The strategic procedure of employee training and development needs to encourage creativity, ensure inventiveness and shape the entire organisational knowledge that provides the organisation with uniqueness and differentiates it from the others.

Education is no longer the duty and privilege of those in higher positions and skilled labour, but it is becoming the duty and need of everyone. The larger the organisations, the more funds they spend on education and provide their employees with greater and diverse possibilities of education and development. Understanding the tremendous significance of education for the modern organisation and confident that it represents a good and remunerative investment, present day organisations set aside more and more resources for this activity. Most of the organisations invest 3 to 5% of their revenue into adult education. It is estimated that the organisations that desire to keep the pace with changes need to provide their employees with 2% of total annual fund of working hours for training and education. Thus, it is necessary to accept the model of permanent, continuous learning. That truth has been known for more than two centuries. Denis Diderot, a French philosopher and literate of the Age of Enlightenment, wrote the following: "Education shouldn't be finished when an individual leaves school, it should encompass all the ages of life...to provide people in every moment of their life with a possibility to maintain their knowledge or to obtain new knowledge".

The only way for present day organisations to survive is the imperative to innovate or perish. Since this depends on the knowledge the organisation possesses, this imperative could be read as: learn faster than competition. The logical sequence is: knowledge creation – innovation – competitive advantage. If knowledge is good, is it not true that the more knowledge we have, the better we are? Many organisations which consider knowledge as a good thing are trapped into the pitfall of gathering as much knowledge as possible. Knowledge that is not necessary is exactly what it is: unnecessary. And the efforts to obtain it are wasted efforts. The only important knowledge is the knowledge with strategic importance to the company, knowledge that helps to increase the value of the company, knowledge with significance to the strategy of the company.

It is not about knowledge for the sake of knowledge, but rather knowledge according to the needs, applicable knowledge, to create innovation and competitive advantage. Obtaining knowledge, learning, education, all could have a real effect on the quality of labour only if they are harmonised with the needs of a particular organisation, its goals and the goals of its employees. The further choice of educational contents and educational methods, and the efficiency of educational effectiveness control depend on clearly defined educational goals and needs, answers to the questions of which knowledge is necessary to realise the strategy and the survival of the organisation in general, which employees need to possess this knowledge and will this knowledge solve certain problems.

Employee training and development does not imply only obtaining new knowledge, abilities and skills, but also the possibility to promote entrepreneurship, introduce employees to changes, encourage the changes of their attitude, introduce the employees to important business decisions and involve them actively in the process of decision making. To precisely define expectations and attract skilled workforce, more and more employment advertising offer a certain number of annual hours or days for education. The most wanted resources are the people with particular knowledge, skills and abilities. Managers must learn to manage them, and the organisations to employ and retain them. Knowledge based organisations must preserve their competitive advantage by retaining skilled workforce, workers of knowledge, strengthening their motivation and improving the reward and compensation systems according to the workers' performances.

Within the context of learning organisation, it is not sufficient for the worker only to add value to the organisation based on his knowledge, but he also has to receive knowledge. He gives as much knowledge as he receives. For the present day employees the wage by itself is not a sufficient incentive, but they also need investment into themselves in a sense of investing in their knowledge. Empolyees no longer work for money alone, nor can they be influenced by traditional attractive financial packages.

Learning Organisation

Every individual should appreciate lifelong learning, and every successful organisation has to become a permanently learning organisation. Many successful organisations describe themselves as learning organisation or one of their strategic goals is to become such an organisation. Companies such as Coca-Cola, Motorola, General Electrics and Cisco have assigned vice presidents for knowledge, learning or intellectual capital whose task is to create knowledge management systems that enable them to quickly adopt development tendencies, influencing in that way the customers, competitors, distributors and suppliers.

The organisation is not only the user of knowledge, but also its creator. According to the views of Peter Senge described in the book named "The Fifth Discipline", the learning organisation implies free flow of knowledge, i.e. lifting of all barriers on developing knowledge and new ideas at the very beginning. In the future it will not be possible to "unthread things from above" and for all the others to follow the "big brother's" instructions anymore. The top organisations of the future will be distinguished by their knowledge about how to encourage engagement and develop the learning potential on each organisational level. Peter Senge's model of a learning organisation is very interesting since it recognises the organisation as a whole, i.e., in his organisation, through their functions and sectors within the organisation, all the employees influence the course of business procedures, and the knowledge creation, consequently the creation of new values both for the organisation and its customers. With this definition, Senge has made significant qualitative progress compared to the classical organisation, since he emphasised the necessity of ability development through the process of learning.

Besides Senge, Chris Argyris was a great populariser of a learning organisation as well. In his book "Teaching smart people how to learn", he says: "Any company that aspires to succeed in the tougher business environment must first resolve a basic dilemma: success in the marketplace increasingly depends on learning, yet most people don't know how to learn. What's more, those members of the organisation that many assume to be the best at learning are, in fact, not very good at it. I am talking about the well-educated, high-powered, highly committed professionals who take up key leadership positions in the modern corporation."

Organisations learn only through the learning individuals. Individual learning does not guarantee organisational learning. But without it there is no organisational learning as well. The ability to learn faster than the competitors may be the only sustainable competitive advantage. Thus, the learning organisation is the organisation that learns and encourages people to learn in the organisation. It motivates information exchange between employees and creates staff with different knowledge. Chris Argiris explains this: "On the other hand, there is a problem of existence of individuals within the organisation who know how to learn, but that doesn't create automatically conditions for the organisation to learn as well. This is due to the indisputable view that knowledge is still the only private property the man owns. This means that individual learning, and even learning of all the employees, doesn't imply the existence of a learning organisation. To have a learning organisation, it is necessary to know how to transfer individual into organisational knowledge, i.e. into organisational learning."

The starting point of knowledge management concept is in the fact that power does not come from knowledge, but from the exchange of knowledge. It starts from the synergic effect. By exchanging knowledge, combining individual knowledge, we get much more qualitative knowledge than the individual knowledge. Obtaining and sharing knowledge is the core of the learning organisation.

The reasons to become a learning organisation are the following: people are developing (greater motivation, flexibility of employees, people are more creative, improved social interaction), better working teams and groups (knowledge sharing, mutual dependence), benefiting organisations (greater work productivity, more qualitative products/services/ procedures, competitive advantage, profit).

Training and Development within Organisation

Unfortunately, the procedures of employee training and development within the organisations are undeveloped. They are mainly performed occasionally, and not connected with organisational strategy, nor do they have some strategic significance. They are mostly enforced when such business problems occur or are perceived that are considered relivable or solvable by organising a training, course or seminar for some of the employees. Employees view the training as an imposed obligation, rather than a way to maximise their potential and they do not realise that by improving their performances and innovation of their knowledge they may contribute to better business results of the organisation they belong to. Unfortunately, top managers do not realise this as well. From their relationship with the employees it is plain to see that the employees are still treated as an expense, rather than an investment worthy of investing.

Many of the managers are under the influence of prejudices such as: training is expensive, training is an expense burdening the current business, it is not rewarding, training is for the young, etc. Knowledge *is* expensive, but ignorance is even more expensive. Human possibilities to learn are unlimited, unless individuals do not limit their abilities within their minds. Many studies have shown that investing in employee training and development has larger business effects than investing in equipment and other material resources. The organisations must harmonise their approach to employee development with the changes. Employee training and development has to be connected with the organisational goals and strategy, they need to fulfil the new reqiurements of the environment. Employee training and development needs to become a managerial function. It is a managerial challenge to consider the employees of the organisation from a strategic perspective (future orientedness) and constantly monitor and encourage the development of new skills and knowledge as the foundation of organisational development.

This is not about assigning the employees to appropriate jobs, but rather about the constant dynamic of encouraging and discovering new possibilities. This is a new type of leadership, significantly different from the classical model of organisational management. The leaders are no longer expected to be all-knowing bosses and supervisors, but rather moderators and inspirators. Since people do not share the information which is the source of their power instictively, the leaders need to recognise, attract and release knowledge in the organisation. One of the main challegnes of modern organisations therefore is how to manage the process of knowledge transfer. "The answer is that wisdom, just because it is the most important, doesn't need to be located inside a tall building where the chief executive and his main assistants hang their hats (and soon their heads as well – unless they join the revolution of the mind). This pictoresque answer of Tom Peters refers to decentralisation and substantivity of employees (turning every workplace into business), which implies a high degree of employee competence and orientation toward the participative style of management.

The process of democratisations, transitions, opening towards the EU, privatisations and arrival of foreign companies and praxis contributed considerably to transformation of approach to employee training and development within our organisations, from the ad hoc processes that originate from the goals and strategies, to a modern approach where human resources and their knowledge are gaining more and more significance.

Knowledge Management and Organisational Learning

As a growing focus of concern within management, knowledge management is an area of research and practice that is still searching for a stable set of core concepts and practical applications. It considers two fundamental philosophical orientations to knowledge management—the "tacit" or *personal knowledge* orientation *versus* the "explicit" or *organisational knowledge* orientation.

The growing stream of articles on and consulting approaches to knowledge management practice today reveals a wide range of recommended processes and techniques. Unfortunately—especially for managers looking for insights to guide knowledge management practices—many of these recommendations often seem disconnected from each other, and in the worst cases, various recommended approaches even seem to be contradicting each other. Analysis of current recommendations, however, suggests that the many ideas for knowledge management being advanced today can be grouped into one of two fundamentally different views of the nature of knowledge itself and of the resulting possibilities for managing knowledge in organisations. These two views are characterised here as the *personal knowledge* approach and the *organisational knowledge* approach. The basic premises and the possibilities for knowledge management practice implied by each of these two approaches are discussed below. Table 1 summarises the fundamental differences in the assumptions underlying the two approaches).

Some important advantages and disadvantages of the two approaches to knowledge management are then discussed.

Personal Knowledge Approach

The personal knowledge approach to knowledge management derives from the fundamental assumptions that knowledge is essentially personal in nature and that knowledge is therefore very difficult (perhaps impracticably so) to extract from the minds of individuals. In effect, this approach to knowledge management assumes, often implicitly, that the knowledge within an organisation essentially consists of "tacit" *personal knowledge* in the minds of individuals in the organisation.

Table 1. Basic Assumptions in Personal versus Organisational Knowledge Management Approaches

Personal Knowledge Approach	*Organisational Knowledge Approach*
Knowledge is personal in nature and very difficult to extract from people.	Knowledge can be articulated and codified to create organisational knowledge assets.
Knowledge must be transferred by moving people within or between organisations.	Knowledge can be disseminated (using information technologies) in the form of documents, drawings, best practice models, etc.
Learning can only be encouraged by bringing the right people together under the right circumstances.	Learning processes can be designed to remedy knowledge deficiencies through structured, managed, scientific processes.

Working from the premise that knowledge is inherently personal in nature and will therefore largely remain tacit in the minds of individuals, the personal knowledge approach generally offers recommendations for knowledge management practice that focus on managing people as individual generators and carriers of knowledge. To manage the personal knowledge of individuals, managers are typically urged to identify the kinds of knowledge possessed by various people in an organisation and then to arrange appropriate interactions between knowledgeable individuals. For example, the personal knowledge approach views the dissemination of knowledge in an organisation as a task that can best be accomplished by transferring people as "knowledge carriers" from one part of an organisation to another. Further, in this approach, a usual recommendation for stimulating organisational learning is to bring knowledgeable individuals together under circumstances that encourage them to share their ideas. These interactions are intended to encourage knowledgeable individuals to apply their knowledge constructively together, to share their knowledge with each other in order to move knowledge from one part of the organisation to another, and hopefully through their interactions to create new knowledge that may be useful to the organisation.Some examples illustrate how the personal knowledge approach to knowledge management may be applied in practice.

Most managers of organisations today do not have a clear view of the specific kinds of knowledge that individuals in their organisation have. This common state of affairs is reflected in the comment usually attributed to executives of Hewlett-Packard in the 1980s: "If we only knew what we know, we could conquer the world." As firms become larger, more knowledge intensive, and more globally dispersed, the need for managers to "know what we know" is becoming acute. A common kind of initiative within the personal knowledge approach is therefore an effort to improve understanding of *who* knows about *what* in an organisation. The creation within Philips, the global electronics company, of an intranet-based "yellow pages" listing experts with different kinds of technical knowledge within Philips' many business units is an example of such an effort. Today Philips employees can type in key words for a specific knowledge domain—say, for example, knowledge about the "design of optical pickup units" for CD/DVD players and recorders—and the yellow pages will retrieve a listing of the people within Philips worldwide business units who claim to have such knowledge. Contact information is also provided for each person listed, so that anyone in Philips who needs the kind of knowledge that an individual claims to have can get in touch with those individuals.

Toyota provides an example of a personal knowledge approach to transferring knowledge within a global organisation. When Toyota builds a new factory and wants to transfer knowledge about its production system to the new employees in the factory, Toyota typically selects a core group of two to three hundred new employees and sends them for several months training and work on the assembly line in one of Toyota's existing factories. After several months of studying the production system and working alongside experienced Toyota assembly line workers, these trained workers are sent back to their new factory site to become the core of production teams formed with other new employees. When they are repatriated, these trained workers are also accompanied by two hundred or so long-term, highly experienced Toyota production workers, who then work alongside all the new employees in the new factory to assure that knowledge of how

Toyota's production process works is fully transferred to all employees in the new factory.

Toyota's use of Quality Circles also illustrates a personal knowledge approach to creating new knowledge. At the end of each work week, groups of Toyota production workers spend one to two hours analysing the performance of their stage in the production system to identify actual or potential problems in quality, productivity, safety, etc. Through their discussions, each group proposes "countermeasures" to correct identified problems, and discusses the results of countermeasures taken during the previous week to address problems identified in earlier Quality Circle discussions. Through such interactions, Toyota employees share their ideas for improvement, devise steps to test new ideas, and assess the results of their tests. This knowledge management practice, which is repeated weekly as an integral part of the Toyota production system, progressively identifies, eliminates, and even prevents sources of process errors. Improvements developed and implemented by Quality Circles over many years have transformed Toyota's production system into one of the highest quality production processes in the world.

Advantages and Disadvantages

A main advantage of the personal knowledge approach is that it offers some relatively simple steps to begin managing knowledge. A basic first step is to identify what each individual in the organisation believes is the specific kind of knowledge that he or she has. Such statements of claimed expertise can help managers do a better job of matching individuals' knowledge with the knowledge requirements of various tasks in the organisation—for example, making more effective assignments of individuals to specific tasks that they will be good at performing, or composing teams with appropriate sets of knowledge to carry out a project. As Philips found with its intranet-based "yellow pages," the relatively little effort needed to create a database listing the expertise claimed by individuals in the organisation may greatly facilitate knowledge sharing among individuals. These easy-to-implement personal knowledge management practices may also avoid some of the practical and motivational challenges that may arise when an organisation asks individuals to make their knowledge explicit.

Although relatively easy to begin, the personal knowledge approach, if used exclusively by an organisation, has some important long-term limitations and disadvantages. One disadvantage is that individuals in an organisation may claim to have personal knowledge that they do not actually have. Moreover, if knowledge only remains tacit in the minds of individuals in an organisation, then the *only* way to move critical knowledge within the organisation is to move people who claim to have such knowledge. Moving people is often costly and time-consuming, and some individuals may resist moves that would disrupt their current work or family life. Even when knowledgeable individuals are willing to be moved, an individual can only be moved one place at a time and can only work so many hours per day, thereby limiting the reach and the speed with which an organisation can practically hope to transfer an individual's knowledge. Further, people in other parts of the organisation may not accept the knowledge of a newly transferred person or may otherwise fail to establish sufficient rapport with transferred individuals to allow the desired knowledge transfer to take place.

Perhaps an even more serious concern in many organisations is that leaving knowledge in tacit form in the minds of key individuals creates a risk that the organisation may lose important knowledge if an individual becomes incapacitated, leaves the organisation, or joins a competing organisation.

Organisational Knowledge Approach

In contrast to the personal knowledge approach, the organisational knowledge approach assumes that knowledge is something that can be made explicit—i.e., can be articulated and explained by individuals who have knowledge, even though some effort and assistance may sometimes be required to help individuals articulate what they know. As a result, the organisational knowledge approach fundamentally assumes that much, if not all, of the knowledge of individuals that is useful to an organisation can be articulated and thereby made explicit and available to others.

Working from this premise, the organisational knowledge approach generally advocates the creation and use of formal organisational processes to encourage and help individuals articulate the important knowledge they have—and thereby to create *organisational knowledge assets.* The organisational knowledge approach also addresses ways that organisational knowledge assets can be disseminated within an organisation, usually through documents, drawings, standard operating procedures, manuals of best practice, and the like. In this regard, information systems are seen as providing a critical means to disseminate organisational knowledge assets over company intranets or between organisations via the internet.

Along with the assumption that knowledge can be made explicit and managed explicitly goes the belief that new knowledge can be created through definable, manageable learning processes. The organisational knowledge approach generally suggests that experiments and other forms of structured, targeted learning processes can be used to remedy important organisational knowledge deficiencies, or that market transactions or strategic partnering may be used to obtain specific forms of needed knowledge or to improve an organisation's existing knowledge assets.

Given these assumptions, the recommendations for knowledge management practice proposed by researchers and consultants working within the organisational knowledge approach typically focus on designing organisational processes for generating, articulating, categorising, and systematically leveraging organisational knowledge assets.

Some examples may help to illustrate the organisational knowledge management approach.

In the 1990s, Motorola was the global leader in the market for pagers (also known as "beepers"). To maintain its leadership position, Motorola introduced new generations of pager designs every 12-15 months. Each new pager generation was designed to offer more advanced features and options for customisation than the preceding generation. To produce its rapidly evolving lines of pagers, Motorola also designed and built a new factory with higher-speed, more flexible assembly lines for each new generation of pager.

To sustain this high rate of product and process development, Motorola formed teams of product and factory designers to co-develop each new generation of pager and the factory for producing the new generation of pager. At the beginning of each project, each new team of designers received a manual of development methods and techniques from the team that had developed the previous generation of pager and its factory.

The new development team would then have three deliverables at the end of their project:

i) an improved and more highly configurable next-generation pager design,

ii) the design of a more efficient and more flexible assembly line for the factory that would produce the new pager, and

iii) an improved design manual that extended the development methods provided to the team in the manual it received by including improved development methods that the team had developed to meet the more demanding product and production goals for its project.

This improved development manual would then be passed on to the next development team given the task of developing the next generation pager and its factory. In this way, Motorola sought to make explicit and disseminate the knowledge developed by its engineers during each project, and thereby to systematically leverage that knowledge in launching the work of the next project team.

In addition to Toyota's personal knowledge management approach that transfers employees around its factories to transfer knowledge about its production system, Toyota also follows highly disciplined organisational knowledge management practices that document in detail the tasks that each team of workers and each individual worker are asked to perform on its assembly lines. These documents provide a detailed description of the content, timing, sequence, and output of each task—how each task is to be performed, how long each task should take, the sequence of steps to be followed in performing each task, and the steps to be taken by each worker in checking his or her own work. As problems arise and are analysed on the assembly line or in employees' weekly Quality Circle meetings, suggestions for improving Toyota's processes are evaluated by Toyota's production engineers and then formally incorporated in revised task description documents.

In addition to documenting process descriptions for repetitive tasks like factory work, some organisations have also created organisational knowledge management approaches to support more creative tasks, such as developing new products. For example, Chrysler's "platform teams" of development engineers have responsibility for creating the next generation platformson which Chrysler's families of automobiles will be based. Each platform team is free to evaluate and select its own design solutions for the many different technical aspects of its vehicle platform. However, each platform team is also required to place its design solutions in a "Book of Knowledge" on Chrysler's intranet. All platform teams can then consult this catalogue of developed design solutions as they carry out their development processes, so that good design solutions developed by one platform team can be located, evaluated, and possibly used by other platform teams.

Other firms have taken an organisational knowledge management approach in product development processes even further. For example, GE Fanuc Automation, one of the world's leading industrial automation firms, develops detailed, company-specific design methodologies for the design of new kinds of components for their factory automation systems. In effect, instead of letting each engineer use his or her own personal knowledge to create new component designs, GE Fanuc's engineers must work together to define standard design methodologies for each type of component the firm uses. Many of these design methodologies are then programmed so that the design of new component variations can be automated, and GE Fanuc's computers then automatically generate design solutions for new components. In this way, GE Fanuc tries to make explicit the best design knowledge of all its engineers—and then to systematically re-use that knowledge by automating new component design tasks.

Advantages and Disadvantages

In many key respects, the advantages and disadvantages of the organisational knowledge approach present a "mirror image" of the advantages and disadvantages of the personal knowledge approach. The organisational knowledge approach is usually much more challenging to start, but may offer significantly greater potential benefits in the long term. I first consider some important potential advantages of the organisational knowledge management approach, and then address some key challenges in starting and sustaining organisational knowledge management approaches in an organisation.

The most fundamental advantage of organisational knowledge approaches is that once an individual's knowledge is articulated in an explicit form (a document, drawing, process description, or other kind of organisational knowledge asset), information systems can usually be used to quickly disseminate that knowledge throughout an organisation. In effect, converting personal knowledge into organisational knowledge creates a knowledge asset that can be made available anytime and anywhere it is needed in an organisation—in effect, freeing an organisation from the limitations of time and space that constrain the dissemination of personal knowledge by moving individuals.

Moreover, once important forms of knowledge are made explicit within an organisation, they can be codified and thereby made easier to leverage than knowledge left in tacit personal form. To *codify knowledge* is to place knowledge in categories that allow important interrelationships between different kinds of knowledge within an organisation to be identified. For example, forms of knowledge in an organisation that share similar theoretical or practical knowledge bases can be identified, so that networks for knowledge sharing can be organised among people working with similar kinds of knowledge. Once important forms of an organisation's knowledge are articulated and codified, knowledge created in one part of an organisation can also be proactively delivered through information systems to people in other parts of the organisation that can benefit from having such knowledge. For example, in the late 1990s AT+T created an IT-based global knowledge network linking common processes in its factories worldwide. New knowledge developed in one factory that would be useful in improving similar processes in other factories could be entered into AT+T's IT system and proactively sent to all other AT+T factories that had similar processes.

A further advantage of the organisational knowledge approach is that once organisational knowledge is made explicit and disseminated to other individuals who have expertise in the same knowledge domain, an organisation's organisational knowledge becomes "visible" and can be discussed, debated, tested further, and improved, thereby stimulating organisational learning processes. (Such processes may also help to identify which individuals in the organisation who claim to have important knowledge are actually capable of making significant contributions to the organisation's knowledge base, and which are not.)

By systematically making its current knowledge base more visible and analysable, an organisation can greatly improve its ability to identify deficiencies in its knowledge base. In effect, by making what it knows explicit, an organisation can begin to see more clearly what it does not know, and then take steps to develop or acquire important forms of knowledge that it does not have or that are not developed to a sufficient level within the organisation.

Finally, an organisation that articulates, codifies, and disseminates its important knowledge assets may thereby minimise the risk that vital knowledge of key individuals may become unavailable if those individuals become incapacitated or leave the organisation.

A number of significant organisational challenges must be overcome, however, to obtain these potential benefits of an organisational knowledge management approach. These challenges primarily arise in managing processes for articulating, evaluating, applying, and protecting organisational knowledge.

Not uncommonly, some individuals in an organisation may lack the skill or motivation to *articulate* their useful knowledge. Individuals may vary greatly in their abilities to articulate their knowledge, and significant organisational support and facilitation may be required to help some individuals with important knowledge to adequately articulate their knowledge and contribute to the creation of organisational knowledge assets. Providing organisational support to individuals who have difficulty articulating their knowledge may involve significant time and financial cost.

An even more fundamental challenge arises when an individual resists articulating his or her knowledge, even though requested by his or her organisation to do so. Such resistance may commonly occur if an individual believes that his or her job security depends on the personal knowledge that he or she has that is important to the organisation.

Individuals may fear that revealing such knowledge would lead to dismissal or loss of influence in an organisation, usually because they believe they would subsequently be less necessary or important to the organisation. Overcoming such fears may call for a redefinition of the employment relationship within an organisation, especially with regard to its key knowledge workers. New employment relationships and incentives may have to be defined to encourage key knowledge workers to engage in continuous learning, to make their knowledge explicit, and to help disseminate their knowledge to others in the organisation.

Organisations must also find ways to systematically *evaluate* knowledge that has been made explicit by various individuals. For example, individuals with different educational backgrounds and professional experience may have come to different conclusions about the most effective way to do something. Such differences will usually be revealed in the process of making their individual knowledge explicit. Organisational processes must be established for evaluating the knowledge that individuals have made explicit and for resolving conflicting knowledge beliefs of individuals. The people involved in making such evaluations must be respected within the organisation for their expertise, objectivity, and impartiality—and in most organisations, such people are usually in short supply, and their time is difficult to obtain. Involving such people in processes for evaluating organisational knowledge may impose significant costs on an organisation—although the resulting benefits may far outweigh the costs.

Since knowledge is useful to an organisation only when it is *applied* in action, a further challenge in implementing organisational knowledge management approaches is assuring that knowledge articulated in one part of the organisation is not rejected or ignored by other parts of the organisation because of an intra-organisational "not invented here" syndrome. One organisational knowledge management approach to this concern is requiring that "best practice models" (such as those defined by panels of experts) be followed throughout an organisation. As various groups within the organisation apply current best practice models, they may develop new knowledge about ways to improve the current best practice, and then report their findings to a panel of experts for their process area, so that their findings can be evaluated and possibly lead to modification of the organisation's current best practice models. Implementing such an organisational knowledge management process, however, requires a high degree of organisational motivation and discipline in systematically contributing to and applying an organisation's current best knowledge and best practice models.

Finally, to assure that organisational knowledge assets remain within the boundaries of the organisation and do not "leak" to competitors, security measures of the type most organisations now routinely use to secure their databases must also be extended to *protecting* an organisation's explicit knowledge assets.

Combining Personal and Organisational Approaches

Personal and organisational knowledge management approaches involve quite different emphases and practices, but both kinds of knowledge management processes are likely to be needed in any organisation. Each approach has important advantages, and in many respects the advantages of one approach can be used to help offset the disadvantages of the other. The objective for knowledge managers is therefore to create knowledge management processes that synthesise the "right" combination and balance of the personal and organisational knowledge management practices. What the "right" combination and balance may consist of will vary with a number of factors specific to each organisation and the way it tries to compete in its markets. However, some basic guidelines can be suggested.

As a rule, personal knowledge management initiatives that bring key knowledge workers face to face are likely to be necessary to build a climate of personal trust and respect among individuals who have important knowledge. Face-to-face meetings may also stimulate exchanges of ideas and speculations that people may be reluctant to contribute through more formalised, IT-based knowledge management processes. Thus, personal knowledge management practices are likely to be vital to *generating* significantly new ideas and thereby to introducing new knowledge to an organisation. By contrast, a key advantage of organisational knowledge practices is their capacity for more efficient, faster dissemination of knowledge, especially through IT systems. In addition, an organisational knowledge approach to disciplined use of best practices and common processes can create "learning platforms" that enable the systematic sharing of new learning that can be used throughout an organisation.

Organisations that have not previously implemented systematic knowledge management approaches should in most cases begin with relatively inexpensive, fast to implement, and less challenging personal knowledge management practices, such as those discussed above. Such practices often create surprising organisational interest in and energy for developing more extensive knowledge management practices. Personal knowledge management practices should evolve to include organisational knowledge management approaches in the long run, however, because organisations that implement effective organisational knowledge management approaches are likely to be much more effective at leveraging their knowledge, and may also become better at systematically generating organisational learning. The first steps in implementing personal knowledge management practices within an organisation should therefore be communicated as only the first step in an evolving knowledge management process that will eventually include more formal and systematic organisational knowledge management practices.

When the respective advantages of personal and organisational knowledge management practices can be combined, an organisation should be able to develop and apply new knowledge considerably faster and more extensively than organisations that do not try to manage knowledge or that use only personal knowledge management practices or only organisational knowledge management practices.

Essential Processes in Knowledge Management

Whether personal or organisational knowledge management practices are used, there are three basic and essential organisational processes that must function well in order for knowledge management to be effective:

i) maintaining learning loops in all organisational processes,

ii) systematically disseminating new and existing knowledge throughout an organisation, and

iii) applying knowledge wherever it can be used in an organisation. Let us consider each of these processes.

A learning loop is any learning process that tries to improve another process, whether incrementally or radically. Quality Circles are an example of an incremental learning loop designed to steadily raise the quality of a production process. More radical learning loops are possible, however—such as regular efforts to "think outside the box" in re-conceptualising how a firm competes in its markets. Whether incremental or radical in intent, learning loops should be designed into *all* organisational processes. The reasoning behind this prescription has much to do with the current emphasis on the "lean organisation." In today's competitive world, only lean organisations that are focused on and excel at key value adding activities (and that outsource other necessary processes) are likely to meet today's rising demands for higher performance and lower price. Every process in a lean organisation is therefore important and worthy of continuous improvement through organisational learning processes—i.e., learning loops.

Once learning loops are in place in an organisation, the next challenge is to *systematically disseminate* existing knowledge and new knowledge generated through learning loops throughout an organisation. Whether accomplished by moving people with personal knowledge or by disseminating new explicit knowledge over IT systems, new knowledge must find its way to other locations in the organisation where it can be used. Such dissemination processes can be either need-driven or proactive. Need-driven dissemination processes use passive systems (like the Philips internal yellow pages) to help individuals find explicit knowledge or other knowledgeable individuals when they feel the need for further knowledge. Proactive dissemination systems classify organisational knowledge and the kinds of people and processes that would benefit from various kinds of knowledge, and then proactively direct new knowledge to people and processes that can benefit from that kind of knowledge.

Knowledge has value to organisations only when it is applied in action within an organisation's processes. Thus, the basic goals of knowledge management practice are not just generating new knowledge, but also assuring that new and existing knowledge is actually applied in all processes where the knowledge can be used throughout an organisation. Achieving this objective is likely to require new incentives and new monitoring processes to assure that new knowledge created elsewhere does not fall victim to a "not invented here" syndrome in which new knowledge is rejected or ignored by groups in whose processes the new knowledge would actually be useful. As a general rule, achieving high performing processes for knowledge generation, dissemination, and application will require substantial redesign of both incentives and monitoring systems in most organisations.

References

Argyris, Chris and Donald Schoen (1978). *Organisational Learning: A Theory of Action Perspective.* Reading, MA: Addison-Wesley.

Merali, Yasmin (2001). "Building and developing capabilities: A cognitive congruence framework," 41-62 in *Knowledge Management and Organisational Competence,* Ron Sanchez, Editor. Oxford: Oxford University Press.

Nelson, Richard and Sidney Winter (1982). *An Evolutionary Theory of Economic Change.* Cambridge, MA: Harvard University Press.

Sanchez, Ron (2001). "Managing knowledge into competences: The five learning cycles of the competent organisation," 3-37 in *Knowledge Management and Organisational Competence,* Ron Sanchez, Editor. Oxford: Oxford University Press.

Sanchez, Ron (1997). "Managing articulated knowledge in competence-based competition," 163-187 in *Strategic Learning and Knowledge Management,* Ron Sanchez and Aimé Heene, Editors. Chichester: John Wiley & Sons.

Spear, Steven, and H. Kent Bowen (1999). "Decoding the DNA of the Toyota production system," *Harvard Business Review,* September-October 1999, 97-106.

Stein, Johan, and Jonas Ridderstråle (2001). "Managing the dissemination of competences," 63-76 in *Knowledge Management and Organisational Competence,* Ron Sanchez, Editor. Oxford: Oxford University Press.

van de Ven, Andrew (1986). "Central problems in the management of innovation," *Management Science,* 32 (5).

Bibliography

Aaker, D.A. (1989). 'Managing assets and skills: the key to sustainable competitive advantage', *California Management Review,* 31, No. 2, pp. 91-106.

Ackoff R. (1999). *Re-Creating the Corporation*, Oxford University Press, New York, Oxfrod.

Alfred W Clark (1976). *Experimenting with organisational life: the action research approach.* New York: Plenum Press.

Allen, David (2001). *Getting things done: the Art of Stress-Free Productivity.* New York: Viking.

Andersen Consulting Company (2000) *Skills Needed for the E-Business Environment.* Andersen Consulting.

Argyris, Chris and Donald Schoen (1978). *Organisational Learning: A Theory of Action Perspective.* Reading, MA: Addison-Wesley.

Bain, Joe S. (1968). *Industrial Organisation.* Wiley, New York.

Barnett, William P (1997). 'The dynamics of competitive intensity'. *Administrative Science Quarterly* 1. 1997.

Barney, Jay B. (1995). 'Looking inside for competitive advantage'. Vol. 9, *The Academy of Management Executive*, 11-01-1995, pp 49ff.

Bass, Bernard (1990). *Handbook of Leadership: Theory, Research, and Managerial Applications.* (3rd Edition) New York: Macmillan.

Beede, David N. and Kan H. Young. (1996). *Patterns of Advanced Technology Adoption and Manufacturing Performance: Employment Growth, Labor Productivity, and Employee Earnings.* U.S. Department of Commerce, Washington, DC.

Boyatzis, Richard E. (1982). *The Competent Manager.* New York: Wiley.

Bresnahan, Timothy F., Erik Brynjolfsson, and Lorin M. Hitt. (1998). *How Do Information Technology and Work Place Organisation Affect Labor Demand? Firm-Level Evidence.* Unpublished manuscript.

Cappelli, Peter. (1993). "Are Skill Requirements Rising? Evidence From Production and Clerical Jobs." *Industrial and Labor Relations Review* 46, no. 3: 515-30.

Chris Argyris (1957). *Personality and organisation; the conflict between system and the individual*. New York: Harper & Row. pp. 47–54.

Churchman C., (1997), *The Systems Approach and Its Enemies,* Basic Books, New York.

Cox, Taylor H. and Ruby L. Beal (1997) *Developing Competency to Manage Diversity*. San Francisco: Barrett-Koehler.

Daniel Katz; Robert Louis Kahn (1966). *The social psychology of organisations*. New York: Wiley. pp. 18–33.

Dervitsiotis K., (2007), Guiding Human Organisations to Climb the Spiral Stages of Performance Improvement, *TQM & Business Excellence, Vol. 19, n 7 & 8.*

Ferris, Gerald R., Perrewe′, Pamela L., Anthony, William P., & Gilmore, David C., (2000), "Political skill at work," *Organisational Dynamics*, 28(4), 25–37.

Fiore, Neil A (2006). *The Now Habit: A Strategic Program for Overcoming Procrastination and Enjoying Guilt- Free Play*. New York: Penguin Group.

Fry, Louis W., "Towards a theory of spiritual leadership," *The Leadership Quarterly*, 14(6), (Dec 2003), 693–727.

Gharajedaghi J., (1999), *Systems Thinking*, Butterworth Heinemann, Boston, MA

Hamel G., (2007), *The Future of management*, Harvard Business School Press, p.9.

Harvey, Edward, & Mills, Russell, (1970), *Patterns of organisational adoption: A political perspective*, Nashville, TN: Vanderbilt University Press, , 181-213.

Henry P Knowles; Börje O Saxberg (1971). *Personality and leadership behavior*. Reading, Mass.: Addison-Wesley Pub. Co.

Holzer, Harry J. (1996). "Employer Skill Needs and Labor Market Outcomes by Race and Gender." *Discussion Paper No. 1087-96*, Institute for Research on Poverty.

Howell, David R. and Edward Wolff. (1991)."Trends in the Growth and Distribution of Skills in the US Workplace, 1960-1985." *Industrial and Labor Relations Review* 44, no. 3: 486-502.

John E Jones; J William Pfeiffer (1973). *The 1973 annual handbook for group facilitators*. San Diego, Calif.: University Associates. pp. 106–109.

Kast F. E. and Rosenzweig J. A., (1985), *Organisation & Management*, McGraw-Hill Inc.

Kenneth Kaye (1994). *Workplace Wars and How to End Them: Turning Personal Conflict into Productive Teamwork.* New York: AMACOM.

Kotter, John, P., *The leadership factor*. Free Press, New York, 1988.

Laszlo E. (1996), *The Systems View of the World*, Hampton Press, Inc., Cresskill, NJ

Le Blanc, Raymond (2008). *Achieving Objectives Made Easy! Practical goal setting tools & proven time management techniques.*. Maarheese: Cranendonck Coaching.

Levenson, Alec R., Elaine Reardon, and Stefanie Schmidt. (1999). *Welfare Jobs and Basic Skills: The Employment Prospects of Wefare Recipients in the Most Populous U.S. Counties.* National Center for Adult Learning and Literacy, Report #10. Cambridge, MA.

Merali, Yasmin (2001). "Building and developing capabilities: A cognitive congruence framework," 41-62 in *Knowledge Management and Organisational Competence,* Ron Sanchez, Editor. Oxford: Oxford University Press.

Nadler D.A., Gerstein M.S., Shaw R.B., (1992), *Organisational Architecture —Designs for Changing Organisations*, Jossey – Bass Publishers, S. Francisco.

Nelson, Richard and Sidney Winter (1982). *An Evolutionary Theory of Economic Change.* Cambridge, MA: Harvard University Press.

Patrick J. Montana (2008). *Management.* New York: Barron's Educational Series. p. 265.

Paul S. Adler. (1986). New Technologies, New Skills. *California Management Review* 9–28.

Peled, Alon, (2000), "Politicking for success: The missing skill," *Leadership and Organisation Development Journal*, 21(1), 20–29.

Pfeffer, Jeffery, (1992), "Understanding power in organisations," *California Management Review*, 35, 29–50.

Quinn, Robert E. (1988) *Beyond Rational Management.* San Francisco: Jossey-Bass.

Richard Arvid Johnson (1976). *Management, systems, and society : an introduction.* Pacific Palisades, Calif.: Goodyear Pub. Co.. pp. 148–142.

Rigby, Darrell (1998) *Management Tools and Techniques*. Boston: Bain and Company.

Sanchez, Ron (1997). "Managing articulated knowledge in competence-based competition," 163-187 in *Strategic Learning and Knowledge*

Management, Ron Sanchez and Aimé Heene, Editors. Chichester: John Wiley & Sons.

Sanchez, Ron (2001). "Managing knowledge into competences: The five learning cycles of the competent organisation," 3-37 in *Knowledge Management and Organisational Competence,* Ron Sanchez, Editor. Oxford: Oxford University Press.

Secunda, Al (1999). *The 15 second principle : short, simple steps to achieving long-term goals.* New York: New York : Berkley Books. pp. 157.

Spear, Steven, and H. Kent Bowen (1999). "Decoding the DNA of the Toyota production system," *Harvard Business Review,* September-October 1999, 97-106.

Stein, Johan, and Jonas Ridderstråle (2001). "Managing the dissemination of competences," 63-76 in *Knowledge Management and Organisational Competence,* Ron Sanchez, Editor. Oxford: Oxford University Press.

Theodore M Mills (1967). *The Sociology of Small Groups.* Englewood Cliffs, N.J.: Prentice-Hall. pp. 14–17

Thompson, James D. (1967). *Organisations in Action.* New York: McGraw-Hill.

van de Ven, Andrew (1986). "Central problems in the management of innovation," *Management Science,* 32 (5).

Vance, Charles M. (1993) *Mastering Management Education.* Newbury Park, CA: Sage.

Veliyath, Rajaram / Fitzgerald, Elizabeth (2000). 'Firm capabilities, business strategies, customer preferences, and hypercompetitive arenas'. *Competitiveness Review,* 10, 2000: 56-82. Indiana.

von Bertalanffi L., (1969), *General Systems Theory,* George Braziller, New York.

Weick, Karl E., & Quinn, Robert E., (1999), "Organisational change and development," *Annual Review of Psychology,* 50, 361–386.

Whetten, David A., & Cameron, Kim S. (1983) "Management skill training; A needed addition to the management curriculum." *Organisational Behavior Teaching Journal,* 8: 10-15.

Wood, Adrian. (1995). "How Trade Hurt Unskilled Workers." *The Journal of Economic Perspectives* 9, no. 3: 57-80.

Index